GPU Pro 360

Guide to Shadows

GPU Pro 360

Guide to Shadows

Edited by Wolfgang Engel

CRC Press
Taylor & Francis Group
Boca Raton London New York

CRC Press is an imprint of the
Taylor & Francis Group, an **informa** business
AN A K PETERS BOOK

CRC Press
Taylor & Francis Group
6000 Broken Sound Parkway NW, Suite 300
Boca Raton, FL 33487-2742

© 2019 by Taylor & Francis Group, LLC
CRC Press is an imprint of Taylor & Francis Group, an Informa business

International Standard Book Number-13: 978-0-8153-8248-5 (Hardback) 978-0-8153-8247-8 (Paperback)

Library of Congress Cataloging-in-Publication Data

Names: Engel, Wolfgang F., editor.
Title: GPU pro 360 guide to shadows / [edited by] Wolfgang Engel.
Description: First edition. | Boca Raton, FL : CRC Press/Taylor & Francis Group, 2018. | Includes
    bibliographical references and index.
Identifiers: LCCN 2018020470 | ISBN 9780815382485 (hardcover : alk. paper) | ISBN 9780815382478
    (pbk. : alk. paper) | ISBN 9781351208352 (ebook)
Subjects: LCSH: Computer graphics. | Shades and shadows—Computer simulation. | Graphics
    processing units—Programming.
Classification: LCC T385 .G688874 2018 | DDC 006.6—dc23
LC record available at https://lccn.loc.gov/2018020470

Visit the eResources: https://www.crcpress.com/9780815382478

Visit the Taylor & Francis Web site at
http://www.taylorandfrancis.com

and the CRC Press Web site at
http://www.crcpress.com

Contents

9 Mipmapped Screen-Space Soft Shadows 129
Alberto Aguado and Eugenia Montiel

10 Efficient Online Visibility for Shadow Maps 147
Oliver Mattausch, Jiri Bittner, Ari Silvennoinen, Daniel Scherzer, and
Michael Wimmer

11 Depth Rejected Gobo Shadows 157
John White

12 Real-Time Deep Shadow Maps 163
René Fürst, Oliver Mattausch, and Daniel Scherzer

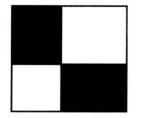

Introduction

In this book we cover various algorithms that are used to generate shadow data. Shadows are the dark companion of lights and although both can exist on their own, they shouldn't exist without each other in games. Achieving good visual results in rendering shadows is still considered one of the particularly difficult tasks of graphics programmers.

The chapter "Fast Conventional Shadow Filtering," by Holger Gruen, covers an algorithm that can be used to reduce the number of necessary percentage closer filtering (PCF) texture operations roughly to a third. This allows the usage of larger filter kernels and therefore results in a softer penumbra that is necessary to reduce the perspective aliasing of shadow pixels along the view frustum.

Holger Gruen's second chapter has a similar target. In "Hybrid Min/Max Plane-Based Shadow Maps," he shows a way to derive a secondary texture from a normal depth-only shadow map that can be used to speed up expensive shadow filtering kernels. He stores a plane equation or min/max depth data for a block of pixels of the original shadow map. Both techniques are especially tailored to rendering shadows on the upcoming generation of graphics hardware.

Hung-Chien Liao demonstrates in his chapter "Shadow Mapping for Omnidirectional Light Using Tetrahedron Mapping" a new way to store shadow data. Instead of using a cube or dual-paraboloid map, he proposes using a tetrahedron projection and storing the data in a two-dimensional map. He also compares his method to cube and dual-paraboloid shadow mapping and concludes that it is faster than cube shadow maps and more accurate compared to dual-paraboloid shadow maps.

In "Screen Space Soft Shadows," Jesus Gumbau, Miguel Chover and Mateu Sbert describe a soft shadow map technique that is built on Randima Fernando's "Percentage-Closer Soft Shadows" and improves on the original idea in speed and flexibility. They use a screen-aligned texture that contains the distance between the shadow and potential occluders and then use this to run an adjustable anisotropic Gauss filter kernel over the original shadow data. This method is quite efficient and has a robustness that makes it suitable for game usage.

"Variance Shadow Maps Light-Bleeding Reduction Tricks," by Wojciech Sterna, covers techniques to reduce light bleeding. There is also an example application that shows the technique.

Pavlo Turchyn covers fast soft shadows with adaptive shadow maps—as used in *Age of Conan*—in his chapter "Fast Soft Shadows via Adaptive Shadow Maps." The chapter describes the extension of percentage-closer filtering to adaptive shadow maps that was implemented in the game. Turchyn proposes a multiresolution filtering method in which three additional, smaller shadow maps with sizes of 1024×1024, 512×512 and 256×256 are created from a 2048×2048 shadow map. The key observation is that the result of the PCF kernel over a 3×3 area of a 1024×1024 shadow map is a reasonably accurate approximation for filtering over a 6×6 area of a 2048×2048 shadow map. Similarly, a 3×3 filter kernel of a 256×256 shadow map approximates a 24×24 area of a 2048×2048 shadow map.

The chapter "Adaptive Volumetric Shadow Maps" by Marco Salvi et al. describes a new approach for real-time shadows that supports high-quality shadowing from dynamic volumetric media such as hair, smoke, and fog. Adaptive volumetric shadow maps (AVSM) encode the fraction of visible light from the light source over the interval $[0, 1]$ as a function of depth at each texel. This transmittance function and the depth value are then stored for each texel and sorted front-to-back. This is called the AVSM representation. This AVSM representation is generated by first rendering all visible transparent fragments in a linked list (see the chapter "Order-Independent Transparency Using Per-Pixel Linked Lists" in *GPU Pro 360 Guide to GPGPU* for the description of per-pixel linked lists). In a subsequent pass, those linked lists are compressed into the AVSM representation, consisting of the transmittance value and the depth value.

Another chapter that describes the fast generation of soft shadows is "Fast Soft Shadows with Temporal Coherence" by Daniel Scherzer et al. The light source is sampled over multiple frames instead of a single frame, creating only a single shadow map with each frame. The individual shadow test results are then stored in a screen-space shadow buffer. This buffer is recreated in each frame using the shadow buffer from the previous frame as input. This previous frame holds only shadowing information for pixels that were visible in the previous frame. Pixels that become newly visible in this frame due to camera or object movement have no shadowing information stored in this buffer. For these pixels the chapter describes a spatial-filtering method to estimate the soft shadow results. In other words the main idea of the algorithm described in the chapter is to formulate light-source area sampling in an iterative manner, evaluating only a single shadow map per frame.

"Mipmapped Screen-Space Soft Shadows," by Alberto Aguado and Eugenia Montiel, uses similar ideas as the other two soft shadow chapters. Soft shadows are generated with the help of mipmaps to represent multifrequency shadows for screen-space filtering. The mipmap has two channels; the first channel stores the shadow-intensity values and the second channel stores screen-space penumbra widths. Shadow values are obtained by filtering while penumbrae widths are propagated by flood filling. After the mipmap is generated, the penumbrae values are used as indices to the mipmap levels. Thus, we transform the problem of shadow generation into the problem of selecting levels in a mipmap. This approach is extended by including layered shadow maps to improve shadows with multiple occlusions.

In "Efficient Online Visibility for Shadow Maps" by Oliver Mattausch et al., the authors introduce an algorithm that makes shadow-map rendering efficient, and that is particularly useful for shadow mapping in large-scale outdoor scenes. This algorithm quickly detects and culls the geometry that does not contribute to shadows in final images. The solution presented by Mattausch and his coauthors uses camera-view visibility information to create a mask of potential shadow receivers in the light view, which restricts the area in which shadow casters have to be rendered. There are four main steps in the algorithm: determine the shadow receivers, create a mask of shadow receivers, render shadow casters using the mask for culling, and compute shading. The authors note that their basic principle is easy to integrate into existing game engines.

In "Depth Rejected Gobo Shadows," John White describes a technique to provide soft shadows using a simple texture sample. This approach extends the basic projected gobo texture concept by removing the incorrect projections on objects closer to the light source.

The chapter "Real-Time Deep Shadow Maps" represents the state of the art in real-time deep shadow maps. The chapter covers implementation that only requires a single rendering pass from the light without introducing any approximations. It covers a novel lookup scheme that exploits spatial coherence for efficient filtering of deep shadow maps.

"Practical Screen-Space Soft Shadows," by Márton Tamás and Viktor Heisenberger, describes how to implement a shadow filter kernel in screen space while preserving the shadow color data in layers.

The chapter "Tile-Based Omnidirectional Shadows," by Hawar Doghramachi, shows how to implement efficient shadows in combination with a tiled deferred shading system by using programmable draw dispatches, the programmable clipping unit, and tetrahedron shadow maps.

The last chapter, "Shadow Map Silhouette Revectorization" by Vladimir Bondarev, utilizes MLAA to reconstruct the shadow penumbra, concealing the perspective aliasing with an additional umbra surface. This is useful for hard shadow penumbras.

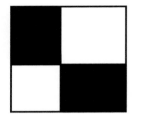

Web Materials

Example programs and source code to accompany some of the chapters are available on the CRC Press website: go to https://www.crcpress.com/9780815382478 and click on the "Downloads" tab.

The directory structure follows the book structure by using the chapter numbers as the name of the subdirectory.

General System Requirements

The material presented in this book was originally published between 2010 and 2016, and the most recent developments have the following system requirements:

- The DirectX June 2010 SDK (the latest SDK is installed with Visual Studio 2012).

- DirectX 11 or DirectX 12 capable GPUs are required to run the examples. The chapter will mention the exact requirement.

- The OS should be Microsoft Windows 10, following the requirement of DirectX 11 or 12 capable GPUs.

- Visual Studio C++ 2012 (some examples might require older versions).

- 2GB RAM or more.

- The latest GPU driver.

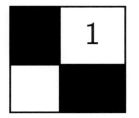

Fast Conventional Shadow Filtering

Holger Gruen

1.1 Overview

This chapter presents ideas on how to reduce the number of hardware-accelerated *percentage closer filtering* (PCF) texture operations for conventional shadow map filtering. A uniform 8×8 filter that would usually be carried out using 49 PCF textures operations can now be carried out with only 16 PCF operations. As the number of texture operations is usually the limiting factor for conventional shadow filtering, the speedup achieved is significant. The techniques described here reduce the number of necessary PCF texture operations from $(N-1) \times (N-1)$ to $(N/2) \times (N/2)$ for uniform(*) and separable shadow filters. Further on, an algorithm to implement box filters with nonseparable unique weights in only $(N-1) \times (N/2)$ instead of $(N-1) \times (N-1)$ PCF texture operations is explained. This algorithm can be used for advanced shadow filtering effects. Please note that the methods described here can also be carried over to filtering color textures.

1.2 Introduction

Conventional shadow filtering works by directly filtering binary visibility results (see [Williams 78]) obtained from a depth-only shadow map. Techniques like [Annen et al. 07], [Donnelly at al. 06], [Dmitriev at al. 07], [Gruen 08], or [Gumbau et al. 10] are not considered to be conventional shadow filtering techniques as they use data in addition to a depth-only shadow map.

Most games still make use of conventional uniform shadow filters. This means that the importance of all shadow map based visibility results (e.g., is the light visible) is equal. In order to achieve soft shadow to light transitions, as a minimal solution four visibility samples, e.g., a 2×2 neighborhood of shadow map samples, are taken into account. These four samples are bi-linearly weighted using sub-texel coordinates to generate a smooth result. This approach is called *percentage closer filtering* (PCF), and is supported by all Direct3D 10.0 class hardware and some Direct3D 9.x class hardware.

A naive way to compute the result of uniformly filtering an $N \times N$ block of shadow map texels is to perform $(N - 1) \times (N - 1)$ PCF shadow map lookups and to divide their sum by $(N - 1) \times (N - 1)$. It is possible though to reduce the number of PCF texture samples to $(N/2) \times (N/2)$. This reduction in texture operation count is achievable by computing shifted texture coordinates for the PCF shadow map lookups. Further the result of each PCF lookup needs to be multiplied by a post texturing weight.

Large uniform filters produce smooth shadows but can blur away fine details. This chapter further describes how to compute higher quality filters that e.g., use a separable Gaussian-like weight matrix to weight each PCF sample. The math behind shifted texture positions and post texturing weights can be used again to implement the separable filter with only $(N/2) \times (N/2)$ PCF samples.

Finally, in order to gain even higher control over the weights in the weights-matrix and to create fully customizable shadow filtering quality, similar math is used to reduce the number of texture operations for nonseparable unique weights from $(N - 1) \times (N - 1)$ to only $(N - 1) \times (N/2)$ for Direct3D.

Note. Since shadow mapping only uses the first data channel of a texture, Shader Model 4.1 or Shader Model 5.0 capable hardware can be used to reduce the number of texture operations to $(N/2) \times (N/2)$ for every conceivable filter for an $N \times N$ pixel block. The reason for this is that the `Gather()` texture operation delivers the values for four adjacent texels. If you are using Direct3D 10.1, Direct3D 11 or above, none of the tricks described below are necessary anymore.

The remainder of the chapter walks through the various conventional shadow filtering techniques. The chapter closes by presenting two exemplary techniques that use a filter matrix with nonseparable weights.

1.3   Uniform Shadow Filtering

As described above, most games still use uniform shadow filters. The naive way to implement these is to carry out $(N - 1) \times (N - 1)$ PCF samples. The following text describes how to get this down to the $(N/2) \times (N/2)$ PCF samples mentioned above.

Please consider the following 4×4 shadow map texel grid in Figure 1.1. Each v_{ij} is a binary visibility [0 or 1] sample derived from the corresponding shadow

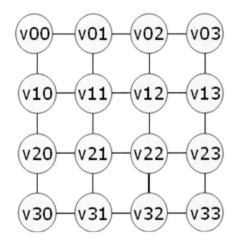
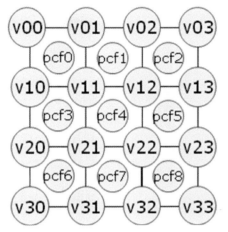

Figure 1.1. $N \times N$ binary visibility samples (0=shadow, 1=full light). A row of weights is applied horizontally first.

Figure 1.2. $N \times N$ binary visibility results are reduced to $(N - 1) \times (N - 1)$ PCF results—the same weights are now applied vertically as well.

map sample (e.g., by comparing each sample with the light space depth of the current pixel).

A uniform PCF sample based filter collapses each 2×2 visibility information block to a PCF filtered visibility result PCF_k by performing a PCF texture lookup as shown in Figure 1.2.

The final filtered result (for $N \times N$ shadow map pixels) is then obtained by computing the term in Equation (1.1):

$$\frac{\sum_{k=0}^{(N-1)\cdot(N-1)} PCF_k}{(N - 1) \cdot (N - 1)}. \tag{1.1}$$

As mentioned above, a naive way to implement this using only Shader Model 4.0 would involve doing $(N - 1) \times (N - 1)$ PCF texture samples. There is a better way though.

The term in Equation (1.1) can also be computed through some ALU shader instructions and only $(N/2) \times (N/2)$ PCF texture instructions as shown in Figure 1.3 for a 4×4 block of visibility results.

In order to understand how this works only one row of visibility samples v_k is considered initially. Assigning weights w_k to each one-dimensional PCF result in that row does produce the term shown in Equation (1.2). Here, x is the sub-texel

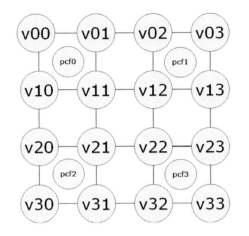

Figure 1.3. It is possible to evaluate the $(N - 1) \times (N - 1)$ PCF-based filter with just $(N/2) \times (N/2)$ PCF sample + some ALU—the unrolled weighted term for bi-linear filtering each 2×2 visibility block.

coordinate ranging from 0.0 to 1.0 (excluding 1.0):

$$\sum_{k=0}^{N-2} (1 - x) \cdot v_k + x \cdot v_{k+1}. \tag{1.2}$$

Equation (1.2) simplifies to Equation (1.3):

$$(1 - x) \cdot v_0 + \left(\sum_{k=1}^{N-2} v_k \right) + x \cdot v_{N-1}. \tag{1.3}$$

To compute shifted texture coordinates x' for PCF texture operations and post texturing weights wp, the following three cases have to be considered:

1. Left border of the filter row (the terms that refer to v01, v02, v11, and v12). The system of equations $(1 - x') \cdot wp \cdot v_0 = (1 - x) \cdot v_0$ and $x' \cdot wp \cdot v_1 = v_1$ is solved by $x' = -\frac{1}{x-2}$ and $wp = 2 - x$.

2. Right border of the filter row. ($N \times N$ binary visibility samples: 0=shadow, 1=full light).The system of equations $(1 - x') \cdot wp \cdot v_{N-2} = v_{N-2}$ and $x' \cdot wp \cdot v_{N-1} = x \cdot v_{N-1}$ is solved by $x' = \frac{x}{x+1}$ and $wp = x + 1$.

3. Central values of the filter row $N \times N$ binary visibility results are reduced to $(N-1) \times (N-1)$ PCF results. The system of equations $(1 - x') \cdot wp \cdot v_k = v_k$ and $x' \cdot wp \cdot v_{k+1} = v_{k+1}$ is solved by $x' = \frac{1}{2}$ and $wp = 2$.

Using these formulas, the filtering for one row can be carried out with only $(N/2)$ PCF samples. Since the filter is symmetric in the y direction, the full box filter can evaluated using only $(N-1) \times (N/2)$ PCF texture samples.

The shaders in Listing 1.1 demonstrate optimized implementations for Direct3D 10.0.

```
#define FILTER_SIZE 8 // 8x8 shadow map samples
#define GS2 ( (FILTER_SIZE-1)/2 )

float shadow_filter( float3 tc )
{
  tc.xyz /= tc.w;

  float  s   = 0.0;
  float2 stc = ( SMAP_size * tc.xy ) + float2( 0.5, 0.5 );
  float2 tcs = floor( stc );
  float2 fc;

  fc     = stc - tcs;
  tc.xy = tc.xy - ( fc * ( 1.0/SMAP_size ) );

  float2 pwAB = ( ( 2.0 ).xx - fc );
  float2 tcAB = ( 1.0/SMAP_size ).xx / pwAB;
  float2 tcM  = (0.5/SMAP_size ).xx;
  float2 pwGH = ( ( 1.0 ).xx + fc );
  float2 tcGH = (1.0/SMAP_size) * ( fc / pwGH );

  for( int row = -GS2; row <= GS2; row += 2 )
  {
    for( int col = -GS2; col <= GS2; col += 2 )
    {
if( row == -GS2 ) // Top row
{
  if( col == -GS2 ) // left
    s += ( pwAB.x * pwAB.y ) * s_smap.SampleCmpLevelZero(
            smp_smap, tc.xy + tcAB, tc.z,
            int2( col, row ) ).x;
  else if( col == GS2 ) // Right
    s += ( pwGH.x * pwAB.y )* s_smap.SampleCmpLevelZero(
            smp_smap, tc.xy + float2( tcGH.x, tcAB.y),
            tc.z, int2( col, row ) ).x;
  else // center
    s += (2.0 * pwAB.y )*s_smap.SampleCmpLevelZero(
            smp_smap, tc.xy + float2( tcM.x, tcAB.y),
            tc.z, int2( col, row ) ).x;
}
else if( row == GS2 )  // Bottom row
{
  if( col == -GS2 ) // Left
    s += ( pwAB.x * pwGH.y ) * s_smap.SampleCmpLevelZero(
```

```
                        smp_smap , tc.xy + float2( tcAB.x, tcGH.y ),
                        tc.z, int2( col, row ) ).x;
            else if( col == GS2 ) // Right
              s += ( pwGH.x * pwGH.y ) * s_smap.SampleCmpLevelZero(
                        smp_smap , tc.xy + tcGH, tc.z,
                        int2( col, row ) ).x;
            else // Center
              s += (       2.0 * pwGH.y ) * s_smap.SampleCmpLevelZero(
                        smp_smap , tc.xy + float2( tcM.x, tcGH.y ),
                        tc.z, int2( col, row ) ).x;
          }
      else // Center rows
      {
        if( col == -GS2 ) // Left
          s += ( pwAB.x * 2.0    ) * s_smap.SampleCmpLevelZero(
                    smp_smap , tc.xy + float2( tcAB.x, tcM.y ),
                    tc.z, int2( col, row ) ).x;
        else if( col == GS2 ) // Right
          s += ( pwGH.x * 2.0    ) * s_smap.SampleCmpLevelZero(
                    smp_smap , tc.xy + float2( tcGH.x, tcM.y),
                    tc.z, int2( col, row ) ).x;
        else // Center
          s += (       2.0 * 2.0    ) * s_smap.SampleCmpLevelZero(
                    smp_smap , tc.xy + tcM, tc.z,
                    int2( col, row ) ).x;
      }
      }
    }

    return s/((FILTERSIZE -1) * (FILTERSIZE -1));
}
```

Listing 1.1. Fast Shader Model 4.0 uniform shadow filter.

1.4   Separable Shadow Filters

Uniform box filters tend to blur out details that should better be preserved. One solution to this problem is to use a Gaussian filter. Gaussian filters are separable. This section therefore takes a closer look at separable shadow filters. Figure 1.4 shows how filter weights that define a separable filter are first used to weight each PCF result in a shadow filter.

The next step is to apply the filter weights vertically, as shown in Figure 1.5.

In order to understand if a separable filter can be implemented with less than the naive $(N-1) \times (N-1)$ PCF operations please consider the weighted bi-linearly filtered visibility results for each 2×2 visibility block as shown in Figure 1.6.

As an example now concentrate on the 2×2 block in orange as shown in Figure 1.7. In order to understand how to select shifted texture coordinates and

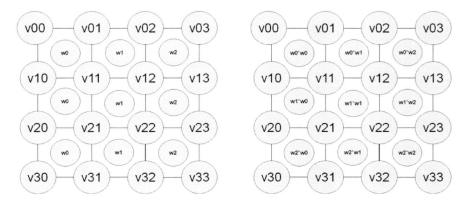

Figure 1.4. A weight is applied to each PCF result.

Figure 1.5.   Shader Model 4.0 needs $(N/2) \times (N-1)$ PCF ops plus some ALU.

post texturing weights, one needs to look at all neighboring 2×2 blocks to find all terms that refer to the visibility block from Figure 1.7.

Assigning terms to each corner of the 2×2 visibility block creates a system of four equations (see Figure 1.8), which needs to satisfy the three unknowns x', y', and p_w.

For a filter that looks at $N \times N$ visibility samples, this means one needs to consider nine cases of equation systems.

For brevity's sake, just the solutions of these equations for the nine cases are presented here.

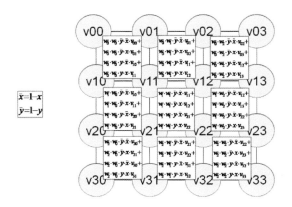

Figure 1.6. Shader Model 4.1 only needs to do $(N/2) \times (N/2)$ gathers plus some ALU.

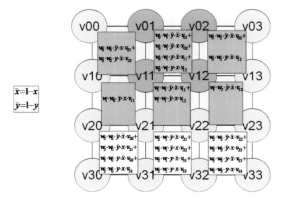

Figure 1.7. Triangle-shaped filter kernel.

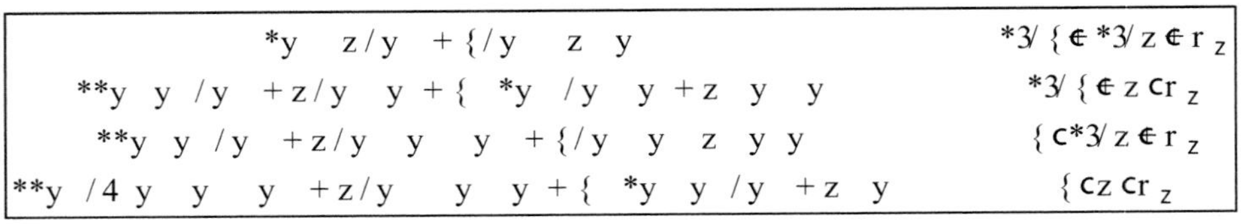

*y z / y + { / y z y			*3/ { € *3/ z € r $_z$
**y y / y + z / y y + { *y / y y + z y y			*3/ { € z cr $_z$
**y y / y + z / y y y + { / y y z y y			{ c *3/ z € r $_z$
**y / 4 y y y + z / y y y + { *y y / y + z y			{ cz cr $_z$

Figure 1.8. Half-moon-shaped kernel.

1. Top left:

$$x' = \frac{(w_1 - w_0) \cdot x - w_1}{w_1 \cdot x - w_1 - w_0},$$

$$y' = \frac{(w_1 - w_0) \cdot y - w_1}{w_1 \cdot y - w_1 - w_0},$$

$$p_w = (w_1^2 \cdot x - w_1^2 - w_0 \cdot w_1) \cdot y + (-w_1^2 - w_0 \cdot w_1) \cdot x + 2 \cdot w_0 \cdot w_1 + w_0^2.$$

2. Top center:

$$x' = \frac{(w_{kx+1} - w_{kx}) \cdot x - w_{kx+1}}{(w_{kx+1} - w_{kx-1}) \cdot x - w_{kx+1} - w_{kx}},$$

$$y' = \frac{(w_1 - w_0) \cdot y - w_1}{w_1 \cdot y - w_1 - w_0},$$

$$\begin{aligned} p_w = &((w_1 \cdot w_{kx+1} - w_1 \cdot w_{kx-1}) \cdot x - w_1 \cdot w_{kx+1} - w_1 \cdot w_{kx}) \cdot y \\ &+ (w_1 + w_0) \cdot w_{kx} + ((-w_1 - w_0) \cdot w_{kx+1} + (w_1 + w_0) \cdot w_{kx-1}) \cdot x \\ &+ (w_1 + w_0) \cdot w_{kx+1}. \end{aligned}$$

3. Top right:

$$x' = \frac{w_{n-1} \cdot x}{w_{n-2} \cdot x - w_{n-1}},$$

$$y' = \frac{(w_1 - w_0) \cdot y - w_1}{w_1 \cdot y - w_1 - w_0},$$

$$\begin{aligned} p_w = &(-w_1 \cdot w_{n-2} \cdot x - w_1 \cdot w_{n-1}) \cdot y + (w_0 + w_1) \cdot w_{n-2} \cdot x \\ &+ (w_1 + w_0) \cdot w_{n-1}. \end{aligned}$$

4. Center left:

$$x' = \frac{(w_1 - w_0) \cdot x - w_1}{w_1 \cdot x - w_1 - w_0},$$

$$y' = \frac{(w_{ky+1} - w_{ky}) \cdot y - w_{ky+1}}{(w_{ky+1} - w_{ky-1}) \cdot y - w_{ky+1} - w_{ky}},$$

$$\begin{aligned} p_w = &((w_1 \cdot w_{ky+1} - w_1 \cdot w_{ky-1}) \cdot x + (-w_1 - w_0) \cdot w_{ky+1} \\ &+ (w_1 + w_0) \cdot w_{ky-1}) \cdot y + (-w_1 \cdot w_{ky+1} - w_1 \cdot w_{ky}) \cdot x \\ &+ (w_1 + w_0) \cdot w_{ky+1} + (w_1 + w_0) \cdot w_{ky}. \end{aligned}$$

5. Center center:

$$x' = \frac{(w_{kx+1} - w_{kx}) \cdot x - w_{kx+1}}{(w_{kx+1} - w_{kx-1}) \cdot x - w_{kx+1} - w_{kx}},$$

$$y' = \frac{(w_{ky+1} - w_{ky}) \cdot y - w_{ky+1}}{(w_{ky+1} - w_{ky-1}) \cdot y - w_{ky+1} - w_{ky}},$$

$$\begin{aligned} p_w =& (((w_{kx+1} - w_{kx-1}) \cdot w_{ky+1} + (w_{kx-1} - w_{kx+1}) \cdot w_{ky-1}) \cdot x \\ &+ (-w_{kx+1} - w_{kx}) \cdot w_{ky+1} + (w_{kx+1} + w_{kx}) \cdot w_{ky-1}) \cdot y \\ &+ ((w_{kx-1} - w_{kx+1}) \cdot w_{ky+1} + (w_{kx-1} - w_{kx+1}) \cdot w_{ky}) \cdot x \\ &+ (w_{kx+1} + w_{kx}) \cdot w_{ky+1} + (w_{kx+1} + w_{kx}) \cdot w_{ky}. \end{aligned}$$

6. Center right:

$$x' = \frac{w_{n-1} \cdot x}{w_{n-2} \cdot x - w_{n-1}},$$

$$y' = \frac{(w_{ky+1} - w_{ky}) \cdot y - w_{ky+1}}{(w_{ky+1} - w_{ky-1}) \cdot y - w_{ky+1} - w_{ky}},$$

$$\begin{aligned} p_w =& ((w_{n-2} \cdot w_{ky-1} - w_{n-2} \cdot w_{ky+1}) \cdot x - w_{n-1} \cdot w_{ky+1} + w_{n-1} \cdot w_{ky-1}) \cdot y \\ &+ (w_{n-2} \cdot w_{ky+1} + w_{n-2} \cdot w_{ky}) \cdot x + w_{n-1} \cdot w_{ky+1} + w_{n-1} \cdot w_{ky}. \end{aligned}$$

7. Bottom left:

$$x' = \frac{(w_1 - w_0) \cdot x - w_1}{w_1 \cdot x - w_1 - w_0},$$

$$y' = \frac{w_{n-1} y}{w_{n-2} \cdot y + w_{n-1}},$$

$$p_w = ((w_1 + w_0) \cdot w_{n-2} - w_1 \cdot w_{n-2} \cdot x) \cdot y - w_1 \cdot w_{n-1} \cdot x + (w_0 + w_1) \cdot w_{n-1}.$$

8. Bottom center:

$$x' = \frac{(w_{kx+1} - w_{kx}) \cdot x - w_{kx+1}}{(w_{kx+1} - w_{kx-1}) \cdot x - w_{kx+1} - w_{kx}},$$

$$y' = \frac{w_{n-1} \cdot y}{w_{n-2} \cdot y - w_{n-1}},$$

$$\begin{aligned} p_w =& ((w_{kx-1} - w_{k+1}) \cdot w_{n-2} \cdot x + (w_{kx+1} + w_{kx}) \cdot w_{n-2}) \cdot y \\ &+ (w_{kx-1} - w_{kx+1}) \cdot w_{n-1} \cdot x + (w_{kx+1} + w_{kx}) \cdot w_{n-1}. \end{aligned}$$

9. Bottom right:

$$x' = \frac{w_{n-1} \cdot x}{w_{n-2} \cdot x + w_{n-1}},$$

$$y' = \frac{w_{n-1} \cdot y}{w_{n-2} \cdot y + w_{n-1}},$$

$$p_w = (w_{n-2} \cdot w_{n-2} \cdot x - w_{n-1} \cdot w_{n-2}) \cdot y + w_{n-2} \cdot w_{n-1} \cdot x + w_{n-1} \cdot w_{n-1}.$$

Using these formulas, the separable filter can now be evaluated using only $(N-1) \times (N/2)$ PCF texture samples using Shader Model 4.0.

The shader in Listing 1.2 demonstrates an optimized implementation for Direct3D 10.0. This shader compiles to binary code that is only slightly slower than the shader in Listing 1.1. There is no reason not to use a separable shadow filter if the additional quality is needed.

```
//#Define SMAP_SIZE 512.
#define INV_SCALE ( 1.0 / SMAP_SIZE )

#define FILTER_SIZE 9 // 8x8 shadow map samples
#define FSH ( FILTER_SIZE/2 )

#if PCF_FILTER_SIZE == 9
static const float SG[9] = { 2,4,6,8,9,8,6,4,2 };
#endif
#if PCF_FILTER_SIZE == 7
static const float SG[7] = { 2,4,6,7,6,4,2 };
#endif
#if PCF_FILTER_SIZE == 5
static const float SG[5] = { 2,4,5,4,2 };
#endif
#if PCF_FILTER_SIZE == 3
static const float SG[3] = { 2,3,2 };
#endif

float shadow_fast_separable( float3 tc )
{
    float   s   = 0.0;
    float   pw;
    float   w= 0.0;
    float2  st;
    float2  stc = ( SMAP_SIZE * tc.xy ) + float2( 0.5, 0.5 );
    float2  tcs = floor( stc );
    float2  fc;
    int     row, col;

    fc    = stc - tcs;
    tc.xy = tc - ( fc * INV_SCALE );

    for( row = 0; row < FILTER_SIZE-1; ++row )
    {
       for( col = 0; col < FILTER_SIZE-1; ++col )
          w += SG[row]*SG[col];
    }

    for( row = -(FSH-1); row <= (FSH-1); row += 2 )
    {
       for( col = -(FSH-1); col <= (FSH-1); col += 2 )
```

```
{
   if( row == -(FSH-1) ) // Top row
{
  if( col == -(FSH-1) ) // Top left
  {
    pw=(SG[1]*SG[1]*fc.x-SG[1]*SG[1]-SG[0]*SG[1])*fc.y+
           (-SG[1]*SG[1]-SG[0]*SG[1])*fc.x+SG[1]*SG[1]+
           2*SG[0]*SG[1]+SG[0]*SG[1];
    st.x=((SG[1]-SG[0])*fc.x-SG[1])/(SG[1]*fc.x-
              SG[1]-SG[0]);
    st.y=((SG[1]-SG[0])*fc.y-SG[1])/(SG[1]*fc.y-
              SG[1]-SG[0]);
  }
  else if( col == (FSH-1) ) // Top right
  {
    pw=(-SG[1]*SG[FILTER_SIZE-2-1]*fc.x-
            SG[1]*SG[FILTER_SIZE-1-1])*fc.y+
           (SG[1]+SG[0])*SG[FILTER_SIZE-2-1]*fc.x+
           (SG[1]+SG[0])*SG[FILTER_SIZE-1-1];
    st.x=(SG[FILTER_SIZE-1-1]*fc.x)/
            (SG[FILTER_SIZE-2-1]*fc.x+SG[FILTER_SIZE-1-1]);
    st.y=((SG[1]-SG[0])*fc.y-SG[1])/
            (SG[1]*fc.y-SG[1]-SG[0]);
  }
  else // Top center
  {
    pw=((SG[1]*SG[col+(FSH-1)+1]-SG[1]*SG[col+
           (FSH-1)-1])*fc.x-SG[1]*
           SG[col+(FSH-1)+1]-SG[1]*SG[col+(FSH-1)])*
           fc.y+((-SG[1]-SG[0])*
           SG[col+(FSH-1)+1]+(SG[1]+SG[0])*SG[col+(FSH-1)
           -1])*fc.x+(SG[1]+SG[0])*SG[col+
           (FSH-1)+1]+(SG[1]+SG[0])*SG[col+(FSH-1)];
    st.x=((SG[col+(FSH-1)+1]-SG[col+(FSH-1)])*
              fc.x-SG[col+(FSH-1)+1])/
              ((SG[col+(FSH-1)+1]-SG[col+(FSH-1)-1])*
              fc.x-SG[col+(FSH-1)+1]-SG[col+(FSH-1)]);
    st.y=((SG[1]-SG[0])*fc.y-SG[1])/(SG[1]*
              fc.y-SG[1]-SG[0]);
  }
   }
   else if( row == (FSH-1) )  // Bottom row
{
  if( col == -(FSH-1) ) // Bottom left
  {
    pw=((SG[1]+SG[0])*SG[row+(FSH-1)-1]-
           SG[1]*SG[row+(FSH-1)-1]*fc.x)*fc.y-
           SG[1]*SG[row+(FSH-1)]*fc.x+
           (SG[1]+SG[0])*SG[row+(FSH-1)];
   st.x=((SG[1]-SG[0])*fc.x-SG[1])/(SG[1]*fc.x-SG[1]-
              SG[0]);
```

```
               st.y=(SG[row+(FSH-1)]*fc.y)/(SG[row+(FSH-1)-1]*
                       fc.y+SG[row+(FSH-1)]);
           }
           else if( col == (FSH-1) ) // Bottom right
           {
              pw=(SG[col+(FSH-1)-1]*SG[row+(FSH-1)-1]*
                      fc.x+SG[col+(FSH-1)]*SG[row+(FSH-1)-1])*fc.y+
                      SG[col+(FSH-1)-1]*SG[row+(FSH-1)]*fc.x+
                      SG[col+(FSH-1)]*SG[row+(FSH-1)];
              st.x=(SG[col+(FSH-1)]*fc.x)/(SG[col+(FSH-1)-1]*fc.x+
                      SG[col+(FSH-1)]);
              st.y=(SG[row+(FSH-1)]*fc.y)/(SG[row+(FSH-1)-1]*fc.y+
                      SG[row+(FSH-1)]);
           }
           else // Bottom center
           {
              pw=((SG[col+(FSH-1)-1]-SG[col+(FSH-1)+1])*
                      SG[row+(FSH-1)-1]*fc.x+(SG[col+(FSH-1)+1]+
                      SG[col+(FSH-1)])*SG[row+(FSH-1)-1])*fc.y+
                      (SG[col+(FSH-1)-1]-SG[col+(FSH-1)+1])*
                      SG[row+(FSH-1)]*fc.x+(SG[col+(FSH-1)+1]+
                      SG[col+(FSH-1)])*SG[row+(FSH-1)];
              st.x=((SG[col+(FSH-1)+1]-SG[col+(FSH-1)])*fc.x-
                      SG[col+(FSH-1)+1])/((SG[col+(FSH-1)+1]-
                      SG[col+(FSH-1)-1])*fc.x-SG[col+(FSH-1)+1]-
                      SG[col+(FSH-1)]);
              st.y=(SG[row+(FSH-1)]*fc.y)/
                      (SG[row+(FSH-1)-1]*fc.y+SG[row+(FSH-1)]);
           }
       }
   else // Center rows
   {
       if( col == -(FSH-1) ) // Center left
       {
          pw=((SG[1]*SG[row+(FSH-1)+1]-SG[1]*
                  SG[row+(FSH-1)-1])*fc.x+(-SG[1]-SG[0])*
                  SG[row+(FSH-1)+1]+(SG[1]+SG[0])*
                  SG[row+(FSH-1)-1])*fc.y+(-SG[1]*
                  SG[row+(FSH-1)+1]-SG[1]*SG[row+(FSH-1)])*
                  fc.x+(SG[1]+SG[0])*SG[row+(FSH-1)+1]+
                  (SG[1]+SG[0])*SG[row+(FSH-1)];
          st.x=((SG[1]-SG[0])*fc.x-SG[1])/(SG[1]*
                  fc.x-SG[1]-SG[0]);
          st.y=((SG[row+(FSH-1)+1]-SG[row+(FSH-1)])*
                  fc.y-SG[row+(FSH-1)+1])/
                  ((SG[row+(FSH-1)+1]-SG[row+(FSH-1)-1])*
                  fc.y-SG[row+(FSH-1)+1]-SG[row+(FSH-1)]);
       }
       else if( col == (FSH-1) ) // Center right
       {
          pw=((SG[col+(FSH-1)-1]*SG[row+(FSH-1)-1]-
```

```
                 SG[col+(FSH-1)-1]*SG[row+(FSH-1)+1])*
                 fc.x-SG[col+(FSH-1)]*SG[row+(FSH-1)+1]+
                 SG[col+(FSH-1)]*SG[row+(FSH-1)-1])*fc.y+
                 (SG[col+(FSH-1)-1]*SG[row+(FSH-1)+1]+
                 SG[col+(FSH-1)-1]*SG[row+(FSH-1)])*fc.x+
                 SG[col+(FSH-1)]*SG[row+(FSH-1)+1]+
                 SG[col+(FSH-1)]*SG[row+(FSH-1)];
        st.x=(SG[col+(FSH-1)]*fc.x/
                 (SG[col+(FSH-1)-1]*fc.x+SG[col+(FSH-1)]);
        st.y=((SG[row+(FSH-1)+1]-SG[row+(FSH-1)])*fc.y-
                 SG[row+(FSH-1)+1])/((SG[row+(FSH-1)+1]-
                 SG[row+(FSH-1)-1]*fc.y-SG[row+(FSH-1)+1]-
                 SG[row+(FSH-1)]);
      }
      else // Center center
      {
        pw=(((SG[col+(FSH-1)+1]-SG[col+(FSH-1)-1])*
                 SG[row+(FSH-1)+1]+(SG[col+(FSH-1)-1]-
                 SG[col+(FSH-1)+1])*SG[row+(FSH-1)-1])*
                 fc.x+(-SG[col+(FSH-1)+1]-
                 SG[col+(FSH-1)])*SG[row+(FSH-1)+1]+
                 (SG[col+(FSH-1)+1]+SG[col+(FSH-1)])*
                 SG[row+(FSH-1)-1])*fc.y+((SG[col+(FSH-1)-1]-
                 SG[col+(FSH-1)+1])*SG[row+(FSH-1)+1]+
                 (SG[col+(FSH-1)-1]-SG[col+(FSH-1)+1])*
                 SG[row+(FSH-1)])*fc.x+(SG[col+(FSH-1)+1]+
                 SG[col+(FSH-1)])*SG[row+(FSH-1)+1]+
                 (SG[col+(FSH-1)+1]+SG[col+(FSH-1)])*
                 SG[row+(FSH-1)];
        st.x=((SG[col+(FSH-1)+1]-SG[col+(FSH-1)])*fc.x-
                 SG[col+(FSH-1)+1])/((SG[col+(FSH-1)+1]-
                 SG[col+(FSH-1)-1]*fc.x-SG[col+(FSH-1)+1]-
                 SG[col+(FSH-1)]);
        st.y=((SG[row+(FSH-1)+1]-SG[row+(FSH-1)])*fc.y-
                 SG[row+(FSH-1)+1])/((SG[row+(FSH-1)+1]-
                 SG[row+(FSH-1)-1]*fc.y-SG[row+(FSH-1)+1]-
                 SG[row+(FSH-1)]);
      }
    }
    s+=pw*g_txShadowMap.SampleCmpLevelZero(g_samShadowMap,
          tc.xy + INV_SCALE * st, tc.z, int2( col, row ) ).x;
    }
  }
  return s/w;
}
```

Listing 1.2. Fast Shader Model 4.0 uniform shadow filter.

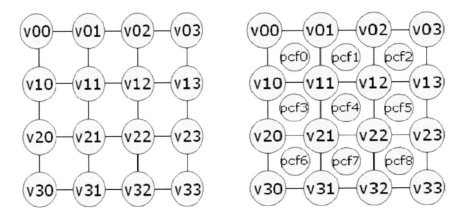

Figure 1.9. Uniformly smooth shadows.   **Figure 1.10.** Contact hardening shadows.

1.5   Nonseparable Unique Weights per PCF Result

Having covered uniform and separable shadow filters this section now looks at filters that are not separable. A nonseparable filter can be used in situations where the filter matrix is dynamic or is, e.g., used to embed the shape of the light source like in [Soler et al. 98].

Consider the 4×4 shadow map texel grid in Figure 1.9. Each v_{ij} is again a binary visibility [0 or 1] sample derived from the corresponding shadow map sample.

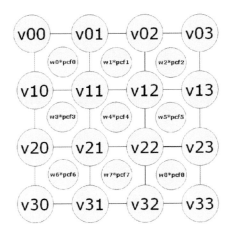

Figure 1.11. Weighted PCF.

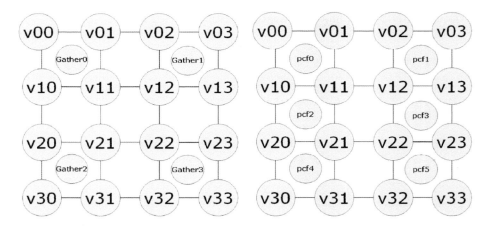

Figure 1.12. Shader Model 4.1/5.0 Implementation of filger shown in Figure 1.13.

Figure 1.13. Shifted Texture Coordinates and post PCF weights.

Now a uniform PCF filter collapses each 2×2 visibility information block to a PCF filtered visibility result PCF_k as shown in Figure 1.10.

A weights matrix now assigns a unique weight w_k to each PCF_k result so one arrives at the situation depicted in Figure 1.11.

The final filtered result (for $N \times N$ shadow map pixels) is then obtained by computing the term in Equation (1.4):

$$\frac{\sum_{k=0}^{(N-1)\cdot(N-1)} w_k \cdot PCF_k}{(N-1) \cdot (N-1)}. \tag{1.4}$$

Using Shader Model 4.1 or Shader Model 5.0 Equation (1.4) can be evaluated through some ALU work and $(N/2) \cdot (N/2)$ `Gather()` instructions as shown in Figure 1.12 for a 4×4 block of visibility results.

Again, the naive way to implement this using only Shader Model 4.0 would involve doing $(N-1) \cdot (N-1)$ PCF texture samples. There is a better way with again fewer PCF instructions as shown in Figure 1.13. Again, shifted texture coordinates and post PCF weights are used to achieve this.

To understand how this works, now consider only one row of visibility samples: v_k. Assigning weights w_k to each one-dimensional PCF result in that row produces the term shown in Equation (1.5). Here x is the sub-texel coordinate ranging from 0.0 to 1.0 (excluding 1.0):

$$\sum_{k=0}^{N-2} (1-x) \cdot v_k \cdot w_k + x \cdot v_{k+1} w_k. \tag{1.5}$$

Equation (1.5) simplifies to Equation (1.6):

$$(1-x) \cdot v_0 \cdot w_0 + \left(\sum_{k=1}^{N-2} v_k \cdot ((w_{k-1} - w_k) \cdot x + w_k) \right) + x \cdot v_{N-1} \cdot w_{N-2}. \quad (1.6)$$

To compute the shifted texture coordinates x' for PCF texture operations and post texturing weights wp, the following three cases need to be considered:

1. *Left border of the filter row.* The system of equations $(1 - x') \cdot wp \cdot v_0 = (1 - x) \cdot w_0 \cdot v_0$ and $x' \cdot wp \cdot v_1 = v_1 \cdot (x \cdot (w_0 - w_1) + w_1)$ is solved by $x' = \frac{(w_1 - w_0) \cdot x - w_1}{w_1 \cdot x - w_1 - w_0}$ and $wp = -w_1 \cdot x + w_1 + w_0$.

2. *Right border of the filter row.* The system of equations $(1 - x') \cdot wp \cdot v_{N-2} = v_{N-2} \cdot (x \cdot (w_{N-2} - w_{N-1}) + w_{N-1})$ and $x' \cdot wp \cdot v_{N-1} = x \cdot w_{N-1} \cdot v_{N-1}$ is solved by $x' = \frac{w_{N-1} \cdot x}{w_{N-2} \cdot x + w_{N-1}}$ and $wp = w_{N-2} \cdot x + w_{N-1}$.

3. *Central values of the filter row.* The system of equations $(1 - x') \cdot wp \cdot v_k = v_k \cdot (x \cdot (w_{k-1} - w_k) + w_k)$ and $x' \cdot wp \cdot v_{k+1} = v_{k+1} \cdot (x \cdot (w_k - w_{k+1}) + w_{k+1})$ is solved by $x' = \frac{(w_{k+1} - w_k) \cdot x - w_{k+1}}{(w_{k+1} - w_{k-1}) \cdot x - w_{k+1} - w_k}$ and $wp = (w_{k-1} - w_{k+1}) \cdot x + w_{k+1} + w_k$.

Using these formulas the filter can now be evaluated using only $(N-1) \times (N/2)$ PCF texture samples using Shader Model 4.0. The PCF samples do only use a modified x-component of the texture coordinates for sampling the shadow map. The y-component stays as it is.

1.6 Advanced Shadow Filtering Techniques

1.6.1 Light Shape-Dependent Shadows for Directional Lights

[Soler et al. 98] describe that a shadow that depends on the shape of the light source can be generated by convoluting an image of the light source and a shadow map. If one assumes that the shape of a light source is rotationally invariant and that the projected size of the light source does not change, one can embed the shape of the light source in the weights matrix used for shadow filtering. Since this weights matrix usually doesn't present a separable filter, one needs to carry out $(N/2) \times (N - 1)$ PCF instructions to carry out the "convolution" of light source and shadow.

Please note that Shader Model 4.1 and Shader Model 5.0 can again get away with $(N/2) \times (N/2)$ `Gather()` texture instructions.

Figures 1.14 and 1.15 show screen shots of a scene renderer with different filter/light shapes.

Figure 1.14. Screen shots of a scene renderer.

Figure 1.15. Screen shots of a scene renderer.

The shader shown in Listing 1.3 contains an implementation of light shape-dependent shadows for a range of light shapes.

```
#define FILTER_SIZE 9
#define GS  ( FILTER_SIZE )
#define GS2 ( FILTER_SIZE / 2 )

// Weight matrices that contain a weight for each pcf
// Result of each 2x2
// pixel block of the shadow map.

#define SM_FILTER_DISC          1
#define SM_FILTER_TRIANGLE        2
#define SM_FILTER_HALFMOON        3

#if FILTER_SIZE == 9
#if FILTER == SM_FILTER_HALFMOON
static const float W[9][9] = {
{ 0.2,1.0,1.0,1.0,1.0,0.0,0.0,0.0,0.0 },
{ 0.0,0.1,1.0,1.0,1.0,1.0,1.0,0.0,0.0 },
{ 0.0,0.0,0.0,0.5,1.0,1.0,1.0,1.0,0.0 },
{ 0.0,0.0,0.0,0.0,1.0,1.0,1.0,1.0,0.0 },
{ 0.0,0.0,0.0,0.0,0.5,1.0,1.0,1.0,0.5 },
{ 0.0,0.0,0.0,0.0,1.0,1.0,1.0,1.0,0.0 },
{ 0.0,0.0,0.0,0.5,1.0,1.0,1.0,0.0,0.0 },
{ 0.0,0.1,1.0,1.0,1.0,1.0,0.0,0.0,0.0 },
{ 0.2,1.0,1.0,1.0,1.0,0.0,0.0,0.0,0.0 }
};
#endif

#if FILTER == SM_FILTER_TRIANGLE
static const float W[9][9] = {
{ 0.0,0.0,0.0,0.0,1.0,0.0,0.0,0.0,0.0 },
{ 0.0,0.0,0.0,0.5,1.0,0.5,0.0,0.0,0.0 },
{ 0.0,0.0,0.0,1.0,1.0,1.0,0.0,0.0,0.0 },
{ 0.0,0.0,0.5,1.0,1.0,1.0,0.5,0.0,0.0 },
{ 0.0,0.0,1.0,1.0,1.0,1.0,1.0,0.0,0.0 },
{ 0.0,0.5,1.0,1.0,1.0,1.0,1.0,0.5,0.0 },
{ 0.0,1.0,1.0,1.0,1.0,1.0,1.0,1.0,0.0 },
{ 0.5,1.0,1.0,1.0,1.0,1.0,1.0,1.0,0.5 },
{ 1.0,1.0,1.0,1.0,1.0,1.0,1.0,1.0,1.0 }
};
#endif

#if FILTER == SM_FILTER_DISC
static const float W[9][9] = {
{ 0.0,0.0,0.0,0.5,1.0,0.5,0.0,0.0,0.0 },
{ 0.0,0.0,1.0,1.0,1.0,1.0,1.0,0.0,0.0 },
{ 0.0,1.0,1.0,1.0,1.0,1.0,1.0,1.0,0.0 },
{ 0.5,1.0,1.0,1.0,1.0,1.0,1.0,1.0,0.5 },
```

```
{ 1.0,1.0,1.0,1.0,1.0,1.0,1.0,1.0,1.0 },
{ 0.5,1.0,1.0,1.0,1.0,1.0,1.0,1.0,0.5 },
{ 0.0,1.0,1.0,1.0,1.0,1.0,1.0,1.0,0.0 },
{ 0.0,0.0,1.0,1.0,1.0,1.0,1.0,0.0,0.0 },
{ 0.0,0.0,0.0,0.5,1.0,0.5,0.0,0.0,0.0 }
};
#endif

#ifdef DX10_1
// 10.1 shader for one unique weight per pcf sample.
// Since it uses Gather(), only (N/2)x(N/2) texture ops
// are necessary. This runs as fast as the uniform or
// separable filter under 10.0.
float shadow_dx10_1( float3 tc )
{
    float4 s = (0.0).xxxx;
    float2 stc = ( SMAP_SIZE * tc.xy ) + float2( 0.5, 0.5 );
    float2 tcs = floor( stc );
    float2 fc;
    int    row;
    int    col;
    float  w = 0.0;
    float4 v1[ GS2 + 1 ];
    float2 v0[ GS2 + 1 ];

    fc.xy = stc - tcs;
    tc.xy = tcs * INV_SCALE;

    for( row = 0; row < GS; ++row )
    {
        for( col = 0; col < GS; ++col )
            w += W[row][col];
    }

    // Loop over the rows.
    for( row = -GS2; row <= GS2; row += 2 )
    {
[unroll]for( col = -GS2; col <= GS2; col += 2 )
    {
      float fSumOfWeights = W[row+GS2][col+GS2];

      if( col > -GS2 )
        fSumOfWeights += W[row+GS2][col+GS2-1];

      if( col < GS2 )
        fSumOfWeights += W[row+GS2][col+GS2+1];

      if( row > -GS2 )
      {
        fSumOfWeights += W[row+GS2-1][col+GS2];
```

```
    if( col < GS2 )
      fSumOfWeights += W[row+GS2-1][col+GS2+1];

  if( col > -GS2 )
    fSumOfWeights += W[row+GS2-1][col+GS2-1];


}

if( fSumOfWeights != 0.0 )
  v1[(col+GS2)/2]=( tc.zzzz <= g_txShadowMap.Gather(
                            g_samPoint, tc.xy,
                            int2( col, row ) ) ) ?
                        (1.0).xxxx : (0.0).xxxx;
else
   v1[(col+GS2)/2] = (0.0f).xxxx;

   if( col == -GS2 )
   {
s.x += ( 1 - fc.y ) * ( v1[0].w *
            ( W[row+GS2][col+GS2] -
              W[row+GS2][col+GS2] * fc.x ) +
          v1[0].z * ( fc.x * (
              W[row+GS2][col+GS2] -
              W[row+GS2][col+GS2+1] ) +
              W[row+GS2][col+GS2+1] ) );
   s.y += (     fc.y ) * ( v1[0].x *
            ( W[row+GS2][col+GS2] -
              W[row+GS2][col+GS2] * fc.x ) +
          v1[0].y * ( fc.x * ( W[row+GS2][col+GS2] -
              W[row+GS2][col+GS2+1] ) +
              W[row+GS2][col+GS2+1] ) );
  if( row > -GS2 )
  {
    s.z += ( 1 - fc.y ) * ( v0[0].x *
            ( W[row+GS2-1][col+GS2] -
              W[row+GS2-1][col+GS2] * fc.x ) +
      v0[0].y * ( fc.x * ( W[row+GS2-1][col+GS2] -
              W[row+GS2-1][col+GS2+1] ) +
              W[row+GS2-1][col+GS2+1] ) );
    s.w += (     fc.y ) * ( v1[0].w *
            ( W[row+GS2-1][col+GS2] -
              W[row+GS2-1][col+GS2] * fc.x ) +
      v1[0].z * ( fc.x * ( W[row+GS2-1][col+GS2] -
              W[row+GS2-1][col+GS2+1] ) +
              W[row+GS2-1][col+GS2+1] ) );
  }
   }
   else if( col == GS2 )
   {
s.x += ( 1 - fc.y ) * ( v1[GS2].w * ( fc.x *
            ( W[row+GS2][col+GS2-1] -
```

```
                       W[row+GS2][col+GS2] ) +
                       W[row+GS2][col+GS2] ) +
               v1[GS2].z * fc.x * W[row+GS2][col+GS2] );
    s.y += (        fc.y ) * ( v1[GS2].x * ( fc.x *
                   ( W[row+GS2][col+GS2-1] -
                     W[row+GS2][col+GS2] ) +
                     W[row+GS2][col+GS2] ) +
               v1[GS2].y * fc.x * W[row+GS2][col+GS2] );

   if( row > -GS2 )
   {
     s.z += ( 1 - fc.y ) * ( v0[GS2].x * ( fc.x *
             ( W[row+GS2-1][col+GS2-1] -
               W[row+GS2-1][col+GS2] ) +
               W[row+GS2-1][col+GS2] ) +
          v0[GS2].y * fc.x * W[row+GS2-1][col+GS2] );
     s.w += (        fc.y ) * ( v1[GS2].w * ( fc.x *
                 ( W[row+GS2-1][col+GS2-1] -
                   W[row+GS2-1][col+GS2] ) +
                   W[row+GS2-1][col+GS2] ) +
            v1[GS2].z * fc.x * W[row+GS2-1][col+GS2] );
   }
       else
       {
     s.x += ( 1 - fc.y ) * ( v1[(col+GS2)/2].w *
                 ( fc.x * ( W[row+GS2][col+GS2-1] -
                 W[row+GS2][col+GS2+0] ) +
                 W[row+GS2][col+GS2+0] ) +
                 v1[(col+GS2)/2].z * ( fc.x *
                 ( W[row+GS2][col+GS2-0] -
                   W[row+GS2][col+GS2+1] ) +
                   W[row+GS2][col+GS2+1] ) );
     s.y += (        fc.y ) * ( v1[(col+GS2)/2].x * ( fc.x *
                 ( W[row+GS2][col+GS2-1] -
                   W[row+GS2][col+GS2+0] ) +
                   W[row+GS2][col+GS2+0] ) +
          v1[(col+GS2)/2].y * ( fc.x *
                 ( W[row+GS2][col+GS2-0] -
                   W[row+GS2][col+GS2+1] ) +
                   W[row+GS2][col+GS2+1] ) );
   if( row > -GS2 )
   {
     s.z += ( 1 - fc.y ) * ( v0[(col+GS2)/2].x * ( fc.x *
                 ( W[row+GS2-1][col+GS2-1] -
                   W[row+GS2-1][col+GS2+0] ) +
                   W[row+GS2-1][col+GS2+0] ) +
          v0[(col+GS2)/2].y * ( fc.x *
                 ( W[row+GS2-1][col+GS2-0] -
                   W[row+GS2-1][col+GS2+1] ) +
                   W[row+GS2-1][col+GS2+1] ) );
     s.w += (        fc.y ) * ( v1[(col+GS2)/2].w * ( fc.x *
```

```
                                    (  W[row+GS2-1][col+GS2-1]  -
                                       W[row+GS2-1][col+GS2+0]  )  +
                                       W[row+GS2-1][col+GS2+0]  )  +
                    v1[(col+GS2)/2].z * ( fc.x *
                                    (  W[row+GS2-1][col+GS2-0]  -
                                       W[row+GS2-1][col+GS2+1]  )  +
                                       W[row+GS2-1][col+GS2+1]  )  );
         }
          }

    if( row != GS2 )
      v0[(col+GS2)/2] = v1[(col+GS2)/2].xy;
      }
    }

    return dot(s,(1.0).xxxx)/w;
}

#endif
// 10.0 shader for one unique weight per pcf sample.
// This shader makes use of
// shifted texture coords and post weights to reduce
// the texture op counts for dx10.0.
// Without this trick, a naive implementation would need
// (N-1)x(N-1) pcf samples.
// This shader only does (N/2)x(N-1) pcf samples instead.
float shadow_dx10_0( float3 tc )
{
    float   s   = 0.0;
    float2 stc = ( SMAP_SIZE * tc.xy ) + float2( 0.5, 0.5 );
    float2 tcs = floor( stc );
    float2 fc;
    int    row;
    int    col;
    float  w = 0.0;

    fc     = stc - tcs;
    tc.xy  = tc - ( fc * INV_SCALE );
    fc.y   *= INV_SCALE;

    for( row = 0; row < GS; ++row )
    {
       for( col = 0; col < GS; ++col )
          w += W[row][col];
    }

    for( row = 0; row < GS; ++row )
    {
       [unroll]for( col = -GS2; col <= GS2; col += 2 )
       {
    if( col == -GS2 )
```

```
{
   if( W[row][col+GS2+1] != 0 ||  W[row][col+GS2] != 0 )
      {
      s += ( ( 1.0 - fc.x ) * W[row][col+GS2+1] +
               W[row][col+GS2] ) *
               g_txShadowMap.SampleCmpLevelZero(
               g_samShadowMap, tc.xy +
               float2( g_vShadowMapSize.z * ( (
               W[row][col+GS2+1] - fc.x * ( W[row][col+GS2+1]
               - W[row][col+GS2] ) ) / ( ( 1.0 - fc.x ) *
               W[row][col+GS2+1] + W[row][col+GS2] ) ),
               fc.y ), tc.z, int2( col, row - GS2 ) ).x;
      }
   else if( col == GS2 )
   {
      if( W[row][col+GS2-1] != 0 ||  W[row][col+GS2] != 0 )
      s += ( fc.x * W[row][col+GS2-1] +
               W[row][col+GS2] ) *
               g_txShadowMap.SampleCmpLevelZero(
               g_samShadowMap, tc.xy +
               float2( g_vShadowMapSize.z * ( ( fc.x *
               W[row][col+GS2] ) / ( fc.x  *
               W[row][col+GS2-1] + W[row][col+GS2] ) ),
               fc.y ), tc.z, int2( col, row - GS2 ) ).x;
   }
   else
   {
      if( ( W[row][col+GS2-1] - W[row][col+GS2+1] ) != 0
            || ( W[row][col+GS2] + W[row][col+GS2+1] ) != 0 )
      s += ( fc.x * ( W[row][col+GS2-1] -
               W[row][col+GS2+1] ) + W[row][col+GS2] +
               W[row][col+GS2+1] ) *
               g_txShadowMap.SampleCmpLevelZero(
               g_samShadowMap, tc.xy +
               float2( g_vShadowMapSize.z *
               ( ( W[row][col+GS2+1] - fc.x *
               ( W[row][col+GS2+1] - W[row][col+GS2] ) ) ) /
               ( fc.x * ( W[row][col+GS2-1] -
               W[row][col+GS2+1] ) + W[row][col+GS2] +
               W[row][col+GS2+1] ) ), fc.y ),
               tc.z, int2( col, row - GS2 ) ).x;
   }
   }
   }
   return s/w;
}
```

Listing 1.3. Light shape-dependent shadow filters.

1.6.2   Contact Hardening Shadows

In order to achieve physically plausible shadows, percentage closer soft shadows
(PCSS) [Fernando 05] were introduced as a real-time method to achieve contact
hardening shadows. Typical implementations of PCSS however suffer from noise
and banding artifacts that result from the use of a poisson disk of samples. This
book introduces a new technique [Gumbau et al. 10] that improves PCSS and
removes the artifacts of the original algorithm. However, as previously stated, it
is not considered a conventional shadow filtering technique as it adds additional
rendering passes and cannot just be dropped into a game engine instead of a
normal PCF-based filter.

The shader in Listing 1.4 now uses a large box (12×12) of shadow map
samples in combination with a non-stationary filter weights matrix to achieve a
transition from sharp to soft shadows. The sample accepts the fact that one needs
to limit the size of the light source in order to achieve high quality results. Since
the sun can usually be treated as a relatively small light source the technique
works well for a directional light.

Figure 1.16. Screenshot of the example in the DirectX SDK with soft shadows.

The Shader Model 5.0 instructions `GatherRed()` and `GatherCmpRed()` are used to accelerate the computation of average-blocker-depth and to accelerate the non-stationary and nonseparable dynamic filter operation.

The screen shots in Figures 1.16 and 1.17 show the difference between shadows that are equally smooth everywhere and shadows that get harder at contact regions.

Blocker search. The search for blockers for an $N \times N$ shadow map filter footprint is carried out using only $(N/2) \times (N/2)$ `GatherRed()` operations. The shader performs 36 of these instructions. A Shader Model 4.0 implementation would need to perform 144 point samples in order to obtain the same information.

Filtering with a dynamic filter matrix. Based on the average blocker depth and the size of the light source, a factor between 0.0 (sharp) to 1.0 (completely blurry) is computed. This factor is used to compute a dynamic weight matrix that results from feeding four matrices into a cubic Bezier function. The math presented above is used to compute the filter, reducing the necessary ALU through the use of `Gat` of `GatherCmpRed()`. Note that the shader from Listing 1.4 can be modified to perform the dynamic filter under Shader Model 4.0 with a reduced set of texture ops.

Figure 1.17. Screenshot of the example in the DirectX SDK without soft shadows.

```
#define FILTER_SIZE    11
#define FS   FILTER_SIZE
#define FS2 ( FILTER_SIZE / 2 )

// Four control matrices for a dynamic cubic bezier filter
// weights matrix.

static const float C3[11][11] =
{ { 1.0,1.0,1.0,1.0,1.0,1.0,1.0,1.0,1.0,1.0,1.0 },
  { 1.0,1.0,1.0,1.0,1.0,1.0,1.0,1.0,1.0,1.0,1.0 },
  { 1.0,1.0,1.0,1.0,1.0,1.0,1.0,1.0,1.0,1.0,1.0 },
  { 1.0,1.0,1.0,1.0,1.0,1.0,1.0,1.0,1.0,1.0,1.0 },
  { 1.0,1.0,1.0,1.0,1.0,1.0,1.0,1.0,1.0,1.0,1.0 },
  { 1.0,1.0,1.0,1.0,1.0,1.0,1.0,1.0,1.0,1.0,1.0 },
  { 1.0,1.0,1.0,1.0,1.0,1.0,1.0,1.0,1.0,1.0,1.0 },
  { 1.0,1.0,1.0,1.0,1.0,1.0,1.0,1.0,1.0,1.0,1.0 },
  { 1.0,1.0,1.0,1.0,1.0,1.0,1.0,1.0,1.0,1.0,1.0 },
  { 1.0,1.0,1.0,1.0,1.0,1.0,1.0,1.0,1.0,1.0,1.0 },
  { 1.0,1.0,1.0,1.0,1.0,1.0,1.0,1.0,1.0,1.0,1.0 },
};

static const float C2[11][11] =
{ { 0.0,0.0,0.0,0.0,0.0,0.0,0.0,0.0,0.0,0.0,0.0 },
  { 0.0,0.2,0.2,0.2,0.2,0.2,0.2,0.2,0.2,0.2,0.0 },
  { 0.0,0.2,1.0,1.0,1.0,1.0,1.0,1.0,1.0,0.2,0.0 },
  { 0.0,0.2,1.0,1.0,1.0,1.0,1.0,1.0,1.0,0.2,0.0 },
  { 0.0,0.2,1.0,1.0,1.0,1.0,1.0,1.0,1.0,0.2,0.0 },
  { 0.0,0.2,1.0,1.0,1.0,1.0,1.0,1.0,1.0,0.2,0.0 },
  { 0.0,0.2,1.0,1.0,1.0,1.0,1.0,1.0,1.0,0.2,0.0 },
  { 0.0,0.2,1.0,1.0,1.0,1.0,1.0,1.0,1.0,0.2,0.0 },
  { 0.0,0.2,1.0,1.0,1.0,1.0,1.0,1.0,1.0,0.2,0.0 },
  { 0.0,0.2,0.2,0.2,0.2,0.2,0.2,0.2,0.2,0.2,0.0 },
  { 0.0,0.0,0.0,0.0,0.0,0.0,0.0,0.0,0.0,0.0,0.0 },
};

static const float C1[11][11] =
{ { 0.0,0.0,0.0,0.0,0.0,0.0,0.0,0.0,0.0,0.0,0.0 },
  { 0.0,0.0,0.0,0.0,0.0,0.0,0.0,0.0,0.0,0.0,0.0 },
  { 0.0,0.0,0.2,0.2,0.2,0.2,0.2,0.2,0.2,0.0,0.0 },
  { 0.0,0.0,0.2,1.0,1.0,1.0,1.0,1.0,0.2,0.0,0.0 },
  { 0.0,0.0,0.2,1.0,1.0,1.0,1.0,1.0,0.2,0.0,0.0 },
  { 0.0,0.0,0.2,1.0,1.0,1.0,1.0,1.0,0.2,0.0,0.0 },
  { 0.0,0.0,0.2,1.0,1.0,1.0,1.0,1.0,0.2,0.0,0.0 },
  { 0.0,0.0,0.2,1.0,1.0,1.0,1.0,1.0,0.2,0.0,0.0 },
  { 0.0,0.0,0.2,0.2,0.2,0.2,0.2,0.2,0.2,0.0,0.0 },
  { 0.0,0.0,0.0,0.0,0.0,0.0,0.0,0.0,0.0,0.0,0.0 },
  { 0.0,0.0,0.0,0.0,0.0,0.0,0.0,0.0,0.0,0.0,0.0 },
};

static const float C0[11][11] =
```

```
{ { 0.0,0.0,0.0,0.0,0.0,0.0,0.0,0.0,0.0,0.0,0.0 },
  { 0.0,0.0,0.0,0.0,0.0,0.0,0.0,0.0,0.0,0.0,0.0 },
  { 0.0,0.0,0.0,0.0,0.0,0.0,0.0,0.0,0.0,0.0,0.0 },
  { 0.0,0.0,0.0,0.0,0.0,0.0,0.0,0.0,0.0,0.0,0.0 },
  { 0.0,0.0,0.0,0.0,0.8,0.8,0.8,0.0,0.0,0.0,0.0 },
  { 0.0,0.0,0.0,0.0,0.8,1.0,0.8,0.0,0.0,0.0,0.0 },
  { 0.0,0.0,0.0,0.0,0.8,0.8,0.8,0.0,0.0,0.0,0.0 },
  { 0.0,0.0,0.0,0.0,0.0,0.0,0.0,0.0,0.0,0.0,0.0 },
  { 0.0,0.0,0.0,0.0,0.0,0.0,0.0,0.0,0.0,0.0,0.0 },
  { 0.0,0.0,0.0,0.0,0.0,0.0,0.0,0.0,0.0,0.0,0.0 },
  { 0.0,0.0,0.0,0.0,0.0,0.0,0.0,0.0,0.0,0.0,0.0 },
};

// Compute dynamic weight at a certain row, column of the matrix.
float Fw( int r, int c, float fL )
{
    return (1.0-fL)*(1.0-fL)*(1.0-fL) * C0[r][c] +
           fL*fL*fL * C3[r][c] +
           3.0f * (1.0-fL)*(1.0-fL)*fL * C1[r][c]+
           3.0f * fL*fL*(1.0-fL) * C2[r][c];
}


#define BLOCKER_FILTER_SIZE    11
#define BFS   BLOCKER_FILTER_SIZE
#define BFS2 ( BLOCKER_FILTER_SIZE / 2 )
#define SUN_WIDTH g_fSunWidth


//================================================================
// This shader computes the contact hardening shadow filter.
//================================================================
float shadow( float3 tc )
{
    float   s   = 0.0f;
    float2 stc = ( g_vShadowMapDimensions.xy * tc.xy ) +
                   float2( 0.5, 0.5 );
    float2 tcs = floor( stc );
    float2 fc;
    int    row;
    int    col;
    float  w = 0.0;
    float  avgBlockerDepth = 0;
    float  blockerCount = 0;
    float  fRatio;
    float4 v1[ FS2 + 1 ];
    float2 v0[ FS2 + 1 ];
    float2 off;

    fc     = stc - tcs;
    tc.xy  = tc - ( fc * g_vShadowMapDimensions.zw );

    // Find number of blockers and sum up blocker depth.
```

```
for( row = -BFS2; row <= BFS2; row += 2 )
{
    for( col = -BFS2; col <= BFS2; col += 2 )
    {
        float4 d4 = g_txShadowMap.GatherRed( g_SamplePoint,
                     tc.xy, int2( col, row ) );
        float4 b4= ( tc.zzzz <= d4 ) ?
                     (0.0).xxxx : (1.0).xxxx;

        blockerCount += dot( b4, (1.0).xxxx );
        avgBlockerDepth += dot( d4, b4 );
    }
}

// Compute ratio using formulas from PCSS.
if( blockerCount > 0.0 )
{
    avgBlockerDepth /= blockerCount;
    fRatio = saturate( ( ( tc.z - avgBlockerDepth ) *
             SUN_WIDTH ) / avgBlockerDepth );
    fRatio *= fRatio;
}
else
{
    fRatio = 0.0;
}

// Sum up weights of dynamic filter matrix.
for( row = 0; row < FS; ++row )
{
    for( col = 0; col < FS; ++col )
    {
        w += Fw(row,col,fRatio);
    }
}

// Filter shadow map samples using the dynamic weights.
[unroll(FILTER_SIZE)]for( row = -FS2; row <= FS2; row += 2 )
{
  for( col = -FS2; col <= FS2; col += 2 )
  {
    v1[(col+FS2)/2] = g_txShadowMap.GatherCmpRed(
                      g_SamplePointCmp, tc.xy, tc.z,
                      int2( col, row ) );

        if( col == -FS2 )
        {
          s += ( 1 - fc.y ) * ( v1[0].w *
              ( Fw(row+FS2,0,fRatio) -
              Fw(row+FS2,0,fRatio) * fc.x ) + v1[0].z *
              ( fc.x * ( Fw(row+FS2,0,fRatio) -
```

```
                  Fw(row+FS2,1,fRatio) ) +
                  Fw(row+FS2,1,fRatio) ) );
          s += (      fc.y ) * ( v1[0].x * (
                  Fw(row+FS2,0,fRatio) -
                  Fw(row+FS2,0,fRatio) * fc.x ) +
                  v1[0].y * ( fc.x*( Fw(row+FS2,0,fRatio) -
                  Fw(row+FS2,1,fRatio) ) +
                  Fw(row+FS2,1,fRatio) ) );
      if( row > -FS2 )
      {
        s += ( 1 - fc.y ) * ( v0[0].x *
              ( Fw(row+FS2-1,0,fRatio) -
                Fw(row+FS2-1,0,fRatio) * fc.x ) +
                v0[0].y *
              ( fc.x * ( Fw(row+FS2-1,0,fRatio) -
                Fw(row+FS2-1,1,fRatio) ) +
                Fw(row+FS2-1,1,fRatio) ) );
          s += (      fc.y ) * ( v1[0].w *
              ( Fw(row+FS2-1,0,fRatio) -
                Fw(row+FS2-1,0,fRatio) * fc.x ) +
                v1[0].z *
              ( fc.x * ( Fw(row+FS2-1,0,fRatio) -
                Fw(row+FS2-1,1,fRatio) ) +
                Fw(row+FS2-1,1,fRatio) ) );
      }
  }
  else if( col == FS2 )
  {
    s += ( 1 - fc.y ) * ( v1[FS2].w * ( fc.x *
          ( Fw(row+FS2,FS-2,fRatio) -
            Fw(row+FS2,FS-1,fRatio) ) +
            Fw(row+FS2,FS-1,fRatio) ) + v1[FS2].z * fc.x *
            Fw(row+FS2,FS-1,fRatio) );
    s += (      fc.y ) * ( v1[FS2].x * ( fc.x *
          ( Fw(row+FS2,FS-2,fRatio) -
            Fw(row+FS2,FS-1,fRatio) ) +
            Fw(row+FS2,FS-1,fRatio) ) + v1[FS2].y *
            fc.x*
            Fw(row+FS2,FS-1,fRatio) );
    if( row > -FS2 )
    {
      s += ( 1 - fc.y ) * ( v0[FS2].x * ( fc.x *
            ( Fw(row+FS2-1,FS-2,fRatio) -
              Fw(row+FS2-1,FS-1,fRatio) ) +
              Fw(row+FS2-1,FS-1,fRatio) ) +
              v0[FS2].y*fc.x * Fw(row+FS2-1,FS-1,fRatio) );
      s += (      fc.y ) * ( v1[FS2].w * ( fc.x *
            ( Fw(row+FS2-1,FS-2,fRatio) -
              Fw(row+FS2-1,FS-1,fRatio) ) +
              Fw(row+FS2-1,FS-1,fRatio) ) +
              v1[FS2].z*fc.x*Fw(row+FS2-1,FS-1,fRatio) );
```

```
                    }
                }
                else
                {
                  s += ( 1 - fc.y ) * ( v1[(col+FS2)/2].w * ( fc.x *
                         ( Fw(row+FS2,col+FS2-1,fRatio) -
                           Fw(row+FS2,col+FS2+0,fRatio) ) +
                           Fw(row+FS2,col+FS2+0,fRatio) ) +
                           v1[(col+FS2)/2].z * ( fc.x *
                         ( Fw(row+FS2,col+FS2-0,fRatio) -
                           Fw(row+FS2,col+FS2+1,fRatio) ) +
                           Fw(row+FS2,col+FS2+1,fRatio) ) );
                  s += (     fc.y ) * ( v1[(col+FS2)/2].x * ( fc.x *
                         ( Fw(row+FS2,col+FS2-1,fRatio) -
                           Fw(row+FS2,col+FS2+0,fRatio) ) +
                           Fw(row+FS2,col+FS2+0,fRatio) ) +
                           v1[(col+FS2)/2].y * ( fc.x *
                         ( Fw(row+FS2,col+FS2-0,fRatio) -
                           Fw(row+FS2,col+FS2+1,fRatio) ) +
                           Fw(row+FS2,col+FS2+1,fRatio) ) );
                  if( row > -FS2 )
                  {
                    s += ( 1 - fc.y ) * ( v0[(col+FS2)/2].x * ( fc.x *
                           ( Fw(row+FS2-1,col+FS2-1,fRatio) -
                             Fw(row+FS2-1,col+FS2+0,fRatio) ) +
                             Fw(row+FS2-1,col+FS2+0,fRatio) ) +
                             v0[(col+FS2)/2].y * ( fc.x *
                           ( Fw(row+FS2-1,col+FS2-0,fRatio) -
                             Fw(row+FS2-1,col+FS2+1,fRatio) ) +
                             Fw(row+FS2-1,col+FS2+1,fRatio) ) );
                    s += (     fc.y ) * ( v1[(col+FS2)/2].w * ( fc.x *
                           ( Fw(row+FS2-1,col+FS2-1,fRatio) -
                             Fw(row+FS2-1,col+FS2+0,fRatio) ) +
                             Fw(row+FS2-1,col+FS2+0,fRatio) ) +
                             v1[(col+FS2)/2].z * ( fc.x *
                           ( Fw(row+FS2-1,col+FS2-0,fRatio) -
                             Fw(row+FS2-1,col+FS2+1,fRatio) ) +
                             Fw(row+FS2-1,col+FS2+1,fRatio) ) );
                  }
                }

                if( row != FS2 )
                {
                    v0[(col+FS2)/2] = v1[(col+FS2)/2].xy;
                }
            }
        }
    }
    return s/w;
}
```

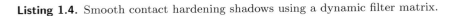

Listing 1.4. Smooth contact hardening shadows using a dynamic filter matrix.

Bibliography

[Annen et al. 07] Thomas Annen, Tom Mertens, Philippe Bekaert, Hans-Peter Seidel, and Jan Kautz. "Convolution Shadow Maps." *Eurographics Symposium on Rendering* 18 (2007).

[Donnelly et al. 06] William Donnelly and Andrew Lauritzen. "Variance Shadow Maps." *SI3D '06: Proceedings of the 2006 Symposium on Interactive 3D Graphics and Games* (2006), 161–165.

[Dmitriev et al. 07] Kirill Dmitriev and Yury Uralsky. "Soft Shadows Using Hierarchical Min-Max Shadow Maps." Presented at Game Developers Conference, San Francisco, March 5–9, 2007. Available at http://developer.download.nvidia.com/presentations/2007/gdc/SoftShadows.pdf.

[Fernando 05] Randima Fernando. "Percentage-Closer Soft Shadows." *International Conference on Computer Graphics and Interactive Techniques* 35 (2005). Available at http://download.nvidia.com/developer/presentations/2005/GDC/Sponsored_Day/Percentage_Closer_Soft_Shadows.pdf.

[Gruen 07] Holger Gruen. "Approximate Cumulative Distribution Function Shadow Mapping." In *ShaderX6 Advanced Rendering Techniques*, edited by Wolfgang Engel. Boston: Charles River Media, 2007, 239–256.

[Gumbau et al. 10] Jesus Gumbau, Miguel Chover, and Mateu Sbert. "Screen-Space Soft Shadows." In *GPUPro Advanced Rendering Techniques*, edited by Wolfgang Engel. Natick, MA: A K Peters, 2010.

[Soler et al. 98] C. Solor and F. Sillion,. "Fast Calculation of Soft Shadow Textures Using Convolution." *Computer Graphics (SIGGRAPH '98 Proceedings)* (1998): 321–32.

[Williams 78] Lance Williams. "Casting curved shadows on curved surfaces." *Computer Graphics (SIGGRAPH '78 Proceedings)* 12 (1978): 270–274.

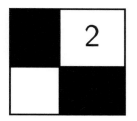

Hybrid Min/Max Plane-Based Shadow Maps
Holger Gruen

2.1 Overview

This chapter presents how to derive a secondary texture from a normal depth-only shadow map. This secondary texture can be used to heavily speed up expensive shadow filtering with big filter footprints. It stores hybrid data in the form of either a plane equation or min/max depth for a two-dimensional block of pixels in the original shadow map. The technique is specifically suited to speeding up shadow filtering in the context of big filter footprint and forward rendering, e.g., when the shadow filtering cost increases with the depth complexity of the scene.

2.2 Introduction

Hierarchical min/max shadow maps [Dmitriev at al. 07] were introduced in order to quickly (hierarchically) reject or accept sub-blocks in a shadow filter footprint that are in full light or in full shadow. For these sub-blocks no additional expensive texture lookup or filtering operations are necessary and this helps to greatly increase the speed of filtering.

Walking the min/max shadow hierarchy does add to the texturing cost. Ideally the texture operations count for quick rejections should be as low as possible. Also min/max shadow maps tend to not always quickly reject pixel blocks for flat features like floor polygons. This is especially true if one pixel in the min/max shadow map maps to a quadrangle of on-screen pixels. To be quickly rejected, one of these on-screen pixels has to either be in front of the minimum depth or behind the maximum depth. Without a big depth bias and all its associated problems

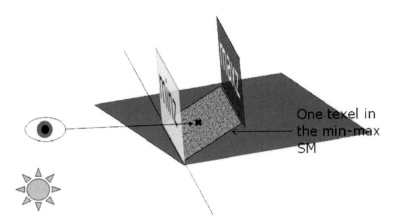

Figure 2.1. One min/max shadow map pixel (noisy quadrangle) can map to many on-screen pixels.

a pixel can usually only be rejected after a deep descent down the min/max hierarchy. This situation is depicted in Figure 2.1.

In order to remedy these shortcomings, this chapter first proposes flattening the min/max texture hierarchy from [Dmitriev at al. 07] to just one min/max texture T that contains the min/max depth data for a block of texels of the original shadow map. This block should be big enough to ideally allow for min/max rejections for all texels of the original shadow map that fall into the block with only one texture lookup.

To also get around losing the quick rejections for planar features, T is used to either store min/max depth data or a plane equation. The plane equation is stored if the block of shadow map pixels that is considered for constructing one min/max pixel lies within a plane. The plane equation allows to decide if a pixel is in front or behind a plane and does not suffer from the need for a high depth bias. Because T stores min/max depth or a plane equation it can be called a *hybrid min/max plane shadow map* (HPSM). A simple form of HPSM has been introduced in [Lobanchikov et al. 09].

The remainder of the text will discuss how to construct an HPSM, how to use the HPSM to quickly reject expensive filter operations, and other uses for HPSMs.

2.3 Construction of an HPSM

If one wants to construct an HPSM from a shadow map, the first thing to decide is what dimension to chose for the HPSM. A typical choice could be to make it 1/4 of the width and 1/4 of the height of the original shadow map.

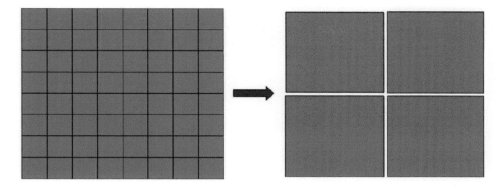

Figure 2.2. A shadow map (left) is converted into an HPSM that is 1/16 the size of the shadow map.

This means that a naive algorithm to construct the HPSM is to just collapse 4 × 4 texels of the shadow map into one pixel of the HPSM (see Figure 2.2).

Unfortunately, since the filter footprint of a shadow filter can also touch neighboring pixels this may not be enough to construct the most efficient HPSM for quickly rejecting pixels as fully lit or fully shadowed. Figure 2.3 shows that with a naive construction method several texture fetches are necessary to get the data for all HPSM texels that touch the shadow map filter.

The target is to get down to only one texture fetch for quick rejections. One solution to reach that target is to not only look at a 4 × 4 block of texels but extend this block on all sides (top, bottom, left and right) by half of the size of the shadow filtering kernel as depicted in Figure 2.4.

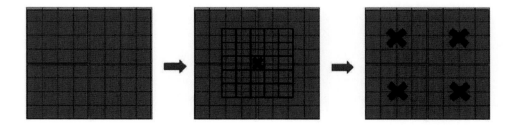

Figure 2.3. A shadow map (left) is converted into an HPSM. The filter footprint of the shadow filter touches more than just one HPSM texel (middle). Instead it can touch four or more neighboring HPSM texels (right).

Figure 2.4. One of the HPSM pixels covering 4×4 shadow pixels is highlighted (left). Extending the box from 4×4 to 10×10 (middle) makes sure that the shadow filter footprint always stays inside the support of the HPSM pixel (right).

It is obvious that one needs to consider quite a lot of shadow map texels to create an HPSM that can reject pixels with only one texture instruction. This can make HPSM construction expensive if only Shader Model 4.0 instructions are available. Direct3D 10.1 and Direct3D 11 support the `Gather()` instruction, which can speed up HPSM instruction enormously since one texture instruction can get four depth values from the shadow map. Further, using Compute Shaders under Direct3D 11 allows facilitating the thread shared memory that significantly speeds up HPSM construction for overlapping construction kernels.

Computing min/max depth of a box of pixels is trivial. How about detecting a plane equation? One way to do this is to convert each shadow map depth value of the construction texel block back to linear a three-dimensional space, e.g., light view camera space:

$$Q = \frac{Z_f}{Z_f - Z_n}, w = \cot\left(\frac{\text{fov}_w}{2}\right), h = \cot\left(\frac{\text{fov}_h}{2}\right).$$
$$Z_{\text{cam}} = \frac{-Q \cdot Z_n}{Z_{\text{sm}} - Q}. \tag{2.1}$$

Equation (2.1) shows how to convert from shadow map depth (Z_{sm}) back to linear light space depth Z_{cam} for a perspective light view used to draw the shadow map. Listing 2.1 now presents a shader function that converts a depth value from the shadow map back to a three-dimensional light space point.

Given Listing 2.1, the pixel shader code for creating an HPSM is presented in Listing 2.2. Please note that the length of the three-dimensional vector stored in the yzw part of the HPSM encodes if an HPSM pixels stores a plane or just min/max depth.

```
// Convert from camera space depth to light space 3d.
// f2ShadowMapCoord is the shadow map texture coordinate for
// fDepth.
float3 GetCameraXYZFromSMDepth(float fDepth,
                              float2 f2ShadowMapCoord )
{
  float3 f3CameraPos;

  // Compute camera Z: see Equation (2.1).
  f3CameraPos.z = -g_fQTimesZNear / ( fDepth - g_fQ );

  // Convert screen coords to projection space XY.
  f3CameraPos.xy = (f2ShadowMapCoord * g_f2ShadowMapSize ) -
                   float2( 1.0f, 1.0f );

  // Compute camera X.
  f3CameraPos.x = g_fTanH * f3CameraPos.x * f3CameraPos.z;

  // Compute camera Y.
  f3CameraPos.y = - g_fTanV * f3CameraPos.y * f3CameraPos.z;

  return f3CameraPos;
}
```

Listing 2.1. A function to convert from shadow map depth to a linear camera space three-dimensional point.

```
float4 main(float4 pos2d : SV_POSITION ) : SV_Target
{
  float2 tc     = pos2d.xy / (g_f2ShadowMapSize / 4 );
  float4 f4MinD = ( 10000.0).xxxx;
  float4 f4MaxD = (-10000.0).xxxx;
  float  fPlane = 1.0f;

  // Call function to gather four depth values from
  // the shadow map: for a Shader Model > 4.0
  // Gather() can be used; otherwise four point samples
  // need to be used.
  float4 f4D  = gather_depth( tc, int2( 0, 0 ) );
  float3 f3P0 = GetCameraXYZFromSMDepth(f4D.x, tc +
               float2( 0,1 ) * 1.0f / g_f2ShadowMapSize );
  float3 f3P1 = GetCameraXYZFromSMDepth(f4D.y, tc +
               float2( 1,1 ) * 1.0f / g_f2ShadowMapSize );
  float3 f3P2 = GetCameraXYZFromSMDepth(f4D.y, tc +
               float2( 1,0 ) * 1.0f / g_f2ShadowMapSize );

  float3 f3N0 = normalize( fP0 - fP1 );
  float3 f3N1 = normalize( fP0 - fP2 );

  // Construct plane normal at central point.
```

```
float3 f3N = cross( fN0, fN1 );

for( int row  = -SHADOW_FILTER_WIDTH/2;
         row  < 4 + SHADOW_FILTER_WIDTH/2;
         row += 2 )
{
  for( int col  = -SHADOW_FILTER_WIDTH/2;
           col  < 4 + SHADOW_FILTER_WIDTH/2;
           col += 2 )
  {
    // Gather four depth values from the shadow map.
    float4 f4D = gather_depth( tc, int2( row, col ) );

    // Min/max construction
    f4MinD = min( f4D, f4MinD );
    f4MaxD = max( f4D, f4MinD );

    // Look at each cam space point.
    float3 f3P = GetCameraXYZFromSMDepth(f4D.x, tc +
               ( float2( 0,1 ) * float2 ( row, col ) ) *
               1.0f / g_f2ShadowMapSize );

    // EPS is the maximum allowed distance from the plane
    // defined by f3P and f3N.
fPlane *= abs( dot( f3P - f3P0, f3N ) ) < EPS ?
               1.0f : 0.0f;

  }
}

// If this is a plane
if( fPlane != 0.0f )
{
  // res.x = distance of plane from origin.
  // res.yzw is normalized normal of plane.
  return float4( length( f3P0 ), f3N );
}
else
{
  // Make sure that length(yzw) is bigger than 1
  return float4( min( min( f4MinD.x, f4MinD.y ),
                      min( f4MinD.z, f4MinD.w ) ),
                 max( max( f4MaxD.x, f4MaxD.y ),
                      max( f4MaxD.z, f4MaxD.w ) ),
                 100.0f, 100.0f );
}
}
```

Listing 2.2. A pixel shader that constructs an HPSM from a normal shadow map.

2.4   Using an HPSM

Having constructed an HPSM, using it is straightforward and demonstrated by
the shader snippet in Listing 2.3.

```
// LSP is the light space position of the current pixel;
// tc.xy is the shadow map texture coordinate for the current
// pixel; tc.z is light space depth of the pixel.
// It is assumed that any necessary depth bias (e.g., to
// deal with the EPS for plane construction) has already been
// add to tc.z.
float shadow(float3 LSP, float3 tc, inout float fLight )
{
  float4 f4HPMS          = g_txHPSM.SampleLevel( s_point, tc.xy,
                                               0 );
  float   fLenSqrNormal = dot( f4HPMS.yzw, f4HPMS.yzw );
  float   fReject = false;

  // Min/max
  if( fLenSqrNormal > 1.1 )
  {
     float fMin = f4HPMS.x;
     float fMax = f4HPMS.y;

     if( tc.z < fMin )
        fLight = 1.0f;
     else if( tc.z > fMax )
        fLight = 0.0f;
     else // call expensive filter
        fLight = filter_shadow( tc );
  }
  else // Plane
  {
     float3 f3P  = f4HPMS.x * f4HPMS.yzw;
     float fDist = dot( f3P - LSP, f4HPMS.yzw );

     if( fDist <= -EPS )
        fLight = 0.0f;
     else // Full light
        fLight = 1.0f;
  }
}
```

Listing 2.3. A pixel shader that uses the HPSM to reject pixels that are in full light or
in full shadow.

2.5   Other Uses for the HPSM

As pointed out in [Lobanchikov et al. 09], HPSM can be used to accelerate all sort of shadow map queries. [Lobanchikov et al. 09] uses a simple form HPSMs to accelerate not only normal shadow filtering but also the rendering of sun shafts. Basically, the shader in question integrates light along a ray from the scene towards the eye. For each point on the ray four PCF shadow map samples are necessary to generate smooth looking sun shafts. Using an HPSM to quickly reject points on a sun shaft ray generates a speedup of $\sim$12% at a resolution of 1600×1200 on an AMD HD4870 GPU versus doing all four PCF samples for every point on the ray.

Bibliography

[Dmitriev et al. 07] Kirill Dmitriev and Yury Uralsky. "Soft Shadows Using Hierarchical Min-Max Shadow Maps." Presented at Game Developers Conference, San Francisco, March 5–9, 2007. Available at http://developer.download.nvidia.com/presentations/2007/gdc/SoftShadows.pdf

[Lobanchikov et al. 09] I. Lobanchikov and H. Gruen, "Stalker: Clear Sky—A Showcase for Direct3D 10.0/1." Presented at Game Developers Conference, San Francisco, March 23–27, 2009. Available at http://www.gdconf.com/conference/Tutorial.

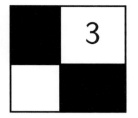

3

Shadow Mapping for Omnidirectional Light Using Tetrahedron Mapping
Hung-Chien Liao

Shadow mapping is a popular method of rendering shadows for a three-dimensional scene. William's original Z-buffer shadow mapping algorithm [Williams 78] is for directional light. We need a different method to approach an omnidirectional light. There are two popular ways to approach omnidirectional light: one is cube mapping [Voorhies and Foran 94] and the other is dual-paraboloid mapping [Heidrich and Seidel 98]. In this paper I present a new shadow mapping technique for omnidirectional lights using tetrahedron mapping.

3.1   Shadow Mapping

The traditional Z-buffer shadow mapping algorithm [Williams 78] consists of two steps. In a first step from the point of view of the camera, the scene is rendered into a shadow map. The shadow map holds then the nearest depth value. In the second step, when the scene is rendered from the point of view of the player camera, the pixels are transformed to light space and compared to the depth values in the shadow map. If the current pixel depth value is larger than the shadow map depth value, then the current pixel is shadowed.

3.2   Tetrahedron Shadow Mapping

A *tetrahedron* is made by four equilateral triangular faces, as depicted in Figure 3.1.

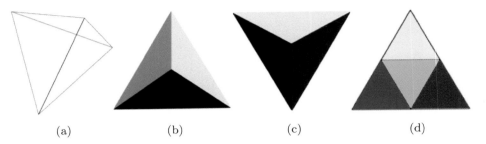

(a)   (b)   (c)   (d)

Figure 3.1. (a) Tetrahedron in a wire frame; (b) solid tetrahedron; (c) solid tetrahedron at a different angle; (d) unwrapped tetrahedron.

There are two main steps. The first is to use tetrahedron mapping to render all objects from the omnidirectional light position to each tetrahedron face and to store the nearest depth value into a two-dimensional texture. The second is to render the scene normally from the player's point of view. During the second step we transform the pixel into the correct light face space to get the depth value and a two-dimensional texture coordinate. Then we use the texture coordinate data to fetch the depth value and compare it with the current pixel depth value.

3.2.1   Step One: Generating Tetrahedron Shadow Map

There are four equilateral triangular faces in a tetrahedron. Consequently, from the center of the tetrahedron to each of its faces, we can get four different frustums that each contain an equilateral triangular face. As shown in Figure 3.2, we use the specific orientation of the tetrahedron in a local light space to generate tetrahedron shadow mapping. We can use any orientation of the tetrahedron to do the same thing, and I will explain why we use this specific orientation of the tetrahedron.

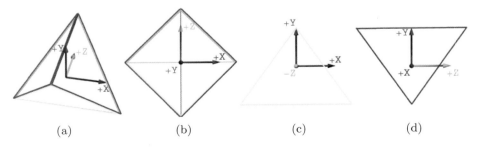

(a)   (b)   (c)   (d)

Figure 3.2. The center of tetrahedron is at the origin of the local light space: (a) perspective view; (b) top view; (c) front view; (d) right view.

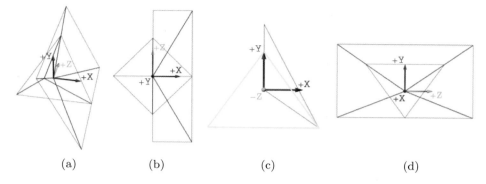

Figure 3.3. (a) Perspective view; (b) top view; (c) front view; (d) right view.

Figure 3.3 is a frustum made from the center of a tetrahedron to the red face and contains the whole red face.

We need to calculate the frustum field of view in the y- and x-directions, as depicted in Figure 3.4.

For the field of view in the y-direction, as depicted in Figure 3.5, Segment C is the distance from the origin to each vertex of the tetrahedron, and each Segment C is the same. Therefore angle α and angle β are the same, too.

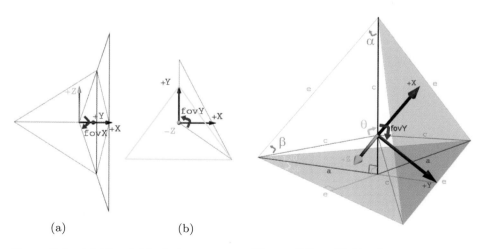

Figure 3.4. (a) The field of view in the x-direction; (b) the field of view in the y-direction.

Figure 3.5. Field of view in the y-direction.

We can compute

$$a = \frac{\left(\frac{e}{2}\right)}{\cos 30°},$$

$$\frac{a}{e} = \sin \alpha.$$

From these two equations we can get:

$$\angle a = \sin^{-1} \frac{1}{2 \times \cos 30°},$$

$$\angle \theta = 180° - 2 \times a.$$

From angle α and β we can get

$$\text{fov}Y = \frac{360° - \theta}{2} = 90° + \alpha \approx 125.26438968°.$$

Then, for the field of view in the x-direction (see Figure 3.6):

$$\frac{\left(\frac{e}{2}\right)}{d} = \tan \frac{\theta}{2}.$$

Therefore,

$$\frac{e}{2} = d \times \tan \frac{\theta}{2};$$

$$\frac{f}{d} = \cos \frac{\text{fov}Y}{2}.$$

Therefore,

$$f = d \times \cos \frac{\text{fov}Y}{2};$$

$$\frac{\left(\frac{e}{2}\right)}{f} = \tan \frac{\text{fov}X}{2}.$$

From these three equations we can get

$$\text{fov}X = 2 \times \tan^{-1} \left(\frac{\left(\frac{e}{2}\right)}{f} \right)$$

$$= 2 \times \tan^{-1} \left(\frac{d \times \tan \frac{\theta}{2}}{d \times \cos \frac{\text{fov}Y}{2}} \right)$$

$$\approx 143.98570868°.$$

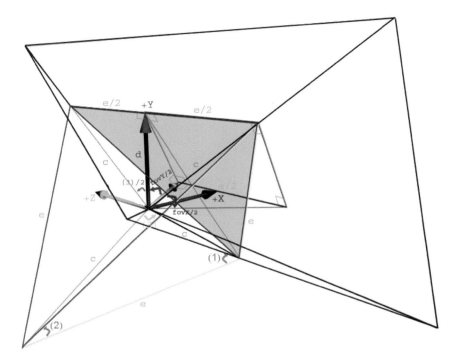

Figure 3.6. The field of view in the X direction.

After we get the field of view in the x- and y-directions, we can then create the frustum perspective matrix. We need to know how big the angle is between the +X-axis and the frustum direction for calculating the view matrix. The angle between +X and frustum direction $= 90° - (fovY/2) \approx 27.36780516°$. In Figure 3.7 you can see four different frustums that contain each equilateral triangular face.

The following is the procedure code for generating a tetrahedron shadow map:

1. Make a two-dimensional render target texture for a tetrahedron shadow map.

2. Set the tetrahedron shadow map as the render target.

3. Set up the field of view of the light face perspective matrix as 143.98570868° in the x-axis and 125.26438968° in the y-axis.

4. For the green face:

   (a) Set up the screen view port, from zero to half the width of the tetrahedron shadow map in the x-axis, and from zero to half height of the tetrahedron shadow map in the y-axis.

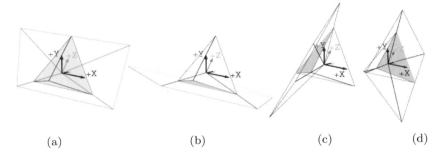

(a)   (b)   (c)   (d)

Figure 3.7. Four frustums that cover all tetrahedron faces: (a) green face; (b) yellow face; (c) blue face; (d) red face.

    (b) Set up the local light view matrix so it corresponds to the green face, from the origin of the local light space to Roll $0.0°$, Pitch $27.36780516°$, and Yaw $0.0°$.

    (c) Render all shadow casting objects that correspond to the green face within light range and store depth value into the tetrahedron shadow map.

5. For the yellow face:

    (a) Set up the screen view port, from half the width of the tetrahedron shadow map to one width of the tetrahedron shadow map in the x-axis, and from zero to half the height of the tetrahedron shadow map in the y-axis.

    (b) Set up the local light view matrix so it corresponds to the yellow face, from the origin of the local light space to Roll $0.0°$, Pitch $27.36780516°$, and Yaw $180.0°$.

    (c) Render all shadow casting objects that correspond to the yellow face within light range and store depth value into the tetrahedron shadow map.

6. For the blue face:

    (a) Set up the screen view port, from zero to half the width of the tetrahedron shadow map in the x-axis, and from half the height of the tetrahedron shadow map to one height of the tetrahedron shadow map in the y-axis.

    (b) Set up the local light view matrix so that it corresponds to the blue face, from the origin of the local light space to Roll $0.0°$, Pitch $-27.36780516°$, and Yaw $-90.0°$.

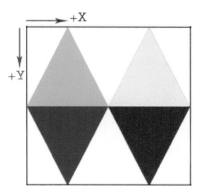

Figure 3.8. Tetrahedron shadow map.

(c) Render all shadow casting objects that correspond to the blue face within light range and store depth value into the tetrahedron shadow map.

7. For the red face:

   (a) Set up the screen view port, from half the width of the tetrahedron shadow map to one width of the tetrahedron shadow map in the x-axis, and from half the height of the tetrahedron shadow map to one height of the tetrahedron shadow map in the y-axis.

   (b) Set up the local light view matrix so that it corresponds to the red face, from the origin of the local light space to Roll $0.0°$, Pitch $-27.36780516°$, and Yaw $90.0°$.

   (c) Render all shadow casting objects that correspond to the red face within light range and store depth value into the tetrahedron shadow map.

After the above steps, you should get a tetrahedron shadow map with depth value, which may look like Figure 3.8.

3.2.2 Step Two: Render the Scene

After we are done rendering the shadow casting object and get the tetrahedron shadow map, it is time to use it. First, we need to combine view, perspective, and texture scale matrix for each face:

$$\text{Offset}X = 0.5/\text{TetrahedronShadowMapWidth},$$
$$\text{Offset}Y = 0.5/\text{TetrahedronShadowMapHeight};$$

$\text{GreenfaceViewPerspectiveTexMatrix}$

$$= \text{GreenfaceViewMatrix} \times \text{LightfacePerspectiveMatrix}$$

$$\times \begin{bmatrix} 0.25 & 0.0 & 0.0 & 0.0 \\ 0.0 & -0.25 & 0.0 & 0.0 \\ 0.0 & 0.0 & 1.0 & 0.0 \\ 0.25 + \text{Offset}X & 0.25 + \text{Offset}Y & 0.0 & 1.0 \end{bmatrix},$$

$\text{YellowfaceViewPerspectiveTexMatrix}$

$$= \text{YellowfaceViewMatrix} \times \text{LightfacePerspectiveMatrix}$$

$$\times \begin{bmatrix} 0.25 & 0.0 & 0.0 & 0.0 \\ 0.0 & -0.25 & 0.0 & 0.0 \\ 0.0 & 0.0 & 1.0 & 0.0 \\ 0.75 + \text{Offset}X & 0.25 + \text{Offset}Y & 0.0 & 1.0 \end{bmatrix},$$

$\text{BluefaceViewPerspectiveTexMatrix}$

$$= \text{BluefaceViewMatrix} \times \text{LightfacePerspectiveMatrix}$$

$$\times \begin{bmatrix} 0.25 & 0.0 & 0.0 & 0.0 \\ 0.0 & -0.25 & 0.0 & 0.0 \\ 0.0 & 0.0 & 1.0 & 0.0 \\ 0.25 + \text{Offset}X & 0.75 + \text{Offset}Y & 0.0 & 1.0 \end{bmatrix},$$

$\text{RedfaceViewPerspectiveTexMatrix}$

$$= \text{RedfaceViewMatrix} \times \text{LightfacePerspectiveMatrix}$$

$$\times \begin{bmatrix} 0.25 & 0.0 & 0.0 & 0.0 \\ 0.0 & -0.25 & 0.0 & 0.0 \\ 0.0 & 0.0 & 1.0 & 0.0 \\ 0.75 + \text{Offset}X & 0.75 + \text{Offset}Y & 0.0 & 1.0 \end{bmatrix}.$$

Second, we can get four center face vectors, one from the center of each tetrahedron, as shown in Figure 3.9. These center vectors are different than the vector of each face view matrix. The green face center vector is $(0.0, -0.57735026, 0.81649661)$; the yellow face center vector is $(0.0, -0.57735026, -0.81649661)$; the blue face center vector is $(-0.81649661, 0.57735026, 0.0)$; and the red face center vector is $(0.81649661, 0.57735026, 0.0)$.

Third, we want to know the corresponding tetrahedron shadow map coordinate given a vertex in local light space. In pseudocode, this looks like Listing 3.1.

Finally, `vResult.x` and `vResult.y` is the (x, y) texture coordinate on the tetrahedron shadow map. We use this texture coordinate to fetch the depth value on the tetrahedron shadow map and compare it with `vResult.z`. If `vResult.z` is bigger this vertex is shadowed; otherwise this vertex is lit.

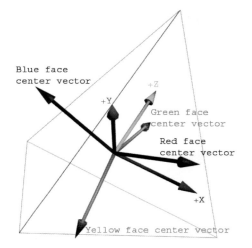

Figure 3.9. Four face center vectors.

```
vector4 vPosition (x, y, z, 1.0);
vector4 vResult;
float g = dot product(vPosition.xyz, green face center vector);
float y = dot product(vPosition.xyz, yellow face center vector);
float b = dot product(vPosition.xyz, blue face center vector);
float r = dot product (vPosition.xyz, red face center vector);
float maximum = max ( max (g, y), max (b, r) );
if (maximum == g)
    vResult = vPosition * green face ViewPerspectiveTexMatrix;
else if (maximum == y)
    vResult = vPosition * yellow face ViewPerspectiveTexMatrix;
else if (maximum == b)
    vResult = vPosition * blue face ViewPerspectiveTexMatrix;
else
    vResult = vPosition * red face ViewPerspectiveTexMatrix;
vResult.x = vResult.x / vResult.w;
vResult.y = vResult.y / vResult.w;
vResult.z = vResult.z / vResult.w;
```

Listing 3.1. Calculate vertex texture coordinate on tetrahedron shadow map and vertex depth to the light.

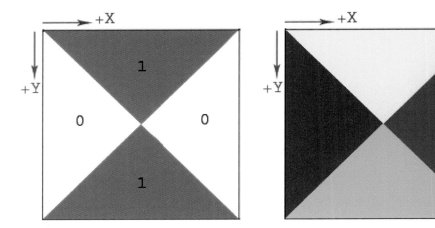

Figure 3.10. Stencil buffer.   **Figure 3.11.**   Tetrahedron shadow map with stencil buffer.

3.3 Optimization

There are some optimizations we can do to further improve tetrahedron mapping. One is using a stencil buffer to improve the quality of the tetrahedron shadow map. In Figure 3.8, we only use half of a tetrahedron shadow map to store the depth value. In order to use a full tetrahedron shadow map to store the depth value, we need to use a stencil buffer. First, we need to initialize the stencil buffer (as shown in Figure 3.10) when we create a depth buffer and stencil buffer. We initialize the gray area to be one, and other area remains zero.

Remember, we do not modify the stencil buffer after we initialize it. After that, we need to roll the view matrix and use a different screen view port when we generate the tetrahedron shadow map. Then we can generate a tetrahedron shadow map like Figure 3.11. In this way, we can use the full tetrahedron shadow map and lose just a little performance.

Another way to optimize is using frustum culling when generating a tetrahedron shadow map for each face. But it is slightly different than the original frustum culling because for each face we project the depth value into a triangle, not a quad. I will use the green face as an example here. First, we test to see if the shadow caster is inside the lighting range or not. Then we use the origin with every two vertices of the green face to generate three planes. After that, we use a plane to a bounding sphere or bounding box collision detection to see if the shadow caster will project into the green face or not. This way we can also reduce the number of draw calls.

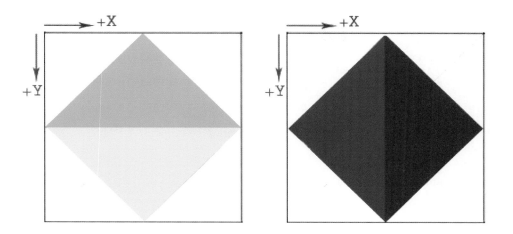

Figure 3.12. Texture Coordinate Group 1.   **Figure 3.13.** Texture Coordinate Group 2.

3.4 Lookup Map

The hardware does not support sampling from a tetrahedron map, but a cube map does. Therefore, we can create a lookup texture by projecting a tetrahedron map into a cube map in order to save some instructions. But it is difficult to linear sample between tetrahedron face boundaries from the lookup cube map. In order to solve this problem, we need to project into two separate sets of texture coordinates as in Figures 3.12 and 3.13.

In Texture Coordinate Group 1, the texture coordinate can be linear sampled correctly between the green and yellow face. It is the same with Group 2. Listing 3.2 shows the actual functions to create the lookup map by using C++ and DirectX 9.

```
void ConvertToViewMatrix(D3DXMATRIX& mOutView,
                         const D3DXMATRIX& mIn)
{
    D3DXMATRIX mTemp(mIn);
    // Right vector for view matrix
    mOutView.m[0][0] = mTemp.m[0][0];
    mOutView.m[1][0] = mTemp.m[0][1];
    mOutView.m[2][0] = mTemp.m[0][2];
    // Up vector for view matrix
    mOutView.m[0][1] = mTemp.m[1][0];
    mOutView.m[1][1] = mTemp.m[1][1];
    mOutView.m[2][1] = mTemp.m[1][2];
    // Look at vector for view matrix
    mOutView.m[0][2] = mTemp.m[2][0];
```

```
    mOutView.m[1][2] = mTemp.m[2][1];
    mOutView.m[2][2] = mTemp.m[2][2];
    // Position for view matrix
    mOutView.m[3][0] = -D3DXVec3Dot( (D3DXVECTOR3*)mTemp.m[0],
        (D3DXVECTOR3*)mTemp.m[3] );
    mOutView.m[3][1] = -D3DXVec3Dot( (D3DXVECTOR3*)mTemp.m[1],
        (D3DXVECTOR3*)mTemp.m[3] );
    mOutView.m[3][2] = -D3DXVec3Dot( (D3DXVECTOR3*)mTemp.m[2],
        (D3DXVECTOR3*)mTemp.m[3] );

    mOutView.m[0][3] = 0.0f;
    mOutView.m[1][3] = 0.0f;
    mOutView.m[2][3] = 0.0f;
    mOutView.m[3][3] = 1.0f;
}

void CreateCubeToTSMCoord(LPDIRECT3DDEVICE9 lpD3DDevice)
{
    const float TSMFaceFOVX = 143.985709f;
    const float TSMFaceFOVY = 125.264389f;
    const float TSMFaceFOVXR = D3DXToRadian(TSMFaceFOVX);
    const float TSMFaceFOVYR = D3DXToRadian(TSMFaceFOVY);
    D3DXMATRIX mTSMFaceViewProj0, mTSMFaceViewProj1,
        mTSMFaceViewProj2, mTSMFaceViewProj3;

    D3DXMATRIX mTexScaleBias(0.5f,  0.0f,  0.0f,  0.0f,
                             0.0f, -0.25f, 0.0f,  0.0f,
                             0.0f,  0.0f,  1.0f,  0.0f,
                             0.5f,  0.25f, 0.0f,  1.0f);

    D3DXMATRIX mLightProjVert, mLightProjHorz;
    D3DXMATRIX mLightView;
    // Calculate all four face direction light-view-projection
    //    matrix for Tetrahedron.
    D3DXMatrixPerspectiveFovLH(&mLightProjHorz, TSMFaceFOVYR,
        tanf(TSMFaceFOVXR * 0.5f) / tanf(TSMFaceFOVYR * 0.5f),
        0.1f, 1000.0f);
    D3DXMatrixPerspectiveFovLH(&mLightProjVert, TSMFaceFOVXR,
        tanf(TSMFaceFOVYR * 0.5f) / tanf(TSMFaceFOVXR * 0.5f),
        0.1f, 1000.0f);

    // ...Calculate the first face light-view-projection matrix.
    D3DXMatrixRotationYawPitchRoll(&mLightView, 0.0f,
        D3DXToRadian(27.3678055f), 0.0f);
    ConvertToViewMatrix(mTSMFaceViewProj0, mLightView);
    D3DXMatrixMultiply(&mTSMFaceViewProj0, &mTSMFaceViewProj0,
        &mLightProjHorz);
    D3DXMatrixMultiply(&mTSMFaceViewProj0, &mTSMFaceViewProj0,
        &mTexScaleBias);
    // ...Calculate the second face light-view-projection matrix.
    D3DXMatrixRotationYawPitchRoll(&mLightView, D3DX_PI,
        D3DXToRadian(27.3678055f), D3DX_PI);
```

```
ConvertToViewMatrix(mTSMFaceViewProj1, mLightView);
D3DXMatrixMultiply(&mTSMFaceViewProj1, &mTSMFaceViewProj1,
    &mLightProjHorz);
mTexScaleBias.m[3][1] = 0.75f;
D3DXMatrixMultiply(&mTSMFaceViewProj1, &mTSMFaceViewProj1,
    &mTexScaleBias);
// ...Calculate the third face light-view-projection matrix.
D3DXMatrixRotationYawPitchRoll(&mLightView, -D3DX_PI * 0.5f,
    -D3DXToRadian(27.3678055f), D3DX_PI * 0.5f);
ConvertToViewMatrix(mTSMFaceViewProj2, mLightView);
D3DXMatrixMultiply(&mTSMFaceViewProj2, &mTSMFaceViewProj2,
    &mLightProjVert);
mTexScaleBias.m[0][0] = 0.25f;
mTexScaleBias.m[1][1] = -0.5f;
mTexScaleBias.m[3][0] = 0.25f;
mTexScaleBias.m[3][1] = 0.5f;
D3DXMatrixMultiply(&mTSMFaceViewProj2, &mTSMFaceViewProj2,
    &mTexScaleBias);
// ...Calculate the fourth face light-view-projection matrix.
D3DXMatrixRotationYawPitchRoll(&mLightView, D3DX_PI * 0.5f,
    -D3DXToRadian(27.3678055f), -D3DX_PI * 0.5f);
ConvertToViewMatrix(mTSMFaceViewProj3, mLightView);
D3DXMatrixMultiply(&mTSMFaceViewProj3, &mTSMFaceViewProj3,
    &mLightProjVert);
mTexScaleBias.m[3][0] = 0.75f;
D3DXMatrixMultiply(&mTSMFaceViewProj3, &mTSMFaceViewProj3,
    &mTexScaleBias);

LPDIRECT3DCUBETEXTURE9 lpCubeToTSM = NULL;
const int CUBE_SIZE = 128;
lpD3DDevice->CreateCubeTexture(CUBE_SIZE, 1, 0,
    D3DFMT_A16B16G16R16F, D3DPOOL_SYSTEMMEM, &lpCubeToTSM,
    NULL);
D3DLOCKED_RECT data;
D3DXVECTOR4 vVertexPos;
for (int iFace = 0; iFace < 6; ++iFace)
{
    lpCubeToTSM->LockRect((D3DCUBEMAP_FACES)iFace, 0, &data,
        NULL, 0);
    LPBYTE lpBits = (LPBYTE)data.pBits;
    for (float fCoordY = CUBE_SIZE * -0.5f + 0.5f;
        fCoordY < CUBE_SIZE * 0.5f; ++fCoordY)
    {
        D3DXFLOAT16 *pTexels = (D3DXFLOAT16*)lpBits;
        lpBits += data.Pitch;

        for (float fCoordX = CUBE_SIZE * -0.5f + 0.5f;
            fCoordX < CUBE_SIZE * 0.5f;
            ++fCoordX, pTexels += 4)
        {
            switch(iFace)
            {
```

```
case D3DCUBEMAP_FACE_POSITIVE_X:
    vVertexPos = D3DXVECTOR4(CUBE_SIZE * 0.5f -
        0.5f, -fCoordY, -fCoordX, 1.0f);
    break;
case D3DCUBEMAP_FACE_NEGATIVE_X:
    vVertexPos = D3DXVECTOR4(CUBE_SIZE * -0.5f +
        0.5f, -fCoordY, fCoordX, 1.0f);
    break;
case D3DCUBEMAP_FACE_POSITIVE_Y:
    vVertexPos = D3DXVECTOR4(fCoordX,
        CUBE_SIZE * 0.5f - 0.5f, fCoordY, 1.0f);
    break;
case D3DCUBEMAP_FACE_NEGATIVE_Y:
    vVertexPos = D3DXVECTOR4(fCoordX,
        CUBE_SIZE * -0.5f + 0.5f, -fCoordY,
        1.0f);
    break;
case D3DCUBEMAP_FACE_POSITIVE_Z:
    vVertexPos = D3DXVECTOR4(fCoordX, -fCoordY,
        CUBE_SIZE * 0.5f - 0.5f, 1.0f);
    break;
case D3DCUBEMAP_FACE_NEGATIVE_Z:
    vVertexPos = D3DXVECTOR4(-fCoordX, -fCoordY,
        CUBE_SIZE * -0.5f + 0.5f, 1.0f);
    break;
}
D3DXVECTOR4 vResult1, vResult2;
// In group 1, we only need to differentiate
//   face 1 and 2.
if (vVertexPos.z > 0.0f)
{
    D3DXVec4Transform(&vResult1, &vVertexPos,
        &mTSMFaceViewProj0);
}
else
{
    D3DXVec4Transform(&vResult1, &vVertexPos,
        &mTSMFaceViewProj1);
}
// In group 2, we only need to differentiate
//   face 3 and 4.
if (vVertexPos.x > 0.0f)
{
    D3DXVec4Transform(&vResult2, &vVertexPos,
        &mTSMFaceViewProj3);
}
else
{
    D3DXVec4Transform(&vResult2, &vVertexPos,
        &mTSMFaceViewProj2);
}
vResult1.x /= vResult1.w;
```

```
                        vResult1.y /= vResult1.w;
                        vResult2.x /= vResult2.w;
                        vResult2.y /= vResult2.w;
                        // Save group 1 texture coordinate info in Red
                        //   and Green channel.
                        D3DXFloat32To16Array(&pTexels[0],
                            &vResult1.x, 1);
                        D3DXFloat32To16Array(&pTexels[1],
                            &vResult1.y, 1);
                        // Save group 2 texture coordinate info in Blue
                        //   and Alpha channel.
                        D3DXFloat32To16Array(&pTexels[2],
                            &vResult2.x, 1);
                        D3DXFloat32To16Array(&pTexels[3],
                            &vResult2.y, 1);
                    }
                }
                lpCubeToTSM->UnlockRect((D3DCUBEMAP_FACES)iFace, 0);
            }
            D3DXSaveTextureToFile("Textures/CubeToTSMCoord2.dds",
                D3DXIFF_DDS, lpCubeToTSM, NULL);
            SAFE_RELEASE(lpCubeToTSM);
    }
```

Listing 3.2. Create lookup map.

After we create the lookup map, we can move forward to use it. Because of the way we align the tetrahedron map, we can calculate the current rendering pixel depth if we are using hardware shadow (see the pseudocode in Listing 3.3).

We can calculate the shadow map coordinate by using the lookup map (see the pseudocode in Listing 3.4).

```
vector3 vPosition (x, y, z);
vector3 vAbsPosition = abs(vPosition);
vector4 vTestPosition(vAbsPosition.x, vPosition.y,
    vAbsPosition.z, 1.0f);
vector4 vResult;
float g = dot product (vTestPosition, green face center vector);
float r = dot product (vTestPosition, red face center vector);
if (g > r)
    vResult=vTestPosition * green face ViewPerspectiveTexMatrix;
else
    vResult = vTestPosition * red face ViewPerspectiveTexMatrix;
vResult.z = vResult.z / vResult.w;
```

Listing 3.3. Rendering pixel depth from the light.

```
vector3 vPosition (x, y, z);
vector3 vAbsPosition = abs(vPosition);
vector4 vTestPosition(vAbsPosition.x, vPosition.y,
    vAbsPosition.z, 1.0f);
vector2 vShadowMapCoord;
float g = dot product (vTestPosition, green face center vector);
float r = dot product (vTestPosition, red face center vector);
if (g > r)
{
    vShadowMapCoord = texCUBE(LookupMap, vPosition).xy;
    vShadowMapCoord.y += 0.5f;
}
else
{
    vShadowMapCoord = texCUBE(LookupMap, vPosition).zw;
    vShadowMapCoord.x += 0.5f;
}
```

Listing 3.4. Rendering pixel texture coordinate on tetrahedron shadow map.

3.5   Conclusion

Table 3.1 is a comparison of dual-paraboloid mapping, cube mapping, and tetrahedron mapping.

Tetrahedron mapping can be used not only on shadow maps but also on environment maps. Prior to the development of tetrahedron mapping, one had to create an extra cube texture or one more two-dimensional texture for an omnidirectional shadow map. Thanks to tetrahedron mapping, one can now save video memory and just use the same two-dimensional texture that is used by the directional and spotlights.

	Dual-Paraboloid Mapping	Cube Mapping	Tetrahedron Mapping
Render Scene	2 times	6 times	4 times
Switch Render Target	2 times	6 times	1 time
Hardware Shadow Map Support (NVIDIA Geforce3 +)	Yes	No	Yes
Accuracy	Not 100% accurate: depends on polygon count.	100%	100%

Table 3.1. Comparison between dual-paraboloid mapping, cube mapping, and tetrahedron mapping.

Figure 3.14. One point light and use dual-paraboloid shadow mapping with two 1024 × 1024 two-dimensional textures.

Figure 3.15. One point light and use cube shadow mapping with one 512 cube texture.

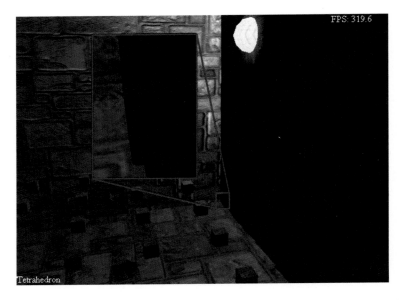

Figure 3.16. One point light and use tetrahedron shadow mapping with one 1024×1024 two-dimensional texture.

Figure 3.17. One point light and use tetrahedron shadow mapping with stencil buffer. The two-dimensional depth texture size is 1024×1024.

Figure 3.18. One point light and use tetrahedron shadow mapping with hardware shadow mapping. The two-dimensional depth texture size is 1024×1024.

Figure 3.19. One point light and use tetrahedron shadow mapping with stencil buffer and hardware shadow mapping. The two-dimensional depth texture size is 1024×1024.

Figure 3.20. Four point lights and use cube shadow mapping with one 512 cube texture.

Figure 3.21. Four point lights and use tetrahedron shadow mapping with stencil buffer and hardware shadow mapping. The two-dimensional depth texture size is 1024×1024.

Performance can improve by twenty percent or more by switching from cube mapping to tetrahedron mapping—even more if you use NVIDIA hardware shadow map and get an extra percentage of closest filtering. Figures 3.14, 3.15, 3.16, 3.17, 3.18, 3.19, 3.20, and 3.21 are screen shots from a test scene.

Bibliography

[Williams 78] Lance Williams. "Casting Curved Shadows on Curved Surfaces." *Computer Graphics (SIGGRAPH '78 Proceedings)* 12.3 (1978): 270–274.

[Voorhies and Foran 94] Douglas Voorhies and Jim Foran. "Reflection Vector Shading Hardware." *Proceedings of SIGGRAPH '94* (1994): 163–166.

[Heidrich and Seidel 98] Wolfgang Heidrich and Hans-Peter Seidel. "View-Independent Environment Maps." *1998 SIGGRAPH / Eurographics Workshop on Graphics Hardware* (1998): 39–46.

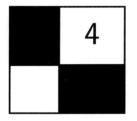

4

Screen Space Soft Shadows
Jesus Gumbau, Miguel Chover, and Mateu Sbert

This work presents a new technique for the real-time rendering of shadows with penumbrae based on shadow mapping. The method uses a screen-aligned texture that contains the distance between the shadow and its potential occluder. This information is used to set up the size of an anisotropic Gaussian filter kernel applied in screen space, which smoothens the standard shadows to create the penumbra. Given that a Gaussian filter is separable, the number of samples required to create the penumbra is much lower than in other soft shadowing approaches. In consequence, higher performance is obtained while also allowing perceptually correct penumbrae to be represented.

4.1   Introduction

Shadows are a very important element in synthetic scenes because they greatly contribute to enhance the realism of the rendered images (see Figure 4.1). Shadow mapping is the most used technique in real-time applications nowadays, because it can be implemented efficiently on the graphics hardware and its performance scales very well. It is also the most active field on shadowing research in the last years.

Unfortunately the standard shadow mapping algorithm is unable to generate shadows with penumbrae (see Figure 4.2 for an example of real-world penumbrae), or soft shadows, as it can not handle area light sources (see Figure 4.3).

In order to generate physically correct penumbrae, we need to determine the amount of light visible from the point being shaded, which is proportional to the size of the penumbra.

A common idea used for representing shadows with penumbrae is to approximate area lights by a set of point light sources, and then to combine the contributions of each single shadow. With this method, the softness of the penumbra is

Figure 4.1. Scene rendered using our method with an 11 × 11 Gaussian anisotropic kernel in screen space. The image shows how the soft shadow becomes sharper as it approaches the occluder.

proportional to the number of virtual light sources used. In practice this method is very expensive, because the shadow casters need to be rendered many times, introducing a huge overhead in geometry-limited scenes. Therefore, more practical solutions are needed in order to be used in real-time applications.

The aim of this work is to introduce a new soft shadow mapping algorithm for generating variable-sized penumbrae that minimizes texture lookups in order to maximize performance. Our technique generates shadows with penumbrae using an anisotropic Gaussian blur filter in screen space with variable size. The idea

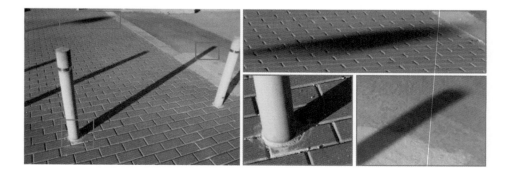

Figure 4.2. Example of real-world penumbrae. Shadows become sharper as they approach the occluder.

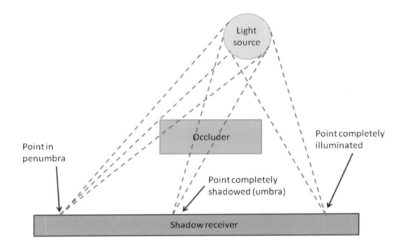

Figure 4.3. The size of the penumbra is determined by the amount of light rays reaching the point being rendered.

behind this work is simple: as a Gaussian filter is separable, it requires far fewer texture accesses than other kernel-based sampling approaches, thus improving performance.

4.2 Previous Work

This paper is an improvement of the traditional shadow mapping technique, which was developed by Williams in 1978 [Williams 78]. It is based on capturing the depth of the shadow casters from the light source. This information is stored into a depth texture that is projected over the scene in order to determine whether a certain pixel is in shadow or not, with a single depth comparison in light space.

In 1987, Reeves [Reeves et al. 87] presented a technique called *percentage closer filtering* (PCF), which makes it possible to reduce the aliasing and to simulate an artificial penumbra of uniform size. The technique was based on performing multiple fetches over the shadow map to determine the amount of light over a given surface.

To allow the rendering of visually pleasant penumbrae, R. Fernando [Fernando 05] introduces percentage closer soft shadows (PCSS) which is able to represent soft shadows with variable-sized penumbrae. This technique is usually combined with a filtering technique like [Donnelly and Lauritzen 06] or [Salvi 07] to reduce the noise. Working source code of this technique can be found at NVIDIA's webpage [Bavoil 08b].

For more information, refer to Hasenfratz et al. [Hasenfratz et al. 03] who presented a survey of techniques for the rendering of penumbrae, which was updated in 2008 by other authors [Bavoil 08a].

4.3   Screen Space Soft Shadows

This work proposes a new method for calculating soft shadows with variable penumbrae in real time. The method is based on blurring the shadows from the observer's point of view by using an anisotropic Gaussian filter of variable size. The aspect ratio of the anisotropic Gaussian filter is determined by using the normal at the point being rendered. The size of the area affected by the filter, which generates softer or sharper penumbrae, varies per pixel and depends on the amount of light potentially received from the area light source. This factor is determined by the visibility of the area light from the point being rendered. The formula used to estimate how much light is received was proposed by [Fernando 05] (see Equation (4.1)).

$$w_{\text{penumbra}} = \frac{(d_{\text{receiver}} - d_{\text{blocker}}) \cdot w_{\text{light}}}{d_{\text{blocker}}}, \tag{4.1}$$

where w_{penumbra} is the final width of the penumbra, d_{receiver}; d_{blocker} are the distances of the receiver and the blocker to the light; and w_{light} is the size of the area light.

Observation reveals that shadows produced by area lights (including the penumbra) are larger than shadows produced by point lights, because the area affected by the penumbra increases with the size of the light source (see Figure 4.4). Therefore our method generates a "dilated" version of the shadow map in order to evaluate the Gaussian filter for those pixels potentially belonging to the area affected by the penumbra. This process is detailed in Section 4.3.1. Without this "dilated" shadow map, we only would be able to render the so-called inner penumbrae.

As a result, this method is able to generate soft shadows with perceptually correct penumbrae, which softens as their distance to the occluder as well as the size of the light source increases (see Figure 4.1).

The following steps describe the process to be performed, for each light source, in order to generate shadow penumbrae with our method:

1. Calculate the standard shadow map (S_{map}) and a "dilated" version (S'_{map}) of the shadow map (see Section 4.3.1 for details).

2. Render the scene from the observer's point of view and calculate the following elements in the same rendering pass: the shadows without penumbrae (or hard shadows), the depth buffer, a normal buffer and the shading of

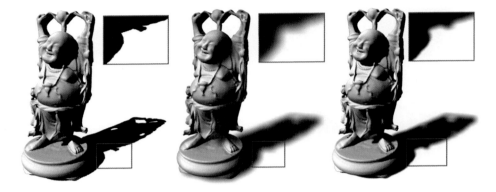

Figure 4.4. Importance of perceptually correct shadows: shadows with no penumbra (left), with uniform penumbra (middle) and with variable penumbra rendered with our method (right). Notice how the penumbra becomes sharper as the shadow approaches the occluder. Notice also the quality of self-shadows compared to uniform penumbra methods.

the scene (without shadows). The distances map is also calculated in the same rendering pass. This map contains the distance from the point being evaluated (P) to the first light occluder, as well as the linear distance to the observer. See Section 4.3.2 for details.

3. Deferred shadowing: render a full screen quad with our custom anisotropic Gaussian blur filter to blur the hard-edged shadows in screen space and to combine them with the shaded scene. The per-pixel size of the area affected by the blurring kernel is calculated using the data in the distances map.

The following are the configuration of the multiple render targets, used to calculate all needed buffers in one rendering pass (step 2):

- MRT0. Diffuse color without shadows.

- MRT1. Normal-depth buffer (RGB: normal's XYZ. Depth is stored in the alpha channel).

- MRT2. Shadow buffer.

- MRT3. Distances map, which contains the following information in the first three channels:

  o R: distance of the shadow caster to the point being rendered (D).

  o G: distance of the observer to the point being rendered (Z).

Figure 4.5. Different intermediate steps of our algorithm. From left to right: the model with hard shadows, the standard shadow map, the dilated shadow map and the final result of blurring the shadows with the anisotropic Gaussian filter.

○ B: mask value determining whether the point is inside the penumbra or not.

4.3.1 Calculating the Shadow Maps

First of all, the standard shadow map is calculated from the light source. It is important to note that this information is insufficient to directly determine the distance to the occluder in order to represent the outter penumbrae.

To solve this problem, we create a coarser version of the shadow map by preprocessing it in the following way: each pixel of the coarse shadow map will approximate a block of pixels of the standard shadow map. The criterion used for this approximation is the minimum value (closest to the light). Take into account that the contents of the coarse shadow map are used as a depth estimation to calculate the distance map, not to generate the shadow itself. We use this criterion because, performing the average of samples of the shadow map without taking into account the shadow receiver, would compute incorrect z-values, and thus incorrect penumbrae.

The dilation is performed in light space, by applying an isotropic min-filter to the original shadow map, after it is computed. Given that this filter is separable, it is computed efficiently as two one-dimensional filters.

The amount of dilation is proportional to the size of the area light source because the size of the penumbra is also proportional to the size of the light source. This is implemented by increasing the radius of the "minimum-value" filter kernel. However, as we are performing the dilation of the shadow map in image space, the shadow receiver cannot be taken into account to calculate the size of the penumbra. As a consequence, the user has to apply a constant factor to the amount of dilation, because the size of the penumbra is also proportional to the distance between the shadow caster and the shadow receiver. This factor is interpreted as the maximum distance to the occluder possible in the scene. If this parameter is too small, penumbrae will not be completely smooth. On the other hand, if the parameter is too large, the resulting penumbrae will be less accurate. In practice, it is not difficult to visually set up this value for a given scene.

Once calculated, the filtered shadow map will allow us to calculate the distances map (see Section 4.3.2) for every point of the penumbrae (including the outer penumbra) in screen space.

4.3.2 Calculating the Distances Map

The distances map is a screen-aligned texture that contains, per pixel, the distance of the shadow to its potential occluder and its distance to the observer. This is computed by rendering a full screen quad so that every pixel in the screen is evaluated. Distances to the occluder are computed by transforming the point being evaluated to the light space. This way, its depth value can be compared directly with the depth of the coarse occluder.

For optimization purposes, the distances map also stores a mask determining which pixels will never receive neither a shadow nor a penumbra. The shadow mask is useful to reduce texture lookups and improve performance.

4.3.3 Applying the Gaussian Filter

Determining the size of the penumbrae. This step generates the penumbra by applying an anisotropic Gaussian blur filter in screen space. The size of the region affected by the kernel varies per pixel depending on:

- The distance of the shadow to the occluder.

- The distance of the light source to the occluder.

- The size of the light source.

To take these factors into account, R. Fernando [Fernando 05] introduced a formula (see Equation (4.1)) that estimates the size of the penumbra by using the parallel planes approach. This assumes that the occluder, shadow receiver, and light sources are parallel. However, in practice it works very well and provides a formula which is not expensive to evaluate.

We derive Equation (4.1) by adding the distance of the pixel to the observer to the computations, because our filter is applied in screen-space and the area affected by the filter diminishes as its distance from the observer increases. Equation (4.2) shows how the previously calculated buffers are now combined in order to determine the size of the area affected by the filter in screen space:

$$w_{\mathrm{penumbra}} = \frac{(d_{\mathrm{receiver}} - d_{\mathrm{blocker}}) \cdot w_{\mathrm{light}}}{d_{\mathrm{blocker}} \cdot d_{\mathrm{observer}}}. \tag{4.2}$$

In Equation (4.2), the size of the penumbra (w_{penumbra}) depends on the following members: ($d_{\mathrm{receiver}} - d_{\mathrm{blocker}}$) represents the distance between the shadow receiver and the shadow caster; d_{observer} is the distance to the observer. These parameters are stored in the distances map; w_{light} is the size of the light source; and d_{blocker} represents the contents of the "coarse" shadow map and stores the distance to the blocker in light space.

Anisotropic filtering. The anisotropic Gaussian filter is a separable filter. One two-dimensional blurring can be performed in two sequential one-dimensional blurring passes: one horizontal and one vertical. This is the key to our method, because applying a Gaussian filter to create the penumbra requires far fewer texture accesses compared to the PCSS approach, which is not separable, allowing the cost of our method to be $O(n + n)$ instead of $O(n^2)$.

For each sample accessed to perform the Gaussian filter, their distance to the observer is taken into account to discard samples whose distance to the current pixel is greater than a certain threshold. This is used to prevent the filter kernel from taking into account parts of the scene that are close in eye space but are far away in world space. It also avoids having to filter the shadows with the contents of the background. The number of samples taken by the Gaussian filter determines both the quality of the shadows and the performance. Therefore this trade-off decision is left to the user as a customizable parameter. An interesting optimization, in order to reduce the number of texture accesses, is to decrease the number of samples as the area affected by the blurring kernel decreases.

To determine the shape of the anisotropic filtering, the normal of the current pixel is fetched from the normal buffer (generated previously using `Multiple RenderTargets`). Using this normal, the local tangent space is calculated and used to determine the local x-, y- and z-axes. Projecting these axes to eye space allows us to determine the shape and orientation of the ellipse which defines the anisotropic filter.

To perform the anisotropic filtering in an efficient way, we use the method presented by [Geusebroek and Smeulders 03]. This work derives the anisotropic Gauss filtering and proposes to apply it as a separable kernel, which can be evaluated efficiently.

Finally, after the vertical blurring pass is performed, the penumbra has already been calculated so the pixel shader combines it with the unshadowed scene C to create the final image, with complete shadows with penumbrae.

4.3.4   Using Average Instead of Minimum Depth

Our technique provides a simplification that allows us to rapidly generate penumbrae, minimizing the number of texture accesses per pixel as based on the minimum depth texture approach. However, while this technique is able to generate plausible soft shadows in most scenes, it may not be completely accurate for some scenes with very complex shadow casters and receivers.

Fernando [Fernando 05] shows how the average depth of the potential occluders is a valid measure to determine the size of the penumbra at a given point. This process, called the *blocker search* step, is accomplished by performing a number of samples over the shadow map in order to determine the average distance of potential occluders. The size of the sampling area is proportional to the size of the light source. On typical scenes, performing 5×5 samples over the shadow map is sufficient to provide accurate results. However, as the size of the light source increases, more samples may be needed for detailed objects to avoid artifacts due to the spacing of the samples in texture space.

Annen et al [Annen et al. 08] introduce an optimization to the blocker search step by performing it as a convolution filter. This way, this step can be done efficiently on the graphics hardware.

Therefore, if desired, a traditional approach based on the blocker search can be implemented to use the average depth instead of the minimum depth, as used in percentage closer soft shadows, while still being able to use our screen-based anisotropic Gaussian filtering to generate the penumbrae.

Obviously the minimum depth texture is not longer necessary when computing the size of the penumbra. Therefore, the step of generating that texture can be safely skipped.

4.4   Results

This section presents performance and quality tests performed using our method with different scene configurations. All tests were run on an Athlon +3500 processor with 3GB of RAM memory and a GeForce 8800GT graphics card. In order to best show the quality of the shadows, quality comparative images were rendered using a black ambient light over untextured surface. This way, shadows can be studied easily.

4.4.1   Quality Tests

The number of samples used by the Gaussian kernel greatly affects the final quality of the penumbra, especially when large light sources are used and large penumbrae must be generated. Figure 4.6 shows a set of shadows generated

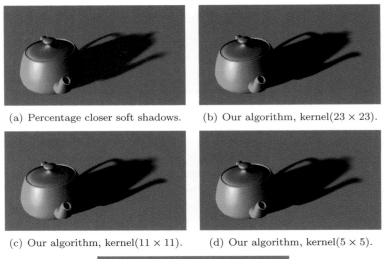

(a) Percentage closer soft shadows.   (b) Our algorithm, kernel(23 × 23).

(c) Our algorithm, kernel(11 × 11).   (d) Our algorithm, kernel(5 × 5).

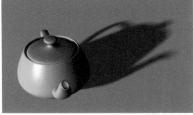

(e) Reference ray-traced shadow.

Figure 4.6. Visual quality comparison between our algorithm (with three different kernel sizes, shown in (b), (c), and (d)) and other approaches: (e) a ray-traced shadow and (a) an implementation of PCSS.

with different kernel sizes in order to show penumbrae quality with different configurations. Three kernel sizes were used: 5 × 5, 11 × 11 and 23 × 23. The image shows how the small 5 × 5 kernel produces some discretization artifacts in the penumbra. The 11 × 11 kernel is useful for the majority of cases, but it can be insufficient when the camera comes close to the penumbra. In these cases a 23 × 23 kernel is more than enough for obtaining good quality.

Figure 4.7 shows the effects of increasing the size of the area light. This figure shows how the size of the penumbra grows proportionally to the size of the light source. Figure 4.7(c) shows that, even with a huge area light, the algorithm is able to represent visually pleasant shadows with perceptually correct penumbrae.

Figure 4.8 shows a complex scene using our soft shadowing technique.

(a) Small light source.   (b) Medium light source.

(c) Large light source.

Figure 4.7. Effects of changing the size of the light source; the size of the penumbra is proportional to the size of the light source.

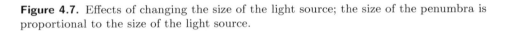

(a) Hard shadows.   (b) Hard shadows.

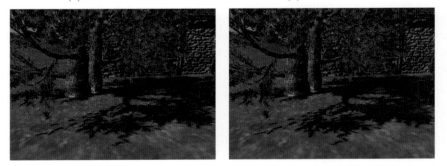

(c) Our algorithm with a 5×5 blur kernel. (d) Our algorithm with a 23×23 blur kernel.

Figure 4.8. Shadows quality in a complex scene with complex shadow casters.

Method	Kernel setup	800×600	1280×1024	1600×1200
standard	*None*	942 fps	595 fps	245 fps
PCF	$PCF(3 \times 3)$	462 fps	230 fps	175 fps
SSSS	$K(5 \times 5)$	553 fps	278 fps	213 fps
	$K(11 \times 11)$	513 fps	256 fps	181 fps
	$K(23 \times 23)$	441 fps	221 fps	155 fps
PCSS	$B_s(5 \times 5) + PCF(5 \times 5)$	504 fps	239 fps	183 fps
	$B_s(5 \times 5) + PCF(11 \times 11)$	251 fps	106 fps	78 fps
	$B_s(5 \times 5) + PCF(23 \times 23)$	122 fps	49 fps	37 fps

Table 4.1. Performance results measured in frames per second (FPS) on the AT-AT scene (200K triangles). SSSS stands for our method (Screen Space Soft Shadows). K refers to the kernel sizes used with each technique. B_s stands for *blocker search*, used in the PCF algorithm.

4.4.2 Performance Tests

Table 4.1 compares performance in the AT-AT scene, using different configurations and techniques. The first and second columns indicate the methods and configurations used, while the rest of the columns show performance (measured in frames per second) for each configuration in both scenes. Standard shadow mapping is used to provide the time needed to calculate shadows without penumbra. In the second row, the time needed to calculate a uniform-sized penumbra is provided. This penumbra is calculated using a percentage closer filter combined with a screen space blur filter that removes artifacts and softens penumbrae. Next, many timings are taken using our method with some different kernel configurations under different screen resolutions. It can be seen that our method performs very well, being that its costs are similar to the uniform-sized penumbrae cost. Finally, percentage closer soft shadows are used in order to provide performance measurements for comparing our technique with a well known soft shadowing method.

As shown in the table, our technique is able to perform very well even at high screen resolutions, outperforming PCSS with similar kernel sizes and screen resolutions. Moreover, it can be seen how performance drops when using PCSS while incrementing the screen resolution and kernel sizes, while performance remains more stable with our algorithm.

4.5 Conclusion

This work presents a new approach for calculating soft shadows with variable-sized penumbrae in real time (see Figure 4.9). To optimize this task, we introduce the concept of distance map, which stores the distance from a pixel potentially

Figure 4.9. Example of penumbrae with different light sizes and different light colors.

affected by the penumbra to the occluder that produces that shadow. This distance is used to generate penumbrae in screen space using an anisotropic Gaussian blurring kernel.

The bottleneck of the PCSS approach is the number of texture accesses required to achieve smooth penumbrae. First, it has to perform a blocker search to determine the overall distance of the shadow to the occluder. Although this step requires at least 3×3 texture reads, it is advisable to use at least 5×5 or even 7×7 to completely avoid artifacts on complex shadow casters. Our method performs the blocker search by just accessing the distances map, which can be generated from a low-resolution coarse shadow map. In addition, PCSS needs to take multiple samples of the shadow map in order to generate the penumbrae. In practice, 13×13 is a good kernel size to achieve smooth shadows with PCSS. Thus, the number of samples required to generate the penumbra with this method is: 5×5 (blocker search) + 13×13 (PCF) = 194 texture reads.

On the other hand, since our algorithm uses a separable filter, the cost of computing the penumbra is $O(n+n)$ instead of $O(n^2)$, as in the PCSS approach. As an example, using an 11×11 kernel with PCSS would require $11 \times 11 = 121$ texture accesses, while by using a separable Gaussian blur it can be performed with only $11+11=22$ texture lookups. This method also proves to be very scalable because increasing the kernel to 17×17 requires only 34 samples with our method and 289 samples with PCSS. This means that even using a massive 50×50 Gaussian filter ($50+50 = 100$ texture lookups), our method would offer better performance compared to PCSS while generating extremely smooth penumbrae.

Moreover, the use of an anisotropic filtering allows our method to take into account the orientation of the surface being shadowed. This way, the screen space filtering is able to deliver precise penumbrae even at grazing angles.

Another advantage of using our method is that it complies with the concept of deferred shading. This shading scheme, which is commonly used in films and postproduction, is becoming popular in the field of real-time graphics. Deferred lighting (see [Engel 08]) uses a similar approach for rendering efficiently a high amount of lights in real time. Our technique is easily integrable in a deferred shading pipeline, performing all the calculations in screen space, taking as input the same buffers used in the deferred shading (except for the distances map). The direct benefits of our approach are that no superfluous calculations are wasted on invisible pixels, as it is applied in screen space over the computed shadow buffer.

On the other hand, this technique presents some limitations. The first limitation is that we are simplifying the blocker search by using a minimum depth filter, which selects the minimum depth from the light source instead of an average depth of the blockers. Another issue is that the coarse shadow map can not take into account the distance of the shadow to the receiver in order to dilate the shadow map, which forces the user to set a fixed safe distance by hand.

However, despite its limitations, our technique is able to deliver perceptually correct penumbrae on controlled scenes, with a performance boost compared with PCSS, almost multiplying by three the performance obtained with large kernels.

Acknowledgments

This work was supported by Ministerio Español de Ciencia y Tecnología (grant TSI-2004-02940 and projects TIN2007-68066-C04-01 and TIN2007-68066-C04-02) and by Bancaja (P1 1B2007-56).

Bibliography

[Annen et al. 08] Thomas Annen, Zhao Dong, Tom Mertens, Philippe Bekaert, Hans-Peter Seidel, and Jan Kautz. "Real-Time, All-Frequency Shadows in Dynamic Scenes." *Proceedings of SIGGRAPH* 3 (2008), 1–8.

[Bavoil 08a] Louis Bavoil. "Advanced Soft Shadow Mapping Techniques." *Game Developers Conference.*

[Bavoil 08b] Louis Bavoil. "Percentage-Closer Soft Shadows." *NVIDIA.* Available online (http://developer.download.nvidia.com/SDK/10.5/direct3d/samples.html).

[Donnelly and Lauritzen 06] William Donnelly and Andrew Lauritzen. "Variance Shadow Maps." In *Proceedings of the 2006 Symposium on Interactive 3D Graphics and Games*, pp. 161–165, 2006.

[Engel 08] Wolfgang Engel. "Designing a Renderer for Multiple Lights: The Light Pre-Pass Renderer." *ShaderX7 : Advanced rendering techniques.*

[Fernando 05] Randima Fernando. "Percentage-Closer Soft Shadows." In *SIGGRAPH '05: ACM SIGGRAPH 2005 Sketches*, p. 35, 2005.

[Geusebroek and Smeulders 03] Jan M. Geusebroek and Arnold W. M. Smeulders. "Fast Anisotropic Gauss Filtering." *IEEE Transactions on Image Processing* 12:8 (2003), 99–112.

[Hasenfratz et al. 03] Jean-Marc Hasenfratz, Marc Lapierre, Nicolas Holzschuch, and François Sillion. "A Survey of Real-Time Soft Shadows Algorithms." *Computer Graphics Forum* 22:4 (2003), 753–774.

[Reeves et al. 87] William T. Reeves, David H. Salesin, and Robert L. Cook. "Rendering Antialiased Shadows with Depth Maps." *SIGGRAPH '87* 21:4 (1987), 283–291.

[Salvi 07] Marco Salvi. "Rendering Filtered Shadows with Exponential Shadow Maps." *ShaderX6 : Advanced rendering techniques.*

[Williams 78] Lance Williams. "Casting Curved Shadows on Curved Surfaces." In *SIGGRAPH '78*, 12, 12, pp. 270–274, 1978.

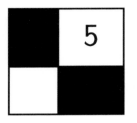

5

Variance Shadow Maps Light-Bleeding Reduction Tricks
Wojciech Sterna

5.1 Introduction

Variance Shadow Maps (VSMs) were first introduced in [Donnelly and Lauritzen 06] as an alternative to bilinear percentage closer filtering (PCF) to speed up rendering of smoothed shadows. The algorithm is relatively inexpensive, easy to implement, and very effective in rendering shadows with large penumbra regions. However, VSM has one major drawback—apparent light-bleeding—which occurs when two or more shadow casters cover each other in light-space. This chapter will show techniques that help to reduce the light-bleeding artifacts in VSM.

5.2 VSM Overview

The idea of variance shadow mapping is to store in the shadow map, instead of a single depth value, a distribution of depth values over some region and to use elementary statistics to evaluate the shadowing term. This approach makes it possible to use filtering methods (bilinear, trilinear, blurring) on the shadow map. A common option is to use Gaussian blur on the shadow map to achieve soft shadows in $O(n)$ time. This is a great advantage over traditional PCF which requires $O(n^2)$ time to achieve the same effect.

To generate the variance shadow map, two values must be written into it. The first is simply a distance from a light source to a pixel, as with traditional shadow mapping (one thing that is important here is that this distance should have a linear metric). The second component of the shadow map is a square of the first component.

Once the shadow map has been prepared (it contains both depth and a square of depth), additional filtering can be applied to it. To achieve good-looking soft shadows, a separable Gaussian filter with 5×5 taps can be used.

To estimate the shadow contribution from such a defined VSM, so-called Chebyshev's inequality (one-tailed version) can be used to estimate the shadowing term:

$$P(O \geq R) \leq p_{\max}(R) \equiv \frac{\sigma^2}{\sigma^2 + (R - \mu)^2}, \quad \text{where} \quad \mu < R \tag{5.1}$$

The variable O is an occluder's depth (shadow map's texel), R is a receiver's depth (distance from a pixel being shaded to a light source), σ^2 is the variance and μ is the mean. The term $P(O \geq R)$ can roughly be interpreted as a probability of a point (at distance R) being lit (unshadowed by a point at distance O), which is the exact value we wish to know, and Chebyshev's inequality gives us an upperbound to this value.

The mean and variance in Equation (5.1) are computed from the first and second statistical moments:

$$\begin{aligned}
M_1 &= E(O) \\
M_2 &= E(O^2) \\
\mu &= M_1 = E(O) \\
\sigma^2 &= M_2 - M_1{}^2 = E(O^2) - E(O)^2
\end{aligned}$$

In fact, the first moment is what is actually stored in the first channel of the shadow map, and the second moment in the second channel of the shadow map. That's why the shadow map can be additionally prefiltered before its use—the moments are defined by the expectation operator which is linear and can thus be linearly filtered.

A sample implementation of standard VSM is shown in Listing 5.1.

```
float VSM(float2 projTexCoord, float depth, float bias)
{
    float2 moments = tex2D(shadowMap_linear, projTexCoord).rg;

    if (moments.x >= depth - bias)
        return 1.0f;

    float variance = moments.y - moments.x*moments.x;
    float delta = depth - moments.x;
    float p_max = variance / (variance + delta*delta);

    return saturate(p_max);
}
```

Listing 5.1. Standard VSM implementation.

Note that the given Chebyshev's inequality (its one-tailed version) is undefined for cases in which $\mu \geq R$. Of course, in such a case a point is fully lit, so the function returns 1.0; otherwise, p_{max} is returned.

5.3   Light-Bleeding

Light-bleeding (see Figure 5.1) occurs when two or more shadow casters cover each other in light-space, causing light (these are actually soft edges of shadows of the objects closest to the light) to bleed onto the shadows of further (from the light) objects. Figure 5.2 shows this in detail.

As can be seen from the picture in Figure 5.2, object C is lit over a filter region. The problem is that when estimating the shadow contribution for pixels of object C over this region, the variance and mean that are used are actually based on the samples from object A (red line) and visible samples from object B (green line) (the shadow map consists of pixels colored by red and green lines), whereas they should be based on samples from object B only (green and blue lines). Moreover, the greater the ratio of distances $\frac{\Delta x}{\Delta y}$ (see Figure 5.2), the more apparent the light-bleeding is on object C.

The VSM is not capable of storing more information (about occluded pixels of object B for instance). This is not even desirable since we want to keep the

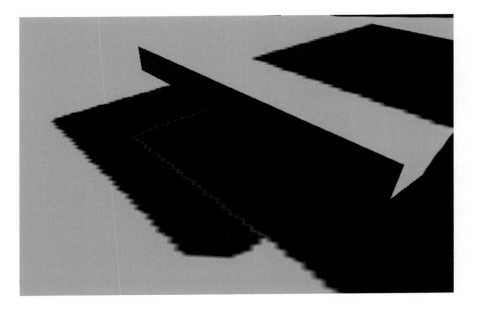

Figure 5.1. Light-bleeding.

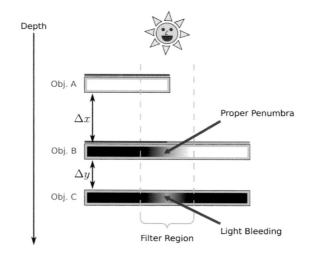

Figure 5.2. How light-bleeding occurs.

algorithm simple and don't want to raise its memory requirements. Fortunately, the following sections in this chapter will present a few very simple tricks that can greatly reduce the problem.

5.4   Solutions to the Problem

5.4.1   Cutting the Tail Off

The first way of reducing light-bleeding was simply cutting off the tail of the p_{max} function. Put simply, it's about subtracting some fixed value from the result of p_{max}. This way, incorrect penumbra regions will get darker but so will the correct ones. However, intensities of incorrect penumbra regions never reach 1 (as shown in [Lauritzen 07]) so the final result can still look good when the cutting value is chosen wisely.

Figure 5.3 shows a side-by-side comparison of standard VSM implementation and the same VSM but with p_{max} cut off by a value of 0.15. Although the light-bleeding is still present it's much less obvious.

As we mentioned earlier, the light-bleeding gets more noticeable when the ratio $\frac{\Delta x}{\Delta y}$ is big. In such a scenario (high depth complexity) it is next to impossible to eliminate the problem by applying only a cutting value. More sophisticated methods are necessary.

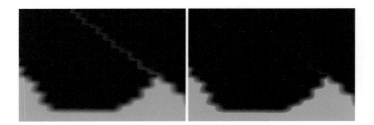

Figure 5.3. VSM and VSM with $p_{\max}$ cut off by 0.15.

5.4.2 Applying VSM to Shadow Boundaries

One of the possibilities for reducing the problem of light-bleeding is, simply to avoid it. The trick is to combine standard depth-comparison shadow mapping with VSM applied only to regions that really need it—shadow boundaries.

The problem with this idea is that the greater the penumbra region, the harder it gets to properly detect shadow boundaries, since more samples are needed. However, if one decides not to blur the shadow map and to rely only on standard hardware linear (or trilinear) filtering, four samples are enough to detect shadow boundaries; light-bleeding free VSM is achieved with the resulting performance comparable to that from standard VSM.

Figure 5.4 shows a side-by-side comparison of standard VSM and the combination of classic shadow mapping with VSM applied only to shadow boundaries.

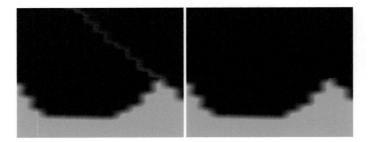

Figure 5.4. VSM and VSM applied to shadow boundaries.

5.4.3 Exponential Variance Shadow Maps

EVSM is a combination of two techniques—variance shadow maps and exponential shadow maps, which were described in [Salvi 08]. The idea was first presented in [Lauritzen 08] and it is surprising that it is not recognized among developers, for it is able to almost completely eliminate the light-bleeding.

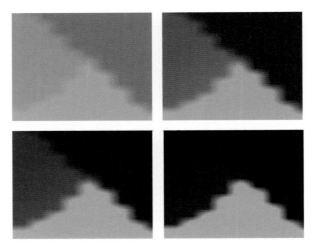

Figure 5.5. ESM with the following constants: 10, 50, 90, 200.

ESMs work similarly to VSMs. A very nice feature of ESM is that it requires only a single-channel shadow map, which stores the first moment. The algorithm also uses statistical methods to estimate the shadowing term and it does so by using the so-called Markov inequality (as opposed to VSM which uses Chebyshev's inequality):

$$P(O \geq R) \leq \frac{E(O)}{R} \tag{5.2}$$

Using Markov inequality as given in Equation (5.2) doesn't provide a good shadow approximation; shadows suffer from a sort of global light-bleeding. However, [Salvi 08] shows that it can be transformed to the following representation:

$$P(e^{kO} \geq e^{kR}) \leq \frac{E(e^{kO})}{e^{kR}} \tag{5.3}$$

Constant k determines how good the approximation is—the greater the value, the better the approximation. Unfortunately, large values cause precision loss, and shadow boundaries become sharper, so a compromise must be found. Figure 5.5 shows a comparison of ESM with different values of constant k.

ESM is simpler, faster, and has a tweakable light-bleeding parameter that makes it more practical than VSM in many cases. However, a very promising idea is the combination of these two techniques—EVSM. Instead of storing depth and a square of depth in the shadow map, we store an exponential of depth and a square of exponential of depth. The exponential function has the effect of decreasing the ratio $\frac{\Delta x}{\Delta y}$ and thus reduces the VSM-like light-bleeding.

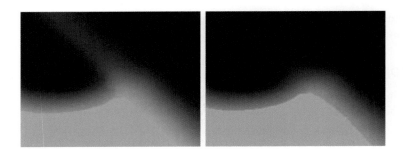

Figure 5.6. VSM and EVSM with p_{max} cut off by 0.05 and $k = 50$.

EVSM suffers from light-bleeding only in cases when both VSM and ESM fail, which rarely happens. A very important feature of EVSM is that the light-bleeding can be controlled by two factors: VSM with the tail cut off and ESM with k constant. Careful adjustment of these two will lead to very pleasing and accurate soft shadows.

Figure 5.6 shows a side-by-side comparison of standard VSM and EVSM.

5.5 Sample Application

In the web materials accompanying this book there is a demo presenting all of the techniques described in this chapter.

Here is the key configuration:

- WSAD + mouse—camera movement;

- Shift—speeding up;

- F1 - F5—change of shadowing technique;

- E/Q—turn on/off shadow map Gaussian blurring;

- R/F—increase/decrease VSM tail cut off parameter;

- T/G—increase/decrease ESM constant k.

The core of the demo are two shader files: `shadow_map.ps` and `light.ps`. Implementations of all algorithms described here can be found in these files.

5.6 Conclusion

Variance shadow mapping has already proven to be a great way of generating soft shadows. The algorithm is easy to implement, fast, and utilizes hardware features of modern GPUs. Despite its advantages, VSM also introduces some problems. The worst one is light-bleeding, which was the subject of discussion in this chapter.

Bibliography

[Donnelly and Lauritzen 06] William Donnelly and Andrew Lauritzen. "Variance Shadow Maps.", 2006. Available online (http://www.punkuser.net/vsm/).

[Lauritzen 07] Andrew Lauritzen. "Summed-Area Variance Shadow Maps." In *GPU Gems 3*, Chapter II.8. Reading, MA: Addison-Wesley, 2007.

[Lauritzen 08] Andrew Lauritzen. Master's thesis, University of Waterloo, 2008.

[Salvi 08] Marci Salvi. "Rendering Filtered Shadows with Exponential Shadow Maps." In *ShaderX^6*, Chapter IV.3. Hingham, MA: Charles River Media, 2008.

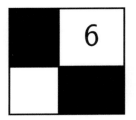

Fast Soft Shadows via Adaptive Shadow Maps

Pavlo Turchyn

We describe a *percentage-closer filtering* (PCF) based extension to an *adaptive shadow maps* (ASM) algorithm [Fernando et al. 01]. Our method enables high-quality rendering of large penumbrae with minimal size of filter-kernel size. It also offers better image quality compared to other PCF-based soft shadows algorithms, such as *percentage closer soft shadows* (PCSS).

6.1 Percentage-Closer Filtering with Large Kernels

Filtering is an important part of every shadow mapping implementation because it serves multiple goals: it reduces aliasing artifacts and allows the creation of soft shadows to improve image realism. Aliasing artifacts manifest themselves when there are either too many shadow map texels per screen area (resulting in the same type of noise that can be observed on regular color textures without mipmapping), or there are too few shadow map texels per screen area, so the shadow map cannot plausibly represent the correct shapes of shadows. However, filtering alone can reduce only the visual impact of undersampling to a certain extent.

PCF is a common method of shadow map filtering. Given shadow map coordinates uv, and depth value d, a PCF computes the following weighted sum:

$$\text{PCF}(\texttt{DepthTexture}, uv, d, n) =$$
$$\sum_{i=1}^{n} \big(\texttt{Weight}[i] * (\texttt{tex2D}(\texttt{DepthTexture}, uv + \texttt{Offset}[i])).\text{r} > d\big).$$

The tables `Weight` and `Offset` hold weights and the texture coordinates offsets, respectively. The choice of `Weight` and `Offset` defines performance and quality of rendering. The computationally fastest way is to use constant tables. In more elaborate schemes, the tables are constructed based on coordinates uv.

Figure 6.1. Soft shadows in *Age of Conan.*

The number of samples n is chosen depending on the size of the area over which the filtering is performed. Summing over the area of $m \times m$ shadow map texels would require at least $n = m^2$ samples if we want to account for all texels. However, such a quadratic complexity of the filter makes PCF impractical for filtering over large areas. For instance, if the size of a shadow map texel's projection onto a scene's geometry is 0.1 m, and the desired penumbra size is about 1.5 meters, then we need to apply PCF over $(1.5/0.1) \times (1.5/0.1) = 15 \times 15$ area, which in turn gives $n = 225$.

It is possible to use PCF with large kernels in time-sensitive applications by decreasing the number of samples, so that $n \ll m^2$, and distributing the samples pseudorandomly over the summation area. Such an approach produces penumbra with noise artifacts as shown in Figure 6.2. A screen-space low-pass filtering can be used for suppressing the noise, but such a post-filtering removes all high-frequency features within penumbra indiscriminately. Moreover, preventing shadows from bleeding into undesired areas in screen space may require the use of relatively expensive filters,(e.g., a bilateral filter).

We propose a *multiresolution filtering* (MRF) method that attempts to alleviate the PCF problem described above. The idea is as follows: When we create the standard shadow map for the scene, we also create versions of it with progressively lower resolutions. For example, if the shadow map's resolution is 2048×2048, we create three additional shadow maps: 1024×1024, 512×512, and 256×256. The key observation is that the result of PCF over a 3×3 area of a 1024×1024 shadow map is a reasonably accurate approximation for filtering over 6×6 area of 2048×2048 map. Similarly, PCF over a 3×3 area of a 256×256 shadow map approximates a 6×6 filter for a 512×512 map, a 12×12 filter for a 1024×1024 map, and a 24×24 filter for a 2048×2048 map. Thus, in order to

Figure 6.2. Filtering comparison. From top to bottom: bilinear PCF; 24 × 24 PCF filter with 32 samples, frame rendering time on Radeon 4870 is 3.1 ms; 24 × 24 PCF filter with 64 samples, 6.7 ms; 24 × 24 MRF filter (3 × 3 PCF), 3.1 ms.

approximate PCF with large kernels, we apply PCF with a small kernel size to a shadow map with reduced resolution.

Approximating arbitrary kernel size. Let us number shadow maps starting with zero index assigned to the shadow map with the highest resolution

```
sampler2D shadowMaps[4] = { shadowMap2048x2048,
    shadowMap1024x1024, shadowMap512x512, shadowMap256x256 };
```

Such a numbering is similar to the numbering of mipmaps of color textures. Suppose we want to approximate an $m \times m$ PCF with an MRF based on nine samples of a 3×3 PCF. The index of the shadow map, which can be used to get an adequate approximation, is computed as

```
float shadowMapIndex = log2( max(1.0, m/3.0) );
```

The value `shadowMapIndex` is a real number (e.g., the value `shadowMapIndex` =2.415 corresponds to a 16×16 kernel), so we have to either round it toward the closest integer, or perform the following interpolation, which is similar to the one used in standard trilinear filtering:

```
float shadowIntensity = lerp(
  PCF(shadowMaps[ floor(shadowMapIndex) ], uv, d, 9),
  PCF(shadowMaps[ ceil(shadowMapIndex) ], uv, d, 9),
  frac(shadowMapIndex) );
```

Pros and cons. MRF enables creating large penumbrae with only a few depth texture samples. Since it is based on a small number of samples, it allows the computiation of shadow intensities using relatively complex filter kernels, which can produce continuous values without the noise inherent to plain PCF kernels with a low number of samples. As a result, MRF does not require any type of postfiltering. Compared to prefiltering methods, (e.g. [Donnelly and Lauritzen 06], [Annen et al. 07], [Annen et al. 08]), MRF does not introduce approximation-specific artifacts, such as light leaking, ringing, or precision deficiencies. Moreover, since MRF is based on a regular PCF, it is possible to utilize existing hardware features, for example hardware bilinear PCF or double-speed depth-only rendering.

6.2   Application to Adaptive Shadow Maps

Adaptive shadow maps (ASM) is a method that addresses perspective and projection aliasing that occurs in standard shadow mapping [Fernando et al. 01]. Another notable advantage of ASM is the ability to exploit frame-to-frame coherency, which was the main reason for implementing the method in Funcom's *Age of Conan*. The algorithm is shown schematically in Figure 6.3. The major steps of the algorithm are explained below.

Creating tiles hierarchy. We start by projecting the view frustum onto the near plane of the light's frustum. The projected frustum is clipped against a grid defined on this plane. This grid is view independent and static (does not change from frame to frame). Each grid cell intersecting with the frustum is called a *tile*. If a tile is closer to the projected frustum's top than a certain threshold distance, we subdivide it into four equal cells (in a quadtree-like fashion). Each resulting cell is tested against the frustum, and the cells intersecting with it are called *child tiles*. We continue the subdivision process to obtain a hierarchy of tiles as shown in Figure 6.3. Note that unlike for example, the cascaded shadow

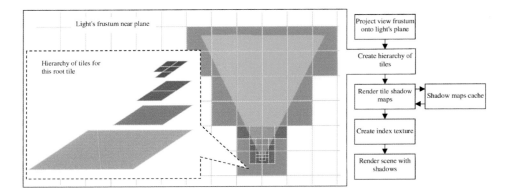

Figure 6.3. Adaptive Shadow Maps.

maps algorithm, here we do *not* subdivide the frustum itself; instead we use the frustum to determine which grid cells it intersects.

Shadow maps rendering. We render a fixed-resolution shadow map (e.g., 256×256) for every tile. Shadow maps are allocated from the single atlas (we use 4096×2048 depth texture in *Age of Conan*). Normally, there could be many tiles (about 100 in *Age of Conan*), but due to frame-to-frame coherency there is a high probability that a given shadow map was already rendered during previous frames. This is controlled through a shadow maps cache with LRU caching policy, (i.e., if the shadow map for a new tile is not present in the cache, then the shadow map which has not been in use for the largest number of frames will be reassigned to this tile).

Scene rendering. Since all shadow maps are equal in size, the shadow map sampling function requires knowledge only of the shadow map's offset within the atlas. These offsets are stored in a small dynamic index texture (we use a 128×128 texture). One can think of index texture as a standard shadow map that covers the entire view range, but instead of depth values, each texel contains the offsets, which are used to locate the actual tile shadow map in the atlas. Shadow map sampling code is given in Listing 6.1. As one can see, the only difference is index-texture indirection.

Pros and cons. ASM enables rendering of highly detailed shadows. Similar shadow mapping quality can be achieved only with standard shadow mapping when using a shadow map of very high resolution (for example, the resolution of an equivalent shadow map in *Age of Conan* is 16384×16384). Unlike projection-modifying approaches, such as [Stamminger and Drettakis 02] or [Martin and Tan 04], ASM does not suffer from temporal aliasing (since the tile's shadow map projection

```
float standardShadowMapSampling(float4 samplePosition)
{
  float4 shadowMapCoords =
    mul(samplePosition, shadowProjectionMatrix);
  return PCF(shadowMapTexture, shadowMapCoords);
}

float shadowMapSamplingASM(float4 samplePosition)
{
  float4 indexCoords =
    mul(samplePosition, shadowProjectionMatrix);
  float3 offset = tex2D(indexTexture, indexCoords.xy);
  float2 C = float2(tileShadowMapSize/atlasSize, 1);
  float3 shadowMapCoords = indexCoords*C.xxy + offset;
  return PCF(atlasTexture, shadowMapCoords);
}
```

Listing 6.1. Standard shadow map sampling vs ASM sampling.

matrices are view independent) and offers an intuitive control over the shadow map's texel distribution.

However, ASM imposes certain restrictions on a scene's granularity. Even though such situations do not occur frequently, in some cases we might need to render a number of shadow maps (we note that in *Age of Conan* we typically render one tile per several frames). As an extreme example, consider a scene that consists of just one huge object; the cost for rendering N shadow maps will be N times the cost of rendering such a scene. On the other hand, imagine a scene that consists of objects so small that they always overlap with just one tile; in this case the cost for rendering N tile shadow maps will be less or equal to the cost of whole scene. Therefore, a preferred scene should consist of a large number of lightweight, spatially compact objects rather than a few big and expensive-to-render geometry chunks.

Provided that granularity of the scene is reasonably fine and there is a certain frame-to-frame coherency, ASM significantly reduces shadow map rendering costs compared to standard shadow mapping. In this regard, one can view ASM as a method for distributing the cost of rendering a single shadow map over multiple frames.

A fundamental shortcoming of ASM is its inability to handle animated objects because such objects require updating the shadow map with every frame, while ASM relies on a shadow maps cache that holds data created over many frames. Similarly, light's position or direction cannot be changed on a per-frame basis because such a change invalidates the cache. In *Age of Conan* we use a separate

1024×1024 shadow map for rendering dynamic objects. Such a shadow map normally contains only a few objects, so it is inexpensive to render. Moreover, one can apply prefiltering techniques, (e.g., variance shadow maps), which may otherwise be problematic from the viewpoint of performance or quality. MRF naturally applies to the hierarchy of shadow maps produced with ASM.

6.3 Soft Shadows with Variable Penumbra Size

PCF with a fixed kernel size does not yield realistic shadows because it produces shadows with fixed penumbrae size, while penumbra in physically correct shadows usually vary greatly across the scene. The larger the light's area is, the bigger the difference should be between shadows from small objects and big objects. Thus, the kernel sizes in PCF should also vary depending on the estimated sizes of penumbrae.

One method for estimating penumbra size is proposed in the *percentage-closer soft shadows* (PCSS) scheme [Fernando 05]. In this method the size of a PCF kernel is a linear function of distance between a shaded fragment and its nearest occluder. The process of estimating the distance, which is called *blocker search*, largely resembles PCF; the difference is that instead of averaging results of depth tests, during blocker search one averages weighted depth values. When a light's area is large, the blocker search has to be performed on a large number of shadow map texels and thus it becomes as expensive as PCF. Attempting to reduce the number of samples may cause visible discontinuities and noise in penumbrae.

We use a faster method to estimate the distance to the occluder. A *depth extent map* (DEM) is a texture that contains minimum and maximum depth values computed over a certain region of the shadow map, which is used for detection of penumbrae regions [Isidoro and Sander 06]. We take the DEM's minimum depth value for the depth of the occluder, thus avoiding expensive blocker search. Since minimum depth value is a noncontinuous function, its use leads to discontinuities in penumbrae (such as clearly visible curves, along which shadows are vastly different). We compute the DEM for a low-resolution shadow map, and then use a single bilinear texture fetch to obtain piecewise-linear depth. The drawback of such an approach is the additional space required for storing the DEM. However, the DEM can be stored at a lower resolution than the resolution of the shadow map.

Occluders fusion. The most outstanding defect of PCF-based soft shadows is incorrect occluder fusion. The larger the penumbra size is, the more the artifacts stand out (see e.g., Figure 6.5(a)). The main source of the problem, illustrated in Figure 6.4, is the inability of a single shadow map to capture information needed

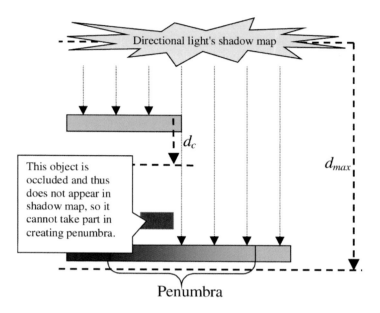

Figure 6.4. Shadow map layering.

to create shadows from area light. Each texel of a shadow map contains visibility information for a single light direction only, though light propagates along a range of directions.

This problem can be reduced relatively easily within the ASM framework. For a small set of tiles, which are closer to the viewer than a certain threshold distance, we render two shadow maps instead of one. First we create a regular shadow map and its corresponding DEM. Let $d_{\max}$ be the shadow map's range. Then, we create a *layer shadow map*, which is identical to the regular one, except that it is constructed using the fragments with depths within the range $[d + d_c, d_{\max}]$ (fragments with depth outside this range are discarded), where d is the corresponding minimum depth value from the DEM constructed for the regular shadow map, and d_c is a constant chosen by user. The penumbra over the scene's objects located within the range $[0; d + d_c]$ will be created using a regular shadow map only, thus occluder fusion will not be correct. However, one can use a layer shadow map to correct the penumbra on the objects located beyond $d + d_c$, as shown in Figure 6.5(b).

Shadow map layering significantly improved image quality in *Age of Conan*, removing a vast majority of occluder fusion artifacts. While theoretically one may utilize more than one layer, in *Age of Conan* one layer appeared to be sufficient. Adding more layers did not lead to any noticeable improvements.

(a) PCSS (from NVIDIA Direct3D SDK 10 Code Samples.)

(b) ASM + MRF + layering.

Figure 6.5. Occluders fusion: PCSS filters out penumbra details, ASM allows keeping them.

6.4 Results

We implemented our soft shadows algorithm in Funcom's MMORPG *Age of Conan*. Figure 6.6 shows in-game benchmark of two shadow mapping methods tested on Intel Core i7 2.66 MHz and AMD Radeon 4850.

Originally, the shadowing method in the released version of *Age of Conan* was standard shadow mapping, and cascaded shadow maps were added a year later with a patch. As shown in Figure 6.6, standard shadow mapping resulted in approximately 30% frame rate drop. The cascaded shadow map performance

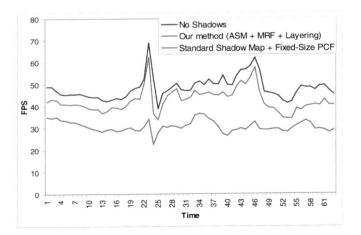

Figure 6.6. Benchmark: fly-by over a level from Age of Conan.

(not shown here) was worse. Implementing ASM-based soft shadows provided not only a substantial increase in image quality, but also a significant performance boost. We use ASM (with MRF and layering) to create shadows from static objects, and a separate 1024×1024 shadow map for dynamic objects, which is filtered with a fixed-size 3×3 PCF kernel.

Bibliography

[Annen et al. 07] Thomas Annen, Tom Mertens, P. Bekaert, Hans-Peter Seidel, and Jan Kautz. "Convolution Shadow Maps." In *European Symposium on Rendering*, pp. 51–60. Aire-la-Ville, Switzerland: Eurographics Association, 2007.

[Annen et al. 08] Thomas Annen, Tom Mertens, Hans-Peter Seidel, Eddy Flerackers, and Jan Kautz. "Exponential Shadow Maps." In *GI '08: Proceedings of Graphics Interface 2008*, pp. 155–161. Toronto, Canada: Canadian Information Processing Society, 2008.

[Donnelly and Lauritzen 06] William Donnelly and Andrew Lauritzen. "Variance Shadow Maps." In *I3D '06: Proceedings of the 2006 Symposium on Interactive 3D Graphics and Games*, pp. 161–165. New York: ACM, 2006.

[Fernando et al. 01] Randima Fernando, Sebastian Fernandez, Kavita Bala, and Donald P. Greenberg. "Adaptive Shadow Maps." In *SIGGRAPH '01: Proceedings of the 28th Annual Cconference on Computer Graphics and Interactive Techniques*, pp. 387–390. New York: ACM, 2001.

[Fernando 05] Randima Fernando. "Percentage-Closer Soft Shadows." In *SIGGRAPH '05: ACM SIGGRAPH 2005 Sketches*, p. 35. New York: ACM, 2005.

[Isidoro and Sander 06] John R. Isidoro and Pedro V. Sander. "Edge Masking and Per-Texel Depth Extent Propagation For Computation Culling During Shadow Mapping." In *ShaderX^5: Advanced Rendering Techniques*. Hingham, MA: Charles River Media, 2006.

[Martin and Tan 04] Tobias Martin and Tiow-Seng Tan. "Anti-Aliasing and Continuity with Trapezoidal Shadow Maps." In *Proceedings of Eurographics Symposium on Rendering*, pp. 153–160. Aire-la-Ville, Switzerland: Eurographics Association, 2004.

[Stamminger and Drettakis 02] Marc Stamminger and George Drettakis. "Perspective Shadow Maps." In *SIGGRAPH '02: Proceedings of the 29th Annual Conference on Computer Graphics and Interactive Techniques*, pp. 557–562. New York: ACM, 2002.

Adaptive Volumetric Shadow Maps

Marco Salvi, Kiril Vidimče, Andrew Lauritzen, Aaron Lefohn, and Matt Pharr

This chapter describes *adaptive volumetric shadow maps* (AVSM), a new approach for real-time shadows that supports high-quality shadowing from dynamic volumetric media such as hair and smoke. AVSMs compute approximate volumetric shadows for real-time applications such as games, for which predictable performance and a fixed, small memory footprint are required (and for which approximate solutions are acceptable).

We first introduced AVSM in a paper at the 2010 Eurographics Symposium on Rendering [Salvi et al. 10]; this chapter reviews the main ideas in the paper and details how to efficiently implement AVSMs on DX11-class graphics hardware. AVSMs are practical on today's high-end GPUs; for example, rendering Figure 7.4 requires 8.6 ms with opacity shadow maps (OSMs) and 12.1 ms with AVSMs—an incremental cost of 3.5 ms to both build the AVSM data structure and to use it for final rendering.

7.1 Introduction and Previous Approaches

Realistic lighting of volumetric and participating media such as smoke, fog, or hair adds significant richness and realism to rendered scenes. Self-shadowing provides important visual cues that define the shape and structure of such media. However, in order to compute self-shadowing in volumetric media, it is necessary to accumulate partial occlusion between visible points and light sources in the scene; doing so requires capturing the effect of all of the volumetric objects between two points and is generally much more expensive than computing shadows from opaque surfaces. As such, while it is common for offline renderers (e.g., those used in film rendering) to compute volumetric shadows, the computation and memory costs required to simulate light transport through participating

Figure 7.1. This image shows self-shadowing smoke and hair, both seamlessly rendered into the same adaptive volumetric shadow map. (Hair model courtesy of Cem Yuksel).

media have limited their use in real-time applications. Existing solutions for real-time volumetric shadowing exhibit slicing artifacts due to nonadaptive sampling, cover only a limited depth range, or are limited to one type of media (e.g., only hair, only smoke, etc.).

Adaptive shadow representations such as deep shadow maps have been used widely in offline rendering [Lokovic and Veach 00, Xie et al. 07]. Deep shadow maps store an adaptive, lossy-compressed representation of the visibility function for each light-space texel, though it is not clear how they can be implemented efficiently enough for real-time performance on today's graphics hardware, due to their high costs in term of storage and memory bandwidth.

Many volumetric shadowing techniques have been developed for interactive rendering. See our paper [Salvi et al. 10] for a detailed discussion of previous approaches; here,in this chapter, we will highlight the most widely known alternatives. A number of approaches discretize space into regularly spaced slices, for example opacity shadow maps [Kim and Neumann 01]. These methods typically suffer from aliasing, with variations specialized to handle small particles that can display view-dependent shadow popping artifacts even with static volumes [Green 08]. Deep opacity maps improve upon opacity shadow maps specifically for hair rendering by warping the sampling positions in the first depth layer [Yuksel and Keyser 08]. Occupancy maps also target hair rendering and use regular sampling, but capture many more depth layers than opacity- or deep-opacity- shadow maps by using only one bit per layer. However, they are limited to volumes composed of occluders with identical opacity [Sintorn and Assarson 09]. Mertens et al. describe a fixed-memory shadow algorithm for hair that adaptively places samples based on a k-means clustering estimate of the transmittance function, assuming density is uniformly distributed within a small number of clusters [Mertens et al. 04]. Recently, Jansen and Bavoil introduced Fourier opacity mapping, which addresses the problem of banding artifacts, but where the detail in shadows is limited by the depth range of volume samples along a ray and may exhibit ringing artifacts [Jansen and Bavoil 10]. Finally, Enderton et al. [Enderton et al. 10] have introduced a technique for handling all types of transparent occluders in a fixed amount of storage for both shadow and primary visibility, generating a stochastically sampled visibility function, though their approach requires a large number of samples for good results.

AVSM generates an adaptively sampled representation of the volumetric transmittance in a shadow-map-like data structure, where each texel stores a compact approximation of the transmittance curve along the corresponding light ray. AVSM can capture and combine transmittance data from arbitrary dynamic occluders, including combining soft media like smoke and well-localized denser media such as hair. It is thus both a versatile and a robust approach, suitable for handling volumetric shadows in a variety of situations in practice. The main innovation introduced by AVSM is a new, streaming lossy compression algorithm that is capable of building a constant-storage, variable-error representation of visibility for later use in shadow lookups.

7.2 Algorithm and Implementation

Adaptive volumetric shadow maps encode the fraction of visible light from the light source over the interval $[0, 1]$ as a function of depth at each texel. This quantity, the *transmittance*, is the quantity needed for rendering volumetric shadows. It is defined as

$$t(z) = e^{-\int_0^z f(x)\, dx},\tag{7.1}$$

where $f(x)$ is an attenuation function that represents the amount of light absorbed or scattered along a light ray (see Figure 7.2).

The AVSM representation stores a fixed-size array of irregularly placed samples of the transmittance function. Array elements, the *nodes* of the approximation, are sorted front-to-back, with each node storing a pair of depth and transmittance values (d_i, t_i). Because we adaptively place the nodes in depth, we can represent a rich variety of shadow blockers, from soft and transmissive particles to sharp and opaque occluders. The number of nodes stored per texel is a user-defined quantity, the only requirement being that we store two or more

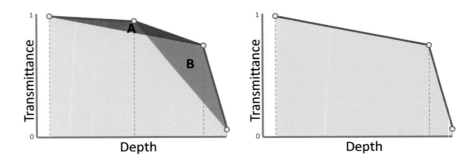

Figure 7.2. AVSM computes a compressed representation of transmittance along a light ray using an area-based curve simplification scheme. This figure depicts compressing a 4-node curve to three nodes. The algorithm removes the node that results in the smallest change in area under the curve, determined by computing the area of the triangle created between the candidate node and its adjacent neighbors (triangles A and B). The right figure shows that we remove the second node from the left because triangle A is smaller than triangle B.

nodes per texel. More nodes allow for a better approximation of transmittance and higher quality shadows, but at the expense of increased storage and computational costs. We have found that, in practice, 8–12 nodes (a cost of 64–96 bytes per texel in the AVSM when full precision is used) give excellent results.

In HLSL code, our AVSM nodes are implemented with a simple structure:

```
#define AVSM_NODE_COUNT 8
#define AVSM_RT_COUNT (AVSM_NODE_COUNT / 4)

struct AVSMData
{
    float4 depth[AVSM_RT_COUNT];
    float4 trans[AVSM_RT_COUNT];
};
```

To simplify our implementation we always store a multiple of four nodes in the AVSM. A group of four nodes fills two render targets (one for depth and one for transmittance). This requirement sets a limit of sixteen nodes per texel since current graphics APIs don't allow binding of more than eight render targets at once.

The following sections will describe first how we generate samples of the full transmittance function, then how these samples are compressed into the AVSM representation, and finally how they are interpolated at rendering time in shading calculations.

7.2.1   Capturing Fragments of Transparent Objects

The first step in the implementation is to render from the light source and capture a per-pixel linked list of all of the transparent fragments visible from the camera at each pixel[1]. A subsequent pass, described in the Section 7.2.3, compresses these linked lists to the compact AVSM representation.

In a manner similar to that of standard shadow maps, AVSMs are created by rendering the scene from the light's viewpoint. AVSM can handle both opaque objects and objects of varying thickness and density. We need to store all of the transparent fragments up to the first opaque fragment, as well as the first opaque fragment itself (if there is one). This information is enough to exactly specify the transmittance curve as seen from the light source. (Transparent fragments behind the first opaque one, as well as any subsequent opaque fragments are irrelevant, since the first opaque fragment immediately drives the transmittance to zero for all depths behind it.)

While it is not strictly necessary, in order to speed up the creation of a volumetric shadow map, we may begin by rendering the opaque objects into a depth buffer to establish the depth beyond which we don't need to capture transparent fragments. We then render a pass that includes the transparent objects, using the already-computed depth buffer for z-tests (with a less-than-or-equal-to test mode), but with z-writes disabled. Each fragment that passes this test is added to a per-pixel linked list of fragments.

The per-pixel linked lists of light-attenuating segments are captured using DX11's support for atomic gather/scatter memory operations in pixel shaders [Yang et al. 10]. The basic idea is that a first r/w buffer is allocated with integer pixel values, each pixel representing a pointer to the head of a list and initially storing a "nil" value (e.g., -1.) These pointers encode offsets into a second larger r/w buffer which stores all lists nodes. A pixel shader then allocates a node from the second buffer by atomically incrementing a globally shared counter (see DirectX11 UAV counters) whose value represents a pointer to a new node. It then inserts at the head of the list the newly allocated node by atomically swapping the previous head pointer with the new one. The content of the new node is updated and its next pointer is set to the previous head of the list.

For our test scenes no more than 20 MB of this buffer is typically needed. Listing 7.1 shows HLSL code for creating these per-pixel linked lists.

---

[1]While AVSM is designed to be a streaming compression algorithm, such an implementation requires support for read-modify-write framebuffer operations in the pixel shader. DirectX11 adds the ability to perform unordered read-modify-write operations on certain buffer types in the pixel shader; however, for AVSM's transmittance-curve-simplification algorithm we need to ensure that each pixel's framebuffer memory is modified by only one fragment at a time (per-pixel lock). Because current DX11 HLSL compilers forbid per-pixel locks, we implement AVSM with variable-memory version that uses the current DX11 rendering pipeline to first capture all transparent fragments seen from the light and then compressing them into the AVSM representation.

```
#define MAX_BUFFER_NODES (1<<24)

RWStructuredBuffer<ListTexNode> gListTexSegmentNodesUAV;
RWTexture2D<uint>               gListTexFirstNodeAddrUAV;

// Allocate a generic node
bool AllocNode(out uint newNodeAddress)
{
    // alloc a new node
    newNodeAddress = gListTexNodesUAV.IncrementCounter();

    // running out of memory?
    return newNodeAddress < MAX_BUFFER_NODES;
}

// Insert a new node at the head of the list
void InsertNode(in int2 screenAddress,
                in uint newNodeAddress,
                in ListTexNode newNode)
{
    uint oldNodeAddress;
    InterlockedExchange(gListTexFirstNodeAddrUAV[screenAddress],
                        newNodeAddress,
                        oldNodeAddress);

    newNode.next = oldNodeAddress;
    gListTexNodesUAV[newNodeAddress] = newNode;
}
```

Listing 7.1. Node allocation and insertion code of a generic list (DirectX11/Shader Model 5).

This process can also be used with transparent objects with finite extent and uniform density in depth—not just billboards. Each object's fragment can store in the list start and end points along the corresponding ray from the light source to define a segment, along with exit transmittance (entry transmittance is implicitly assumed to be set to 1). For example, given billboards representing spherical particles, we insert a segment representing the ray's traversal through the particle; for hair we insert a short segment where the light enters and exits the hair strand; for opaque blockers, we insert a short, dense segment that takes the transmittance to zero at the exit point.

7.2.2 AVSM Compression

After the relevant fragments have been captured in a list at each pixel, we need to compute a compressed transmittance curve in a fixed amount of memory. Doing so not only saves a considerable amount of storage and bandwidth, but makes lookups very efficient. In general, the number of transparent fragments at a pixel will be much larger than the number of AVSM nodes (e.g., Figure 7.6 shows a transmittance curve with 238 nodes and its 12 nodes counterpart compressed with AVSM), therefore, we use a streaming compression algorithm that in a single (post-list-creation) rendering pass approximates the original curve.

Each node of our piecewise transmittance curve maps to an ordered sequence of pairs (d_i, t_i) that encode node position (depth) along a light ray and its associated transmittance. AVSMs store the transmittance curve as an array of depth-transmittance pairs (d_i, t_i) using two single-precision floating-point values[2]. An important ramification of our decision to use a fixed, small number of nodes is that the entire compressed transmittance curve can fit in on-chip memory during compression. As with classic shadow maps we clear depth to the far plane value, while transmittance is set to 1 in order to represent empty space.

We insert each new occluding segment by viewing it as a compositing operation between two transmittance curves, respectively representing the incoming blocker and the current transmittance curve. Given two light blockers, A and B, located along the same light ray, we write the density function $f_{AB}(x)$ as a sum of their density functions $f_A(x)$ and $f_B(x)$. By simply applying Equation (7.1) we can compute their total transmittance:

$$t_{\text{tot}}(z) = e^{-\int_0^z f_{AB}(x)\,dx}$$
$$= e^{-\int_0^z f_A(x)\,dx} e^{-\int_0^z f_B(x)\,dx} = t_A(z)t_B(z). \qquad (7.2)$$

In the absence of lossy compression, the order of composition is not important. More relevantly, this equation shows that the resulting total transmittance is given by the product of the two transmittance functions respectively associated to each light blocker.

Conceptually, our task is to compute a set of nodes that accurately represents the full transmittance curve.[3] For the first few segments in the linked list, up to the fixed number of AVSM nodes that we are storing, our task is straightforward: we insert the segment into the AVSM array. We move the nodes with depths greater than the new ones (a segment maps to two nodes) one element forward, making an opening at the offset into the array, at which the new nodes should be added, and creating new transmittance values for each opening by linearly interpolating neighboring nodes. We then composite this curve with the curve represented by the incoming segment (see Equation (7.2)). Once the (on-chip) array of nodes contains more nodes than can be stored in the AVSM texture, we apply a curve simplification algorithm; our method compresses transmittance

---

[2]It's also possible to use half-precision values for relatively simple scenes without incurring noticeable image artifacts.

[3]The problem of approximating a polygonal curve P by a simpler polygonal curve Q is of interest in many fields and has been studied in cartography, computer graphics, and elsewhere; see our EGSR paper for more references on this topic.

data simply by removing the node that contributes the least to the overall transmittance curve shape. In other words, we remove the node, that once removed, generates the smallest variation to curve integral (see Figure 7.2). Compression proceeds by removing one node at a time until the maximum node count is reached. We apply compression only to internal nodes. In practice, this is a benefit because these uncompressed nodes provide important visual cues such as transition into a volume or the shadows cast from a volume onto opaque surfaces.

Although transmittance varies exponentially between nodes, like deep shadow maps, we assume linear variation to simplify area computations. This allows us to write the transmittance integral I_t for an N node curve as the sum of $N-1$ trapezoidal areas:

$$I_t = \sum_{i=0}^{N-1} \frac{(d_{i+1} - d_i)(t_i + t_{i+1})}{2}.$$

The removal of an internal ith node affects only the area of the two trapezoids that share it. Since the rest of the curve is unaffected we compute the variation of its integral $\triangle_{t_i}$ with a simple, geometrically derived formula:

$$\triangle_{t_i} = |(d_{i+1} - d_{i-1})(t_{i+1} - t_i) - (d_{i+1} - d_i)(t_{i+1} - t_{i-1})|.$$

In practice, due to the lossy compression, the order in which segments are inserted can affect the results. In particular, when generating the per-pixel linked lists in the previous pass, the parallel execution of pixel shaders inserts segments into the linked lists in an order that may vary per-frame even if the scene and view are static. Inconsistent ordering can result in visible temporal artifacts, although they are mostly imperceptible in practice when using eight or more AVSM nodes or when the volumetric media is moving quickly (e.g., billowing smoke). In those rare cases when a consistent ordering cannot be preserved and the number of nodes is not sufficient to hide these artifacts, it is also possible to sort the captured segments by depth via an insertion sort before inserting them. We discuss the cost of this sort in Section 7.3.3.

7.2.3   AVSM Sampling

Sampling AVSMs can be seen as a generalization of a standard shadow-map depth test [Williams 78] of translucent occluders. Instead of a binary depth test, we evaluate the transmittance function at the receiver depth[4].

Due to the irregular and nonlinear nature of the AVSM data, we cannot rely on texture-filtering hardware, and we implement filtering in programmable shaders. For a given texel, we perform a search over the entire domain of the curve to find

---

[4]It's also possible to render opaque blockers into an AVSM. In this case AVSM sampling will behave exactly as the method introduced by [Williams 78].

the two nodes that bound the shadow receiver of depth d, we then interpolate the bounding nodes' transmittance (t_l, t_r) to intercept the shadow receiver.

In order to locate the two nodes that bound the receiver depth (i.e., a segment), we use a fast two-level search; since our representation stores a fixed number of nodes, memory accesses tend to be coherent and local, unlike with variable-length linked-list traversals necessary with techniques like deep shadow maps [Lokovic and Veach 00]. In fact, the lookups can be implemented entirely with compile-time (static) branching and array indexing, allowing the compiler to keep the entire transmittance curve in registers. Listing 7.2 shows an implementation of our AVSM segment-finding algorithm specialized for an eight node visibility curve, which is also used for both segment insertion and sampling/filtering[5].

As we do at segment-insertion time, we again assume space between two nodes to exhibit uniform density, which implies that transmittance varies exponentially between each depth interval (see Equation (7.1)), although we have found linear interpolation to be a faster and visually acceptable alternative:

$$T(d) = t_l + (d - d_l) \cdot \frac{t_r - t_l}{d_r - d_l}$$

This simple procedure is the basis for point filtering. Bilinear filtering is straightforward; the transmittance $T(d)$ is evaluated over four neighboring texels and linearly weighted.

```
struct AVSMSegment
{
    int    index;
    float  depthA;
    float  depthB;
    float  transA;
    float  transB;
};

AVSMSegment FindSegmentAVSM8(in AVSMData data,
                             in float receiverDepth)
{
    AVSMSegment Output;
    int         index;
    float4      depth, trans;
    float       leftDepth, rightDepth, leftTrans, rightTrans;
```

---

[5]Please see the demo source code in the accompanying web materials for a generalized implementation that supports 4-, 8-, 12- and 16-node AVSM textures.

```
//  We start by identifying the render target that..
//  ..contains the nodes we are looking for..
if (receiverDepth > data.depth[0][3]) {
    depth        = data.depth[1];
    trans        = data.trans[1];
    leftDepth    = data.depth[0][3];
    leftTrans    = data.trans[0][3];
    rightDepth   = data.depth[1][3];
    rightTrans   = data.trans[1][3];
    Output.index = 4;
} else {
    depth        = data.depth[0];
    trans        = data.trans[0];
    leftDepth    = data.depth[0][0];
    leftTrans    = data.trans[0][0];
    rightDepth   = data.depth[1][0];
    rightTrans   = data.trans[1][0];
    Output.index = 0;
}
//  ..we then look for the exact nodes that wrap..
//  ..around the shadow receiver.
if (receiverDepth <= depth[0]) {
    Output.depthA = leftDepth;
    Output.depthB = depth[0];
    Output.transA = leftTrans;
    Output.transB = trans[0];
} else if (receiverDepth <= depth[1]) {
    ....
    ....
} else {
    Output.index += 4;
    Output.depthA = depth[3];
    Output.depthB = rightDepth;
    Output.transA = trans[3];
    Output.transB = rightTrans;
}
return Output;
}
```

Listing 7.2. Segment finding code for 8-node AVSM data.

7.3 Comparisons

We have compared AVSM to a ground-truth result, deep shadow maps (DSM), Fourier opacity maps (FOM), and opacity shadow maps (OSM). All techniques were implemented using the DirectX11 rendering and compute APIs.

All results are gathered on an Intel Core i7 quad-core CPU running at 3.33 GHz running Windows 7 (64-bit) and an ATI Radeon 5870 GPU.

```
[unroll] for (i = 0; i < AVSM_NODE_COUNT + 2; ++i) {
    // Compute render target and vector element indices
    const int rtIdx = i >> 2;
    const int elemIdx = i & 0x3;

    float tempDepth, tempTrans;
    // Insert last segment node
    [flatten]if (i == postMoveSegmentEndIdx) {
        tempDepth = segmentDepth[1];
        tempTrans = newNodesTransOffset[1];
    // Insert first segment node
    } else if (i == postMoveSegmentStartIdx) {
        tempDepth = segmentDepth[0];
        tempTrans = newNodesTransOffset[0];
    // Update all nodes in between the new two nodes
    } else if ((i > postMoveSegmentStartIdx) &&
               (i < postMoveSegmentEndIdx)) {
        tempDepth = depth[i-1];
        tempTrans = trans[i-1];
    // Update all nodes located behind the new two nodes
    } else if ((i > 1) && (i > postMoveSegmentEndIdx)) {
        tempDepth = depth[i-2];
        tempTrans = trans[i-2];
    // Update all nodes located in front the new two nodes
    } else {
        tempDepth = depth[i];
        tempTrans = trans[i];
    }

    // Linearly interpolates transmittance along the incoming..
    // ..segment and composite it with the current curve
    tempTrans *= Interp(segmentDepth[0], segmentDepth[1],
                        FIRST_NODE_TRANS_VALUE,
                        segmentTransmittance, tempDepth);

    // Generate new nodes
    newDepth[rtIdx][elemIdx] = d;
    newTrans[rtIdx][elemIdx] = t;
}
```

Listing 7.3. Segment insertion code for AVSMs. Note that there is no dynamic branching nor dynamic indexing in this implementation, which makes it possible for intermediate values to be stored in registers and for efficient GPU execution.

Figure 7.3. A comparison of smoke added to a scene from a recent game title with AVSM with 12 nodes (left) and deep shadow maps (right). Rendering the complete frame takes approximately 32 ms, with AVSM generation and lookups consuming approximately 11 ms of that time. AVSM is 1–2 orders of magnitude faster than a GPU implementation of deep shadow maps and the uncompressed algorithm, yet produce a nearly identical result. (Thanks to Valve Corporation for the game scene.)

Figure 7.4. Comparison of AVSM, Fourier opacity maps, and opacity shadow maps to the ground-truth uncompressed result in a scene with three separate smoke columns casting shadows on each other: AVSM with eight nodes (top left), ground-truth uncompressed (top right), Fourier opacity maps with 16 expansion terms (bottom left), and opacity shadow maps with 32 slices (bottom right). Note how closely AVSM matches the ground-truth image. While the artifacts of the other methods do not appear problematic in these still images, the artifacts are more apparent when animated. Note that the differerent images have been enhanced by 4x to make the comparison more clear.

Figure 7.5. This scene compares (from left to right) AVSM (12 nodes), uncompressed, opacity shadow maps (32 slices), and Fourier opacity maps (16 expansion terms). Note that AVSM-12 and uncompressed are nearly identical and the other methods show substantial artifacts. In particular FOM suffers from severe over-darkening/ringing problems generated by high-frequency light blockers like hair and by less-than-optimal depth bounds. Also note that these images use only bilinear shadow filtering. Using a higher-quality filtering kernel substantially improves the shadow quality.

7.3.1   Qualitative Evaluation

Figure 7.3 shows AVSMs (12 nodes) compared to deep shadow maps (error threshold set to 0.002). There is little perceptible difference between the results, demonstrating that for this real-time scene, our decision to permit variable error per texel is not a problem. The accuracy of AVSM is further validated by inspecting the transmittance curves and seeing that even with eight nodes, AVSM very closely approximates the true transmittance curves. The results for sampling the uncompressed data also look identical. Our experience is that eight nodes results in acceptable visual quality for all views and configurations in this scene. All shadow map sizes in these images are 256^2.

Figure 7.4 shows a visual comparison among 8-node AVSM, 16-term Fourier opacity maps, and 32-slice opacity shadow maps against the ground-truth uncompressed result for a scene with three smoke columns casting shadows on each other. Note how much more closely the AVSM matches the ground-truth uncompressed result. The quality improvements are especially noticeable when animated. A key benefit of AVSM compared with these other real-time methods is that AVSM quality is much less affected by the depth range covered by the volumetric occluders.

7.3.2   Quantitative Evaluation

We validate the AVSM compression algorithm accuracy by inspecting a number of transmittance curves and comparing to the ground-truth uncompressed data as well as the deep shadow map compression technique. Overall, we see that the 4-node AVSM shows significant deviations from the correct result, 8-node AVSM matches closely with a few noticeable deviations, and 12-node AVSM often matches almost exactly.

Figure 7.6 shows a transmittance curve from a combination of smoke and hair (see image in Figure 7.5) with discrete steps for each blonde hair and smooth

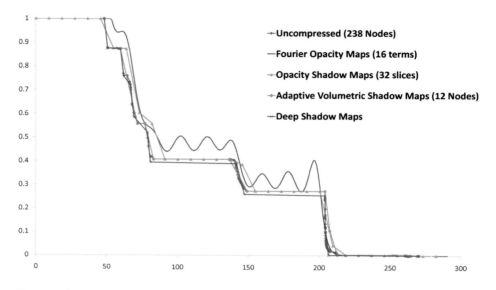

Figure 7.6. Transmittance curves computed for a scene with a mix of smoke and hair for AVSM (12 nodes) and the ground-truth uncompressed data (238 nodes). The hairs generate sharp reductions in transmittance, whereas the smoke generates gradually, decreasing transmittance. AVSM matches the ground-truth data much more closely than the other real-time methods.

transitions in the smokey regions. Note that the 12-node AVSM matches the ground-truth data much more closely than the opacity or Fourier shadow map (both of which use more memory than AVSM to represent shadow data) and is similar to the deep shadow map but uses less memory and is 1–2 orders of magnitude faster.

7.3.3 Performance and Memory

AVSM achieves its goal of adaptively sampling volumetric transmittance curves with performance high enough for real-time rendering throughout the Valve software scene (Figure 7.3). Table 7.1 shows the performance results for the view shown in Figure 7.4 for AVSM compared to opacity shadow maps, Fourier opacity maps, deep shadow maps, and the uncompressed approach. For this scene, AVSM compression takes only 0.5–1.5 ms, AVSM lookups take 3–10 ms depending on the number of AVSM nodes, capturing the segments takes 0.4 ms, and sorting

	AVSM4	AVSM8	AVSM16	OSM32	FOM16	DSM
Compress	0.5 ms	0.7 ms	1.6 ms	1 ms	1.1 ms	193 ms
Filtering	3 ms	5.4 ms	9.5 ms	1.4 ms	8.9 ms	52 ms
Total Time	9.7 ms	12.1 ms	17.43 ms	8.6 ms	15 ms	251 ms
Mem Usage	22(2)MB	24(4)MB	28(8)MB	8 MB	8 MB	40 MB

Table 7.1. Performance and memory results for 256^2 resolution, adaptive volumetric shadow maps (AVSM) with 4, 8 and 16 nodes, opacity shadow maps (OSM) with 32 slices, Fourier opacity maps (FOM) with 16 expansion terms, deep shadow maps (DSM), and the ground-truth uncompressed data for the scene shown in Figure 7.4. The AVSM compression algorithm takes 0.5–1.6 ms to build our representation of the transmittance curve even when there are hundreds of occluders per light ray. The total memory required for AVSM and DSM implementations on current graphics hardware is the size of the buffer used to capture the occluding segments plus the size of the compressed shadow map (shown in parentheses).

the segments (via insertion sort) before compression takes 3 ms[6]. As discussed earlier, the errors arising from not sorting are often imperceptible so sorting can usually be skipped—reducing the AVSM render-time to be nearly identical to that of opacity and Fourier opacity maps.

There are two key sources to AVSM performance. First is the use of a streaming compression algorithm that permits direct construction of a compressed transmittance representation without first building the full uncompressed transmittance curve. The second is the use of a fixed, small number of nodes such that the entire representation can fit into on-chip memory. While it may be possible to create a faster deep shadow map implementation than ours, sampling deep shadow maps' variable-length linked lists is costly on today's GPUs, and it may result in low SIMD efficiency. In addition, during deep shadow map compression, it is especially challenging to keep the working set entirely in on-chip memory.

Table 7.1 also shows the memory usage for AVSM, deep shadow maps, and the uncompressed approach for the smoke scene shown in Figure 7.4. Note that the memory usage for the variable-memory algorithms shows the amount of memory allocated, not the amount actually used per frame by the dynamically generated linked lists.

7.4 Conclusions and Future Work

Adaptive volumetric shadow maps (AVSM) provide an effective, flexible, and robust volumetric shadowing algorithm for real-time applications. AVSMs achieve a high level of performance using a curve-simplification compression algorithm

---

[6]While the AVSM blockers, insertion, and sampling code have received much attention, we don't currently have an optimized list sorting implementation but we expect it is possible to do significantly better than our current method.

that supports directly building the compressed transmittance function on-the-fly while rendering. In addition, AVSM constrains the compressed curves to use a fixed number of nodes, allowing the curves to stay in on-chip memory during compression. As the gap between memory bandwidth and compute capability continues to widen, this characteristic of the algorithm indicates that it is likely to scale well with future architectures.

One limitation of AVSM is the introduction of variable error per texel in exchange for the speed and storage benefits of fixed storage and fast compression. While we show in our test scenes and analysis that this is a valuable trade-off to make for real-time applications insofar as it affords high performance and rarely produces perceptible artifacts, offline rendering users that need absolute quality guarantees may want to continue to use a constant-error compression strategy such as deep shadow maps.

A second limitation is that implementations using current real-time graphics pipelines require a potentially unbounded amount of memory to first capture all occluding segments along all light rays. In addition, the unordered concurrency in pixel shaders means that when working with a low number of AVSM nodes per texel the segments may need to be re-sorted after capture to eliminate certain temporal artifacts. If future graphics pipelines support read-modify-write memory operations with a stable order, such as ordering by primitive ID, this limitation will go away.

Moreover, while our implementation requires DirectX11-compliant hardware, it is interesting to note that sampling and filtering an AVSM requires only DirectX9-compliant hardware. Moreover, since in many cases volumetric shadows exhibit very low spatial frequency and require low resolution shadow maps, it should be possible to implement AVSM on a current game console like Sony PS3® by writing a specialized SPU-based software rasterizer for particles/billboards that build AVSMs on-chip and in a single pass, avoiding locks and per-pixel lists, with AVSM sampling and filtering left to the GPU.

7.5 Acknowledgments

We thank Jason Mitchell and Wade Schin from Valve Software for the Left-for-Dead-2 scene and their valuable feedback; and Natasha Tatarchuk and Hao Chen from Bungie and Johan Andersson from DICE for feedback on early versions of the algorithm. Thanks to the the entire Advanced Rendering Technology team, Nico Galoppo and Doug McNabb at Intel for their contributions and support. We also thank others at Intel: Jeffery Williams and Artem Brizitsky for help with art assets; and Craig Kolb, Jay Connelly, Elliot Garbus, Pete Baker, and Mike Burrows for supporting the research.

Bibliography

[Enderton et al. 10] Eric Enderton, Erik Sintorn, Peter Shirley, and David Luebke. "Stochastic Transparency." In *I3D '10: Proceedings of the 2010 Symposium on Interactive 3D Graphics and Games*, pp. 157–164. New York: ACM, 2010.

[Green 08] Simon Green. "Volumetric Particle Shadows." http://developer. download.nvidia.com/compute/cuda/sdk/website/C/src/smokeParticles/doc/ smokeParticles.pdf, 2008.

[Jansen and Bavoil 10] Jon Jansen and Louis Bavoil. "Fourier Opacity Mapping." In *I3D '10: Proceedings of the 2010 Symposium on Interactive 3D Graphics and Games*, pp. 165–172. New York: ACM, 2010.

[Kim and Neumann 01] Tae-Yong Kim and Ulrich Neumann. "Opacity Shadow Maps." In *Rendering Techniques 2001: 12th Eurographics Workshop on Rendering*, pp. 177–182. Aire-la-Ville, Switzerland: Eurographics Assocaition, 2001.

[Lokovic and Veach 00] Tom Lokovic and Eric Veach. "Deep Shadow Maps." In *Proceedings of ACM SIGGRAPH 2000, Computer Graphics Proceedings, ACS*, pp. 385–392. New York: ACM, 2000.

[Mertens et al. 04] Tom Mertens, Jan Kautz, Philippe Bekaert, and F. van Reeth. "A Self-Shadowing Algorityhm for Dynamic Hair using Clustered Densities." In *Rendering Techniques 2004: Eurographics Symposium on Rendering*. Aire-la-Ville, Switzerland: Eurographics, 2004.

[Salvi et al. 10] Marco Salvi, Kiril Vidimče, Andrew Lauritzen, and Aaron Lefohn. "Adaptive Volumetric Shadow Maps." In *Eurographics Symposium on Rendering*, pp. 1289–1296. Aire-la-Ville, Switzerland: Eurographics Association, 2010.

[Sintorn and Assarson 09] Erik Sintorn and Ulf Assarson. "Hair Self Shadowing and Transparency Depth Ordering Using Occupancy Maps." In *I3D '09: Proceedings of the 2009 Symposium on Interactive 3D Graphics and Games*, pp. 67–74. New York: ACM, 2009.

[Williams 78] Lance Williams. "Casting Curved Shadows on Curved Surfaces." *Computer Graphics (Proceedings of SIGGRAPH 78)* 12:3 (1978), 270–274.

[Xie et al. 07] Feng Xie, Eric Tabellion, and Andrew Pearce. "Soft Shadows by Ray Tracing Multilayer Transparent Shadow Maps." In *Rendering Techniques 2007: 18th Eurographics Workshop on Rendering*, pp. 265–276. Aire-la-Ville, Switzerland: Eurographics Association, 2007.

[Yang et al. 10] Jason Yang, Justin Hensley, Holger Gruen, and Nicolas Thibieroz. "Real-Time Concurrent Linked List Construction on the GPU." In *Rendering Techniques 2010: Eurographics Symposium on Rendering*, pp. 51–60. Aire-la-Ville, Switzerland: Eurographics Association, 2010.

[Yuksel and Keyser 08] Cem Yuksel and John Keyser. "Deep Opacity Maps." *Computer Graphics Forum* 27:2 (2008), 675–680.

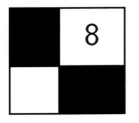

8

Fast Soft Shadows with Temporal Coherence
Daniel Scherzer, Michael Schwärzler, and Oliver Mattausch

8.1 Introduction

In computer graphics applications, soft shadows are usually generated using either a single shadow map together with some clever filtering method (which is fast, but inaccurate), or by calculating physically correct soft shadows with *light-source area sampling* [Heckbert and Herf 97]. Many shadow maps from random positions on the light source are created (which is slow) and the average of the resulting shadow tests is taken (see Figure 8.1).

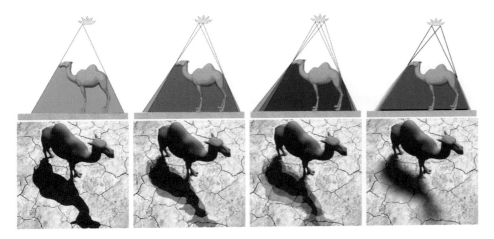

Figure 8.1. Light sampling with one, two, three and 256 shadow maps (*left* to *right*).

We present a soft shadow algorithm that combines the benefits of these two approaches by employing temporal coherence: the light source is sampled over multiple frames instead of a single frame, creating only a single shadow map with each frame. The individual shadow test results are stored in a screen-space (of the camera) *shadow buffer* (see Figure 8.2). Focusing each shadow map on creation can be done because only fragments in the screen space of the camera remain stored in the shadow buffer. This buffer is recreated with each frame using the shadow buffer from the previous frame B_{prev} as input (ping-pong style). The input B_{prev} holds shadowing information only for pixels that were visible in the previous frame. Pixels that become newly visible in the current frame due to camera (or object) movement (so-called disocclusions) have no shadowing information stored in this buffer. For these pixels we use spatial filtering to estimate the soft shadow results.

Our approach is faster as typical single sample soft shadow approaches like PCSS, but provides physically accurate results and does not suffer from typical single-sample artifacts. It also works on moving objects by marking them in the shadow map and falling back to a standard single-sample approach in these areas.

8.2   Algorithm

The main idea of our algorithm is to formulate light-source area sampling in an iterative manner, evaluating only a single shadow map per frame. We start by looking at the math for light-source area sampling: given n shadow maps, we can calculate the soft shadow result for a given pixel $\mathbf{p}$ by averaging over the hard-shadow results s_i calculated for each shadow map. This is given by

$$\psi_n(\mathbf{p}) = \frac{1}{n}\sum_{i=1}^{n} s_i(\mathbf{p}). \tag{8.1}$$

We want to evaluate this formula iteratively by adding a new shadow map at each frame, combining its shadow information with the data from previous frames that have been stored in a so-called shadow buffer B_{prev}, and storing it in a new shadow buffer B_{cur}. With this approach, the approximated shadow in the buffer improves from frame to frame and converges to the true soft shadow result.

Our approach has the following steps (see also Figure 8.2):

1. Create a shadow map SM from a randomly selected position on the area light.

2. Create a new shadow buffer B_{cur} with B_{prev} and SM as input. For each screen pixel we do the following steps:

    (a) Calculate the hard shadow result from SM (see Listing 8.1).

(b) Check if the pixel was visible in the last frame and therefore has associated shadowing information stored in the shadow buffer (see Section 8.2.1):

   Yes: Combine information from the shadow buffer with SM (see Section 8.2.2).

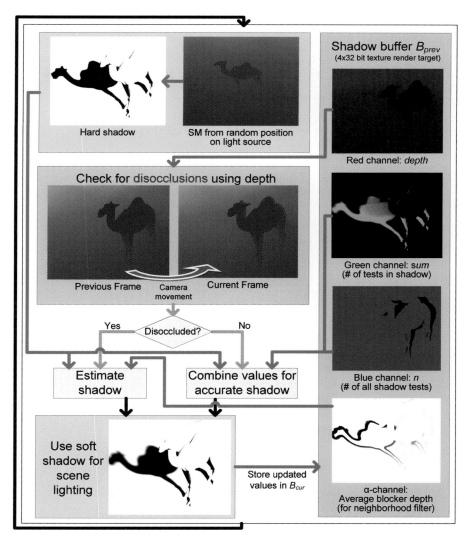

Figure 8.2. Structure of our algorithm.

No: Use a depth-aware spatial filtering approach that incorporates neighboring shadow buffer values to generate an initial soft shadow estimation for this pixel (see Section 8.2.3).

We will now describe the individual steps of this algorithm in more detail (including code fragments from our HLSL 4.0 pixel shader). The first step is straightforward: a random position on the light source is selected. This position is then used as a point light source from which a shadow map is created. For creating the shadow map and evaluating the hard shadow results any algorithm can be used, for instance *LiSPSM* [Wimmer et al. 04] or *silhouette shadow maps* [Sen et al. 03]. Then we start to create the new shadow buffer B_{cur} by using the shadow buffer from the previous frame B_{prev} and SM as input.

```
//shadow map sampling coordinates
const float2 smCoord = texSpace(input.LightPos);
//Linear depth of current pixel in light space
const float fragDepth = input.LightPos.z;
//sample depth in shadow map
const float Depth = getSMtexel(smCoord);
//store hard shadow test result as initial sum
float ShadowSum = shadowTest(Depth,fragDepth);
```

Listing 8.1. Hard shadow test.

8.2.1 Was This Pixel Visible?

We first have to check if the pixel $\mathbf{p}_{cur}$ we are looking at was visible in the previous frame and can therefore be found in B_{prev}. The process to determine this is called *temporal reprojection* [Scherzer et al. 07], We back-project it (thereby accounting for camera movement) into the coordinate system where B_{prev} was created. We transform $\mathbf{p}_{cur}$ therefore, from the post-perspective space of the current view back into the post-perspective space of the previous frame. Since we have the 3D position of our current pixel, we can simply use the view ($\mathbf{V}$) and projection ($\mathbf{P}$) matrices and their inverses of the current frame and the previous frame to do the transformation (see Figure 8.3):

$$\mathbf{p}_{prev} = \mathbf{P}_{prev} * \mathbf{V}_{prev} * \mathbf{V}_{cur}^{-1} * \mathbf{P}_{cur}^{-1} * \mathbf{p}_{cur}$$

To detect pixels that were not visible in the previous frame we first check if $\mathbf{p}_{prev}$ is inside B_{prev} in the x- and y-direction and then we check the z (i.e., the depth) difference between $\mathbf{p}_{prev}$ and the corresponding entry in B_{prev} at position $\mathbf{p}_{prev}$. If this difference exceeds a certain threshold, we conclude that this pixel was not visible in the previous frame (see Listing 8.2 and 8.3).

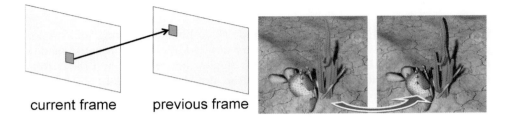

Figure 8.3. Back-projection of a single pixel (left). If we do this for every pixel we virtually transform the previous frame into the current, except for the pixels that were not visible in the previous frame (shown in red (right)).

```
bool outsideTexture(float2 Tex) {
  return any(bool2(Tex.x < 0.0f, Tex.y < 0.0f))
    || any(bool2(Tex.x > 1.0f, Tex.y > 1.0f));
}
```

Listing 8.2. Helper function for checking the validity of texture coordinates.

The obtained position will normally not be at an exact pixel center in B_{prev} except in the special case that no movement has occurred. Consequently, texture filtering should be applied during the lookup in the shadow buffer B_{prev}. In practice, the bilinear filtering offered by graphics hardware shows good results.

```
//previous shadow buffer sampling coordinates:
const float2 shadowBuffTexC = texSpace(input.BufferPos);
//check if the pixel is inside the previous shadow buffer:
if(!outsideTexture(shadowBuffTexC)) {
  //inside of previous data -> we can try to re-use information!
  float4 oldData = getShadowBufferTexel(shadowBuffTexC);
  const float oldDepth = oldData.x;
  //check if depths are alike, so we can re-use information
  if(abs(1-input.BufferPos.z/oldDepth) < EPSILON_DEPTH) {
    //old data available -> use it, see next section
    ...
  }
}
```

Listing 8.3. Test if the data for the current pixel was available in the previous shadow buffer.

8.2.2 Using the Shadow Buffer B_{prev}

In regions where no disocclusions occurred, B_{prev} holds shadowing information gathered over all the previous frames. Every new, additionally generated shadow map SM improves the accuracy of this soft shadow information, and the current result has to be combined, therefore, with the already existing data.

SM allows us to calculate hard shadow results for the current frame, and together with the stored n and sum values in B_{prev}, the accurate shadow can easily be computed by (see Listing 8.4)

1. add the current shadow amount to the sum of all shadows,

2. increase the count n by 1,

3. divide the new sum by the new n.

```
//introduce better names for data from previous shadow buffer
const float oldSum = oldData.y;
const float oldCount = oldData.z;
//add shadow buffer sum to the current sum
ShadowSum += oldSum;
//increment n
float n = oldCount + 1;
//calculate soft shadow
float softShadow = ShadowSum / n;
```

Listing 8.4. Combination of a hard shadow and the data from the shadow buffer.

8.2.3 Soft Shadow Estimation in Disoccluded Areas

If the pixel is not in B_{prev}, we cannot calculate a soft shadow using Equation (8.1) as described in Section 8.2.2, since we have only one shadow-map test result of which to calculate the average. We therefore generate an initial soft shadow estimation for this pixel by a applying a depth-aware spatial filter (bilateral filter) (see Listing 8.5), which takes neighboring pixels (distributed on a Poisson disk) in the shadow buffer B_{prev} into account if they lie on a similar depth.

```
float neighborhoodFilter(const float2 uv,
            const float2 filterRadiusUV,
            const float currentDepth) {
  float sampleSum = 0, numSamples = 0;
  for(int i = 0; i < NUM_POISSON_SAMPLES; ++i ) {
    const float2 offset = poissonDisk[i] * filterRadiusUV;
    const float3 data = getShadowBufferTexel(uv + offset).xyz;
```

```
      const float depth = data.x;
      const float sum = data.y;
      const float n = data.z;
      if(abs(1-currentDepth/depth) < EPSILON_DEPTH) {
        sampleSum += sum/n;
        numSamples++;
      }
    }
  return numSamples > 0 ? sampleSum/numSamples : -1;
}
```

Listing 8.5. Soft shadow estimation by filtering the shadow buffer neighborhood.

If these neighboring pixels have not been recently disoccluded, they are very likely to provide a good approximation of the correct soft shadow value and will help to avoid discontinuities between the shadowed pixels.

The filter radius is calculated using the same penumbra estimation as in the PCSS algorithm [Fernando 05]. The idea is to approximate all occluders in a search area around the pixel by one planer occluder at depth z_{avg}. Using the intercept theorem and the relations between pixel depth $z_{receiver}$ and light source size w_{light} an estimation of the penumbra width $w_{penumbra}$ (see Figure 8.4) is given by

$$w_{penumbra} = w_{light} \frac{\left(z_{receiver} - z_{avg}\right)}{z_{avg}}.$$

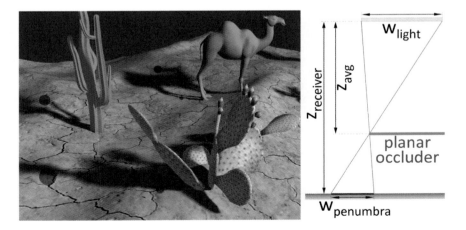

Figure 8.4. The sampling radius of the neighborhood filter depends on the scene depth and an estimated penumbra size (left). The penumbra width can be approximated by using the intercept theorem (right).

The calculation of the average occluder depth is done by searching for potential blockers in the shadow map, and is therefore a computationally costly step—but in contrast to PCSS, we have to do this step only in the case of a disocclusion. Otherwise, we store it in the shadow buffer for further use in consecutive frames (see Section 8.2.4).

In practice, it has been found useful to assign a weight larger than 1 to this approximation (for one hard shadow map evaluation), to avoid jittering artifacts in the first few frames after a disocclusion has occurred. Therefore, we use the number of Poisson samples from the neighborhood filter as weight.

8.2.4 Putting It All Together

In order to avoid visible discontinuities when switching from the estimate generated after a disocclusion and the correct result obtained from the shadow buffer B_{prev}, the two shadow values are blended. This blended shadow is only used to improve the visual quality in the first few frames and is not stored in the shadow buffer. Note that we do not have to estimate the average blocker depth for the neighborhood filter again, as it has been evaluated and stored in the shadow buffer directly after the disocclusion! Additionally, this average blocker depth is refined every frame by adding the additional depth value from the current shadow map SM (see Listing 8.6).

```
//load average blocker depth from the previous frame
const float oldAvgBlockerDepth = oldData.w;
//if first frame after dissoclusion only one depth is available
if(1.0 == ShadowSum) avgBlockerDepth = Depth;
//Update average blocker depth
if(oldAvgBlockerDepth >= 0.0f) {
  if(avgBlockerDepth >= 0.0f) {
    float sum = oldAvgBlockerDepth*(n-1);
    sum += avgBlockerDepth;
    avgBlockerDepth = sum/(n);
  }
  else
    avgBlockerDepth = oldAvgBlockerDepth;
}
```

Listing 8.6. Iterative refinement of the average blocker depth.

To derive a formula for the blending weight we use a statistical approach: we estimate the standard error s of our sampling-based soft shadow solution with a binomial variance estimator

$$s_n(\mathbf{p}) = \sqrt{\frac{\psi_n(\mathbf{p})(1 - \psi_n(\mathbf{p}))}{n - 1}}$$

This formula allows us to estimate the quality of our soft shadow solution after taking n shadow maps (for details see [Scherzer et al. 09]). If this standard error is above a certain user-defined threshold err_{max}, we use only the approach described in Section 8.2.3. If the standard error is below a certain second threshold err_{min}, we use only the sampling-based soft shadow. Between these bounds, we blend the two soft shadow results.

```
//calculate standard error with binomial variance estimator
const float error =
  n == 1.0 ? 1.0 : sqrt(softShadow*(1-softShadow)/(n-1));
//if we have recently disoccluded samples or a large error,
//support the shadow information with an approximation
if(error >= err_min && avgBlockerDepth > 0) {
  //penumbra estimation like in PCSS, but with the average
  //occluder depth from the history buffer
  const float penumbraEstimation = vLightDimensions[0] *
    ((fragDepth - avgBlockerDepth) / avgBlockerDepth);
  //do spatial filtering in the shadow buffer (screen space):
  const float depthFactor = (nearPlaneDist/input.Depth);
  const float shadowEstimate = neighborhoodFilter(
    shadowBuffTexC, vAspectRatio*depthFactor*penumbraEstimation,
    input.Depth);
  //if shadow estimate valid calculate new soft shadow
  if(shadowEstimate > 0.0f) {
    if(inDisoccludedRegion) {
      //disoccluded sample: only estimated shadow
      //define weight for estimate
      const float estimateWeight = NUM_POISSON_SAMPLES;
      ShadowSum = shadowEstimate*estimateWeight;
      n = estimateWeight;
      softShadow = shadowEstimate;
    } else {
      //blend estimated shadow with accumulated shadow
      //using the error as blending weight
      const float weight = (err_max-error)/(err_max-err_min);
      softShadow =
        shadowEstimate * (1-weight) + softShadow * weight;
    }
  }
}
```

Listing 8.7. The standard error decides which method is used.

After having the soft shadow result evaluated for each displayed pixel, the final steps are to

- use the calculated result to modify the scene illumination, and output the shadowed scene on the corresponding render target, and to

- store the current depth, the number of successful shadow tests sum, the number of samples n, and the average blocker depth in the new shadow buffer render target B_{cur}.

```
output.Col1 = float4(input.Depth,ShadowSum,n,avgBlockerDepth);
//output the illuminated and shadowed image
output.Col0.rgb = LightingFunction(..) * (1-softShadow);
return output;
```

Listing 8.8. Store values in shadow buffer and output rendered image.

8.2.5 Moving Objects

Special care must be taken when it is necessary to handle moving objects, since they frequently produce disocclusions. Moreover, only the most recently accumulated shadow tests in the shadow buffer provide valid shadow information: as these shadow-casting objects move on, older shadow tests originate from different spatial scene compositions, and reusing them would lead to strong streaking artifacts.

We therefore identify shadows that are cast by moving objects by storing their depth in the shadow map SM with a negative sign (generating no additional memory cost) and checking whether this value is negative during the lookup in the shadow map. If this is the case (i.e., if we have a shadow that is cast by a moving object), we reduce the corresponding weight by setting sum and n to a low value. This allows new shadow tests to have more impact on the result, and removes the streaking artifacts at the cost of the physical correctness of the shadow. Please note that an example shader, in which moving objects are properly handled, is included in the demo application in the accompanying web materials.

8.3 Comparison and Results

The proposed soft-shadowing algorithm offers a way to render physically accurate, high quality soft shadows in real-time applications at the same speed as today's fastest single-sample methods. Figure 8.5 shows a benchmark that compares our method to a fast PCSS version using only 16 texture lookups for the blocker search and 16 texture lookups for the PCF kernel on a 720p viewport.

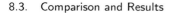

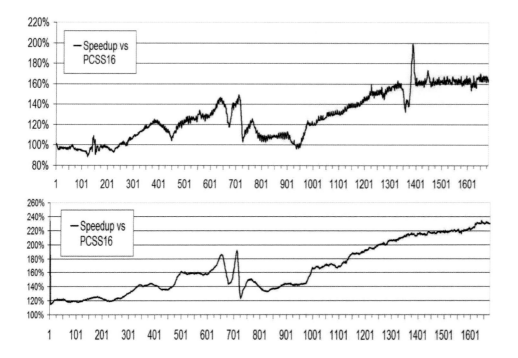

Figure 8.5. Speedup of our new algorithm in comparison to PCSS16 on a GeForce 280GTX (top) and a 9600MGT (bottom).

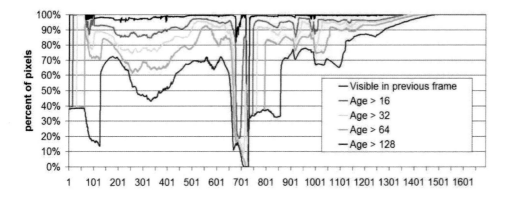

Figure 8.6. The "age" (i.e., the number of reusable shadow tests) of the fragments in our walkthrough scene.

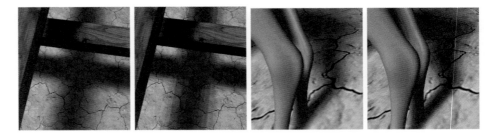

Figure 8.7. Overlapping occluders (our method, PCSS 16/16) and bands in big penumbrae (our method, PCSS 16/16) are known problem cases for single sample approaches left to right:.

Our algorithm tends to have a slower frame rate in cases of numerous disocclusions, because it has to perform the additional blocker search for the penumbra estimation. Due to its higher complexity (more ifs), our shader can be slower than PCSS in such circumstances. As soon as the shadow buffer is exploited and its values can be reused, our approach can unfold its strength and deliver higher frame rates, while PCSS still has to do the shadow map lookups. As can be seen in Figure 8.6, the number of fragments for which buffer data can be reused is usually high enough to obtain frame rates exceedings those that can be obtained with PCSS.

In static scenes, the soft shadows generated with our method are physically accurate and of a significantly better quality than is produced by PCSS, which suffers from typical single-sample artifacts (see Figure 8.7). For moving objects, the shadow buffer can hardly be exploited, and we therefore provide a fallback solution in which spatial neighborhood filtering is applied. Though humans can hardly perceive the physical incorrectness in such cases, there is room for improvement, since some flickering artifacts may remain when dynamic shadows overlap with static shadows that have large penumbrae.

Bibliography

[Fernando 05] Randima Fernando. "Percentage-Closer Soft Shadows." In *ACM SIGGRAPH Sketches*, p. 35. New York: ACM, 2005.

[Heckbert and Herf 97] Paul S. Heckbert and Michael Herf. "Simulating Soft Shadows with Graphics Hardware." Technical Report CMU-CS-97-104, CS Dept., Carnegie Mellon University, 1997.

[Scherzer et al. 07] Daniel Scherzer, Stefan Jeschke, and Michael Wimmer. "Pixel-Correct Shadow Maps with Temporal Reprojection and Shadow Test Confidence." In *Proceedings Eurographics Symposium on Rendering*, pp. 45–50. Aire-la-Ville, Switzerland: Eurographics Association, 2007.

[Scherzer et al. 09] Daniel Scherzer, Michael Schwärzler, Oliver Mattausch, and Michael Wimmer. "Real-Time Soft Shadows Using Temporal Coherence." In *Proceedings of the 5th International Symposium on Advances in Visual Computing: Part II, Lecture Notes in Computer Science (LNCS)*, pp. 13–24. Berlin, Heidelberg: Springer-Verlag, 2009.

[Sen et al. 03] Pradeep Sen, Mike Cammarano, and Pat Hanrahan. "Shadow Silhouette Maps." *ACM Transactions on Graphics (Proceedings of SIGGRAPH)* 22:3 (2003), 521–526.

[Wimmer et al. 04] Michael Wimmer, Daniel Scherzer, and Werner Purgathofer. "Light Space Perspective Shadow Maps." In *Proceedings of Eurographics Symposium on Rendering 2004*. Aire-la-Ville, Switzerland: Eurographics Association, 2004.

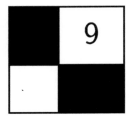

Mipmapped Screen-Space Soft Shadows

Alberto Aguado and Eugenia Montiel

This chapter presents a technique for generating soft shadows based on shadow maps and screen space image filtering. The main idea is to use a mipmap to represent multifrequency shadows in screen space. The mipmap has two channels: the first channel stores the shadow intensity values and the second channel stores screen-space penumbrae widths. Shadow values are obtained by filtering while penumbrae widths are propagated by flood filling. After the mipmap is generated, the penumbrae values are used as indices to the mipmap levels. Thus, we transform the problem of shadow generation into the problem of selecting levels in a mipmap. This approach is extended by including layered shadow maps to improve shadows with multiple occlusions.

As with the standard shadow-map technique, the computations in the technique presented in this chapter are almost independent of the complexity of the scene. The use of the shadow's levels of detail in screen space and flood filling make this approach computationally attractive for real-time applications. The overhead computation compared to the standard shadow map is about 0.3 ms per shadow map on a GeForce 8800GTX.

9.1 Introduction and Previous Work

The shadow map technique is a well-known method for generating real-time shadows [Williams 78]. It is widely used in applications since it is computationally attractive and it is capable of dealing with complex geometry. The original technique determines if a point is in a shadow by comparing the distances to the light and to the camera in two steps. First, the scene is rendered from the camera view point and the distance of the closest point is stored in the texture defining the shadow map. In the second step, the position of a point is transformed into the camera frame, so its distance to the camera can be compared to the shadow-map value. This comparison determines if a point is occluded or not; thus points are either fully shadowed or fully illuminated. The binary nature of the comparison produces hard shadows, reducing the realism of the scene. As such, previous works have extended the shadow-map technique to produce soft shadows.

The technique presented in this chapter filters the result of the shadow map test. This approach was introduced in the percentage closer filtering (PCF) [Reeves et al. 87] technique. PCF determines the shadow value of a pixel by projecting its area into the shadow map. The shadow intensity is defined by the number of values in the shadow map that are lower than the value at the center of the projected area. Percentage closer soft shadows (PCSS) [Fernando 05] extended the PCF technique to include shadows of different widths by replacing the pixel's area with a sampling region whose area depends on the distance between the occluder and the receiver.

The PCSS technique is fast and it provides perceptually accurate soft shadows, so it has become one of the most often used methods in real-time applications. However, it has two main issues. First, since it requires sampling a region per pixel, it can require an excessive number of computations for large penumbrae. The number of computations can be reduced by using stochastic sampling, but it requires careful selection of the sampling region in order to avoid artifacts. Second, to determine the region's size, it is necessary to estimate an area in which to search for the blockers. In general, it is difficult to set an optimal size, since large regions lead to many computations and small regions reduce the shadows far away from the umbra.

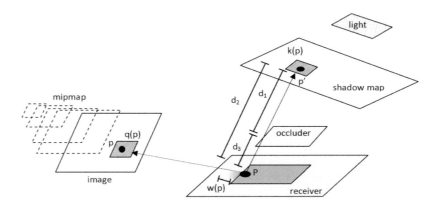

Figure 9.1. The mipmap in image space is built by using the result of the shadow map test and the distances between the occluder and the receiver.

In [Gambau et al. 10], instead of filtering by sampling the shadow map, soft shadows are obtained by filtering the result of the shadow-map comparison in screen space. The technique in this chapter follows this approach and it introduces a mipmap to represent multiple-frequency shadow details per pixel. As such, the problem of filtering is solved by selecting a mipmap level for each pixel. Filtering via mipmapping has been used in previous shadow-map techniques such as convolution shadow maps [Annen et al. 08] and variance shadow maps [Donnelly and Lauritzen 06]. In the technique presented in this chapter, mipmapping is used to filter screen-space soft shadows. In addition to storing multi-frequency shadows, the mipmap is exploited to propagate occlusion information obtained from the occluder and the shadowed surface. Occlusion information is used to select the shadow frequency as an index to a level in the mipmap. The efficiency of the mipmap filtering and the screen-space computations make it possible to create penumbrae covering large areas, expending little computational overhead, and performing no stratified sampling.

9.2 Penumbra Width

Figure 9.1 illustrates the geometry of the scene, the camera, and the shadow map. A point P in a surface is mapped to the point p in the image and to the point p' in the shadow map by the inverse of the camera and light transformations, respectively. The shadow map stores the closest distance to any surface from the light viewpoint. This is the distance denoted as d_1 in Figure 9.1. Thus, p will be in shadow when the distance in the shadow map is lower than the distance to the point P. That is, the shadow intensity of the pixel p is zero if $d_1 < d_2$, and 1 otherwise.

Soft shadows can be generated by filtering the result of the shadow-map comparison in a region $k(p)$ in the shadow map. Using PCF, the region is defined by the projection of the area of the pixel p into the shadow map. With PCSS, the region is determined based on the estimation of the penumbrae sizes and it is implemented in two steps. The first step searches for the occluder of the point P by averaging the values in the shadow map close to p'. In general, there is no way to determine the size of the search region and it is set as a parameter according to the scene. Once the distance to the occluder has been determined, the second step estimates the penumbra width by considering the geometry of the occluder, the receiver, and the light. This is defined as

$$w(p) = \frac{d_2(p) - d_1(p)}{d_1(p)} L \; .$$

Here, the value of L represents the size of the light and it is used to control the penumbrae; by increasing L, shadows in the scene become softer. Once the penumbra width is computed, the shadow can be filtered by considering a region

$k(p)$ whose size is proportional to it. That is, PCSS uses a proportional constant to map the penumbra width to the shadow map region $k(p)$.

The technique presented in this chapter is based on the PCSS penumbra estimation, but the values are computed only for the points that pass the shadow-map test. This is because, for these points, it is not necessary to compute averages to obtain the occluders' distances; they can be obtained by fetching the value for the point p' in the shadow map. That is, d_1 is simply defined by the shadow map entry. Another difference from PCSS is that the penumbra estimation is not used to define a filter of the values in the shadow map, but it is used to define a filter in image space.

9.3 Screen-Space Filter

An estimate of the penumbra width in image space can be obtained by projecting $w(p)$ into the image plane. That is,

$$q(p) = \frac{f}{z} w(p).$$

Here, f is the focal length and z is the depth of the fragment. Thus, f/z accounts for the perspective scale. The focal length is a constant parameter that defines the distance between the center of projection and the image plane. In general, the area will be dependent also on the orientation between the camera and the surface. However, since we use isotropic filters, we cannot transform the area using particular directions.

The computation of $q(p)$ can be performed during the shadow map test as shown in Listing 9.1. In this implementation, the variable "pos" stores the position of the fragment in the world space, and it is used to compute the position in light space. The world-space and light-space positions are then used in the shadow-map test and in the computation of the penumbra width. The result of the shadow map is stored in the red channel of the render target and the penumbra width is stored in the blue channel. Notice that the implementation does not compute occlusion values for all the pixels, but some will have the 0×FFFFFFFF value.

```
void main(INPUT input, inout OUTPUT output)
{
    // Position in light space
    float4 light_pos = mul (pos, light_matrix)

    // Shadow map value
    float shadow_map_val = tex2D(shadowmap_texture0, light_pos);

    // Shadow map test
    output.color.r = shadow_map_val < light_pos.z - shadow_bias;
```

```
    // Penumbra width
    output.color.b = 0xFFFFFFFF;
    if(output.color.r == 1.0f) {
            float distance_factor =
                (light_pos.z / shadow_map_val) - 1.0f;
            output.color.b = distance_factor * L * f * A / pos.z;
    }

    // Tag the region for region filling
    output.color.g = output.color.r
}
```

Listing 9.1. Performing the shadow test and computing the penumbrae widths in two different texture channels.

Figure 9.2 shows examples of the penumbrae values. The image on the left shows an example scene. The image in the middle shows the penumbrae widths. The white pixels are points without penumbrae widths. That is, they are points without occlusions. The pixels' intensities represent penumbrae widths and they show the dependency between the occluder and the receiver positions. Occluders that are far away from the receiver have lighter values than occluders that are closer. Lighter values indicate large smooth shadows while dark values indicate that shadows should have well-delineated borders. The image on the right shows the result of the shadow-map test computed in Listing 9.1. The pixels in this image have just two intensities that define hard shadows.

Notice that the code in Listing 9.1 computes penumbrae estimations only for pixels in the hard shadow region. However, in order to compute soft shadows, it is necessary to obtain estimates of the points that will define the umbra of the shadow. The penumbrae widths for these pixels can be obtained by searching for the closer occluder. Here, the search is performed by a flood-filling technique implemented in a mipmap. In this approach, each level of the mipmap is manually

Figure 9.2. Example scene (left). Penumbra widths, light values indicate large penumbrae (middle). Hard shadows (right).

created by rendering a single quad. The pixel shader sets as render target the mipmap level we are computing, and it takes as resource texture the previous mipmap level. The advantage of this approach is that the reduction in resolution at each level causes an increase in the search region. Thus, large regions can be searched with a small number of computations.

The flood-filling implementation requires distinguishing between pixels that have been filled and pixels that need to be filled. This can be efficiently implemented by using a single bit in a texture. To simplify the presentation, the implementations in Listing 9.1 and Listing 9.2 use an extra channel on the texture. In Listing 9.1 the pixels that define the filled region are tagged by setting the green channel to one. This channel is used, when the mipmap level is created, as shown in Listing 9.2 to distinguish pixels that should be used during the flood fill. In Listing 9.2, the value of a pixel is obtained by averaging the values that form the fill region using a 5×5 window in the source texture. The implementation averages distances so pixels so that are close to several occluders do not produce sharp shadow discontinuities.

```
void main(INPUT input, inout OUTPUT output)
{
    // The sum of all values in the region
    float sum = 0.0f;

    // Number of points in the region
    float num = 0.0f;

    // Flood fill using a window 5x5
    for (int i = 0; i<5; i++) {
        for (int j = 0; j<5; j++) {
            float4 t = float4( uv.x - target_shift.x
                                       * (-2.5f + i),
                               uv.y - target_shift.y
                                       * (-2.5f + j),
                               0, previous_level);

            // Read input level
            float4 val = tex2Dlod(samMipMap, t);

            // Flood fill averaging region pixels only
            if(val.g == 1.0f){
                sum += val.b;
                num++;
            }

        }
    }

    // Output flood fill value
    if( num>0.0f ) {
```

```
            // Pixel should be flood
            output.color.b = sum / num;
            output.color.g = 1.0f;
    }
    else{
            // Pixel is not in the flood region
            output.color.b = 0xFFFFFFFF;
            output.color.g = 0.0f;
    }
}
```

Listing 9.2. The mipmap level generation. Flood filling for occlusion values.

Figure 9.3 shows an example of the results of the flood-filling implementation. At each level the penumbrae widths are propagated, covering large regions in the image. Since each level has half-resolution, a pixel covers four times the area of the previous level. Thus, large regions are covered using few levels.

Figure 9.3. Mipmap levels obtained by flood filling. The flood fill propagates information from hard shadows to outer regions.

9.4 Filtering Shadows

The penumbrae widths in the mipmap define the filtering that should be applied to the hard shadows in order to obtain soft shadows. Although it is possible to apply a filter for each pixel, a more efficient implementation can be obtained by using a multi-frequency representation. The main advantage is that frequency filtering can be used to reduce the data, so filters of large regions can be performed with small kernels applied to few pixels. That is, large filters correspond to small kernels in low-resolution images.

```
void main(INPUT input, inout OUTPUT output)
{
    // The sum of all values in the region and number of points
    float sum = 0.0f;
    float num = 0.0f;

    // Stores result of filter
    output.color.b = 0.0f;
```

```
            // Evaluate using a window 5x5
        for (int i = 0; i<5; i++) {
            for (int j = 0; j<5; j++) {
                float4 t = float4(uv.x - target_shift.x
                                  * (-2.5f + i),
                                  uv.y - target_shift.y * (-2.5f + j),
                                  0, previous_level);
                // Read input level
                float4 val = tex2Dlod(samMipMap, t);

                // Flood fill averaging region pixels only
                if(val.g == 1.0f){
                    sum += val.b;
                    num++;
                }
                // Gaussian filter
                output.color.b += val.r * kernel[i][j];
            }
        }
        // Output flood fill value
        if( num>0.0f ) {
            output.color.b = sum / num;
            output.color.g = 1.0f;
        }
        else{
            output.color.b = 0xFFFFFFFF;
            output.color.g = 0.0f;
        }
    }
```

Listing 9.3. Mipmap level generation including the filter of the shadow map test values. The red channel stores the shadow intensity, the blue channel stores the penumbra width and the green channel is used to tag the filled region.

When creating a multi-frequency representation, it is important to select the cutoff frequencies to avoid aliasing [Bracewell 00]. Since the resolution of the mipmap is reduced by half at each level, aliasing is avoided by reducing the frequency by half. This cutoff frequency is obtained by a Gaussian filter with standard deviation set to one. In the implementation, the filter is computed at the same time as the flood-filling in Listing 9.2, but on a different texture channel. Listing 9.3 includes the filtering to the mipmap level generation shader. The kernel matrix defines the normalized coefficients of the Gaussian filter.

Figure 9.4 shows an example of the results obtained when applying the filtering. The top row shows the mipmap levels. Notice that high resolutions give fine detail with well-delineated shadow borders while coarse resolutions have soft borders. The images in the bottom row were obtained by using the shadows defined on the corresponding image on the top row. That is, the same filter size is used for the whole image, so penumbrae have the same widths. This example shows that

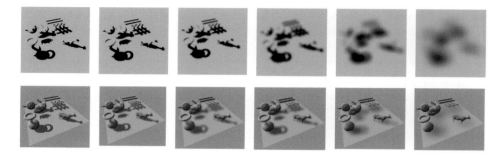

Figure 9.4. Mipmap levels obtained by filtering the result of the shadow map test (top). Shadows defined at each mipmap level (bottom).

image-space filters can be used to generate shadows with different penumbrae; however, to obtain compelling shadows in the image, we should select different frequencies for different pixels. That is, we have changed the problem of shadow generation into a problem of selecting levels in a mipmap.

9.5   Mipmap Level Selection

The flood-fill and filtering processes create a mipmap with two channels: the first channel contains shadows filtered with different cutoff frequencies and the second channel contains penumbrae widths. Small penumbrae widths values indicate close contact points or close lights, so the shadows should be well delineated. That is, the pixel should be rendered using the shadows on the first levels of the mipmap. Large values indicate that the distance between the occluder and the receiver is significant with respect to the distance and size of the light. Thus, pixels should use the shadows in the low-resolution levels; the penumbrae width determines the frequency content in each pixel.

In order to select the mipmap level for each pixel, we relate the penumbrae widths to filter sizes by considering the fact that since filters are applied at each resolution, the size of the filter is squared on each level. That is, the width of the filter at level i is

$$s = 2^i.$$

Thus, if we consider that the width of the penumbra is defined by the size of the filter, then a penumbra width will be generated at the level

$$i = \log_2\left(q\left(p\right)\right).$$

Notice that this equation does not give integer levels; we should not be limited by the values in the mipmap levels, and we can generate shadows for intermediate values. In the implementation, we use bilinear interpolation to compute the shadows between mipmap levels. This generates a variation of shadows and produces smooth transitions in the penumbrae.

```
void main(INPUT input, inout OUTPUT output)
{
    // Init shadow intensity
    float shadow = 1.0f;

    // Fetch mipmap levels
    float4 val[8];
    for( int level =0; level < 8; level++ ){
        val[level]= tex2Dlod(g_samMipMap, float4(uv,0,level);
    }

    // Find q(p)
    float q = 0;
    for( int level = 0; level < MAX_LEVELS {\&}{\&} q == 0 ;
      level++ ){
        if (val[level].y != 0) q = val[level].z;
    }

    if( q>0.0f )
    {
        // Selected level
        if(q<1) q = 1;
        float l = log2(q);
        if(l > MAX_LEVELS) l = MAX_LEVELS - 0.1f;

        // Interpolate levels
        int down = floor(l);
        int up = down + 1;
        float interp = l-down;

        // Shadow intensity
        shadow = (1.0f - lerp(val[down].x,val[up].x,interp));
    }
    output.color = shadow;
}
```

Listing 9.4. Shadow intensity computation from the mipmap.

The selection of levels implementation is outlined in Listing 9.4. The code starts by fetching all the levels of the mipmap. The fetching step uses interpolation, so we obtain smooth shadow values. The value of $q(p)$ is obtained by looking for the first penumbra value in the mipmap levels. This value is then used to compute the shadow intensity by interpolating a pair of selected levels.

The shadow intensity should be added to the final rendering of the scene. The way this is performed depends on the rendering type. Figure 9.5 illustrates

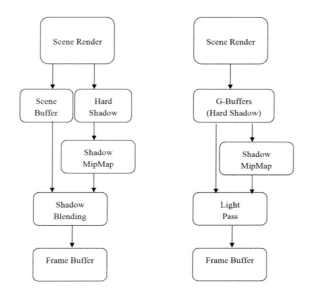

Figure 9.5. Mipmapped shadows implemented using the main scene rendering. Forward rendering (left). Deferred rendering (right).

how shadows can be added to the scene in forward and deferred rendering. In forward rendering, as shown in Figure 9.5 (left), hard shadows are computed during the main rendering of the scene, and they are stored in the bottom level of the mipmap. Thus, the scene buffer does not contain any shadows. Afterward the mipmap is constructed and subsequently the scene is shadowed by a shadow blending post-processing. The post-processing computes the shadow intensities and it combines the scene buffer and the shadow intensity by rendering a single quad. In the deferred rendering illustrated in Figure 9.5 (right), hard shadows are stored in a G-buffer and the shadow map can be used during the lighting pass.

Figure 9.6 shows some examples of soft shadows generated by using the mipmap technique. The first two images were obtained by changing the light's area, so shadows become smoother. The third image shows a close-up view to highlight contact shadows. As with any other shadow-map techniques, accurate shadows at contact point and self-shadows require an appropriate bias in the shadow map test. The first image in the bottom row shows how shadows change depending on the distance between the occluder and the receiver. Shadows are blurred and smooth for distant points whilst they are well delineated close to contact points. The final two images show the result on textured surfaces.

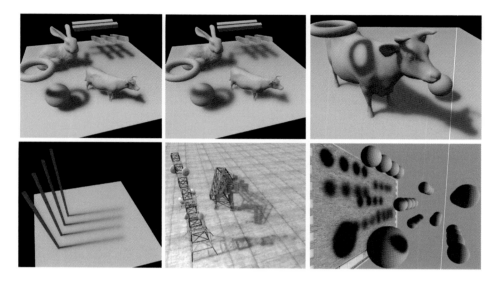

Figure 9.6. Examples of soft shadows.

9.6   Multiple Occlusions

In general, shadow-map techniques can suffer from light bleeding. This is because the shadow map stores a single value that represents the distance to the closest surface. Thus, when a surface has multiple occluders, the distance to the closest occluder cannot be computed. This is illustrated in Figure 9.7, which highlights two points on the receiver; one point has one occluder and the other has two occluders. For the dark point, the distance to the occluder is determined by subtracting the distance to the light from the distance in the shadow map (i.e., $d_2 - d_1$). This gives a good estimate of the occluder's distance. For the lighter point, the shadow map stores the distance to the closest occluder (i.e., d'_1). Thus, the occluder's distance is computed as $d_2 - d'_1$ and, consequently, the shadow will be overestimated. In some cases, as shown in Figure 9.6, the variations of shadow intensity may not produce notable changes in intensities. However, in several cases the difference between shadows can be very noticeable. This problem is more significant for semitransparent objects.

A straightforward approach to computing a better estimate of the distances between the receiver and the occluders is to perform a ray-tracing search; however, this will impose important computational constraints. An alternative approach is to store several values in the shadow map, so we can search for the closest occluder. A simple implementation of this approach can be developed using layered shadow maps.

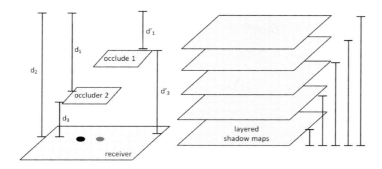

Figure 9.7. Light bleeding caused by multiple occlusion.

Layered shadow maps define an array of shadow maps that store the distances to the closest point for slices parallel to the light. In our implementation, each shadow map is obtained by rendering the scene multiple times, changing the near clip of the camera to cover the regions illustrated in Figure 9.7 (right). That is, the first shadow map covers a small region far from the light and the next shadow maps cover regions that increase in size approaching the camera.

In order to use layered shadow maps, the shadow-map test in Listing 9.1 should be changed to search for occluders in an array of textures. This is implemented in Listing 9.5. Here, the test is performed on each of the layer textures and the first layer that passes the shadow-map test is used to compute the occluder distance. It is important to mention that if multiple occluders are close to each other, then they will be located in the same shadow map. However, if they are close, then the distance error is low and the shadows are similar. That is, layers will not guarantee the correct distance computation, but they will mitigate problems caused by multiple occluders at far distances.

Figure 9.8 shows two examples that compare renderings with and without layered shadow maps. The images in the top row were obtained with a single shadow map while the images on the bottom row have eight layers. In the example shown in the images on the left, there are two multiple occlusions caused by the brick blocks and containers. Since the distance between the bricks and the container on the left is small relative to their distance to the light, shadows caused by both objects merge without causing artifacts. However, the large distance between the bricks and the container at the right causes a light shadow under the container. As shown in the image on the bottom row, these problems are reduced by using layered shadow maps.

The example in the top-right image in Figure 9.8 shows light bleeding caused by a semitransparent object. Shadows for semitransparent objects can be created by changing the intensity of the shadows according to the transparency value of the albedo texture of the occluder. This modification can be implemented

```
void main(INPUT input, inout OUTPUT output)
{
    float4 light_pos = mul (pos4,light_matrix)

    // For each layer
    float2 shadow_map_val[8]
    shadow_map_val[0] = GetShadowMap(0,light_pos); // :
    shadow_map_val[7] = GetShadowMap(7,light_pos);

    // Shadow map test. Look for first occluder
    output.color.r = 0.0f;
    float distance = 0.0f;

    for( index =0; index<7;index++){
        if(shadow_map_val[index].x < light_pos.z - shadow_bias) {
            output.color.r = shadow_map_val[index].y;
            distance = shadow_map_value[index].x;
            index = 8;
        }
    }

    float distance_factor =
                     (light_pos.z / distance)--1.0f;
    output.color.b = distance_factor * L * f * A / pos.z;
}
```

Listing 9.5. Performing the shadow test and computing the penumbrae widths for layered shadow maps and transparency.

during the shadow-map test, so it does not add any significant computational overhead; it requires changing the shadow-map generation and the shadow-map test. The shadow-map creation should be modified so that the shadow map keeps the distance to the closest object and the alpha value of the albedo texture. The alpha value can then be used as shown in Listing 9.5 to determine the intensity of the shadow.

The computation of transparency, using values in the shadow map, is computationally attractive; however it can produce light bleeding for multiple occluders. This is illustrated in Figure 9.8 (top right). Here, the bin is causing a multiple occlusion with the bus stop glass. Thus, the shadow cast by the bin uses the transparency of glass and produces a very weak shadow. This is because a single shadow map stores only the alpha of the closest object to the light. As shown in Figure 9.8 (bottom right), layered shadow maps can alleviate this problem. However, if the occluders are moved close to each other, the layer strategy may fail to store multiple values and objects can produce incorrect shadows.

Figure 9.8. Examples of layered shadows. Light bleeding caused by incorrect computation of the distance between the occluder and the receiver (top). Layered shadow maps can reduce occluder problems (bottom).

9.7 Discussion

Compared with standard shadow maps, the technique presented in this chapter uses an extra texture to store the mipmap and one texture for each layer for the layered version. In terms of processing, it adds a computational overhead caused by: (i) the computations of the penumbra width during the shadow-map test (Listing 9.1); (ii) the creation of the mipmap (Listing 9.3); and (iii) the mipmap lookup during shadow blending (Listing 9.4).

The rendering times of the technique are shown in Table 9.1. The columns in the table show the frames per second when: rendering without shadows, rendering using standard shadow maps, rendering using the mipmap, and when using layers. The results were obtained for a test scene with 13K faces and by using a GeForce 8800GTX with a 720×480 display resolution. The implementation used a 512×512 shadow map and six mipmap levels. The frame time increases about 0.3 ms when the mipmap is used to generate soft shadows. This increase is mainly because of the time spent during the generation of the mipmap. In

	No Shadows	Standard Shadow Map (hard shadows)	Mipmap Shadows	Layered Shadow Maps
Frame Rate	345	340	305	230
Frame Time	2.89ms	2.94ms	3.27ms	4.34ms

Table 9.1. Frame rate for different implementations.

the layered version, the increase in rendering time is mainly due the multiple rendering required to create the shadow map for each layer. The time shown in Table 9.1 was obtained by considering six layers.

The computational load is adequate for real-time applications and the results show compelling smooth shadows. However, multiple occlusions can produce light bleeding. This is more evident as the light's area increases, since shadows with significantly different intensities can be created. This problem can be mitigated by saturating the intensity of the shadows or by using layered shadow maps. Nevertheless, when dealing with complex scenes and large-area lights, there still may be variations of intensities on multiple occlusion zones. As such, the technique could benefit from more elaborate layer placements or peeling layer strategies. Finally, it is important to mention that this technique relies on shadow maps, so it inherits those computational advantages, but it is also prone to inherent problems such as z-fighting for incorrect depth bias.

Bibliography

[Annen et al. 08] Thomas Annen, Zhao Dong, Tom Mertens, Philippe Bakaert, Hans-Peter Seidel and Jan Kautz. "Real-Time All-Frequency Shadows in Dynamic Scenes." *ACM Transactions on Graphics (Proc SIGGRAPH)* 27:3 (2008), 34:1–34:8

[Bracewell 00] Ronald Bracewell. *The Fourier Transform and its Applications*. Singapore: McGraw-Hill International Editions, 2000.

[Donnelly and Lauritzen 06] William Donnelly and Andrew Lauritzen. "Variance Shadow Maps." In *Symposium on Interactive 3D Graphics and Games*, pp. 161-165. New York: ACM, 2006.

[Fernando 05] Randima Fernando. "Percentage-Closer Soft Shadows." In *Proc SIGGRAPH Sketches*, pp. 35. New York: ACM, 2005.

[Gambau et al. 10] Jesus Gambau, Miguel Chover and Mateu Sbert. "Screen Space Soft Shadows." In *GPU Pro Advanced Rendering Techniques*, edited by Wolfgang Engel, pp. 477–491. Natick, MA: A K Peters, 2010.

[Reeves et al. 87] William Reeves, David Salesin and Robert Cook. "Rendering Antialised Shadows with Depth Maps." *Computer Graphics (Proc. SIGGRAPH)* 21:4 (1987), 283-291.

[Williams 78] Lance Williams. "Casting Curved Shadows on Curved Surfaces." *Computer Graphics (Proc. SIGGRAPH)* 12:3 (1978), 270–274.

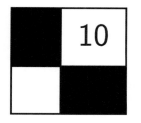

10

Efficient Online Visibility for Shadow Maps

Oliver Mattausch, Jiri Bittner, Ari Silvennoinen, Daniel Scherzer, and Michael Wimmer

10.1 Introduction

Standard online occlusion culling is able to vastly improve the rasterization performance of walkthrough applications by identifying large parts of the scene as invisible from the camera and rendering only the visible geometry. However, it is of little use for the acceleration of shadow-map generation (i.e., rasterizing the scene from the light view [Williams 78]), so that typically a high percentage of the geometry will be visible when rendering shadow maps. For example, in outdoor scenes typical viewpoints are near the ground and therefore have significant occlusion, while light viewpoints are higher up and see most of the geometry.

Our algorithm remedies this situation by quickly detecting and culling the geometry that does not contribute to the shadow in the final image. Note that from the geometry visible from the light, only a small fraction will remain (for

Figure 10.1. The shadow-map geometry rendered for a particular *Left 4 Dead* view (left) and the corresponding light-view visualization (right), where the rendered shadow casters are shown in red.

example, the red parts in Figure 10.1). The main idea is to use camera-view visibility information to create a mask of potential shadow receivers in the light view, which restricts the areas where shadow casters have to be rendered. This algorithm makes shadow-map rendering efficient by providing the important property of *output sensitivity* (i.e., the complexity depends only on what is visible from the camera and not the size of the scene).

The method is easy to integrate into an existing rendering engine that already performs occlusion culling for rasterization. It is orthogonal to the particular occlusion-culling algorithm being used. We used the CHC++ algorithm [Mattausch et al. 08] in our implementation, but in principle any state-of-the-art occlusion-culling algorithm can benefit from our method. Likewise, our method does not pose any restriction on the shadow-mapping algorithm being used. It was tested successfully with different algorithms like uniform shadows, LiSPSM, or cascaded shadow maps.

Our method is particularly useful for shadow mapping in large-scale outdoor scenes. In terms of overall render time (i.e., the whole pipeline until the final shaded image is rendered), the algorithm achieves a speedup of up to ten in real-world city scenes compared to the naïve use of occlusion culling. It also brings a significant speedup of up to two in real game scenes (e.g., a *Left 4 Dead* level as shown in Figure 10.1).

10.2 Algorithm Overview

The algorithm consists of the following four main steps, as also shown in Figure 10.2. Steps 1 and 4 constitute the standard approach for deferred shading (including shadow mapping); the main contributions of our algorithm are Steps 2 and 3.

Step 1: Determine shadow receivers. First we use occlusion culling to render the scene from the camera. This gives us the visible geometry, which corresponds to the potential shadow receiver geometry. Such an initial depth pass is a common practice in rendering engines. Our implementation uses a deferred shading approach, where other attributes like the geometry normals are stored in separate render targets for subsequent shading together with the depth buffer. We use a bounding volume hierarchy over the geometry as input to our occlusion-culling algorithm, and the potential shadow receivers correspond to the leaves of this hierarchy. Note that this step provides a conservative estimate of the visible geometry.

Step 2: Create a mask of shadow receivers. Next we render the potential receivers from the light view to generate a so-called receiver mask. During shadow-map rendering, shadow map updates are restricted to this mask. We can further tighten the receiver mask and restrict shadow-map rendering to only those shadow map texels that correspond to visible receiver

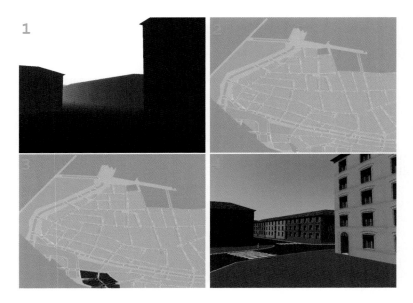

Figure 10.2. Steps of our algorithm. (1) Determine the potential shadow receivers and compute the depth buffer. (2) In light view, create a mask from the potential receivers containing only those fragments that contribute to a pixel in camera view (shown in green). (3) Determine visible subset of shadow casters using occlusion queries against the mask, and rasterize them into a shadow map. (4) Shade image using the depth buffer and the shadow map.

pixels. For this purpose, we make an additional lookup into the camera depth buffer when rendering into the shadow map (this step can be seen as a *reverse shadow test*).

Step 3: Render shadow casters using the mask for culling. After using the potential receivers for mask creation, we rasterize the rest of the scene geometry in order to complete the shadow map, i.e., the *potential shadow casters*. Our receiver mask allows us to quickly reject geometry that does not contribute to the final image, and significantly reduces the number of rendered shadow casters. This is done using hierarchical occlusion culling from the light view, issuing fast hardware occlusion queries to test if a node affects any masked pixels. Note that the speedup of our method is achieved in this step.

Step 4: Compute shading. Finally, we use the shadow map generated in the previous step to perform shadow mapping to find those pixels that are visible from the light source, and shade them accordingly. Note that this step is not altered by our approach.

10.3   Detailed Description

10.3.1   Determine Shadow Receivers

The first step of our algorithm consists of rendering the scene using an online occlusion-culling algorithm, which efficiently detects and culls the geometry that is not visible from the camera. Occlusion queries are issued on cheap proxy geometry (e.g., a bounding box) in order to determine the visibility of the contained complex geometry. Luckily a hardware implementation of occlusion queries is available [Cunniff et al. 07], which returns the number of visible fragments after a small latency.

Occlusion-culling algorithms usually employ front-to-back rendering, and make heavy use of temporal coherence for efficiency and minimizing the query overhead. Culling becomes particularly efficient if it employs a spatial hierarchy to quickly cull large groups of shadow casters, e.g., a bounding volume hierarchy in the case of the CHC++ algorithm. Occlusion culling is less effective for extreme bird's eye views, as much of the scene is visible from such views. Hence, for a typical light view (consider shadows cast from the sun) it is not feasible to use naïve occlusion culling.

Besides determining the depth buffer, such an occlusion pass also gives a good estimate of the geometry visible in the current frame and hence the potential shadow receiver geometry (as of course we are only interested in shadowing the visible geometry). We will use both depth buffer and visible geometry as input to our receiver-masking algorithm.

10.3.2   Create a Mask of Shadow Receivers

The general idea of our method is to create a mask of visible shadow receivers, i.e., those objects determined as visible in the first camera-rendering pass (Step 1). In order to create the mask, we rasterize the actual geometry of the visible shadow receivers into a render target. The creation of the mask happens in a separate pass before rendering the shadow map, but already generates parts of the shadow map itself as well, simplifying the subsequent shadow-map rendering pass. Note that this method alone would already create a valid receiver mask (shown in Figure 10.3 (left)).

However, we can do even better and create a tighter mask by considering the fact that not all of the potential receiver fragments are visible from the camera view. This is because visibility in the camera view is only determined on a per-object basis, while for some objects, only a few pixels are actually visible. The invisible pixels can be detected and discarded using a *reverse shadow test* (see Listing 10.1[1]), leaving only the fragments actually visible in the camera view (depicted in orange in Figure 10.3 (left)). The shader tests whether the current

---

[1]Note that all code segments are given in the Cg shading language.

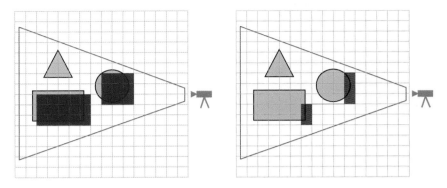

Figure 10.3. The mask is created by rasterizing the potential receiver geometry from the light view (dark-blue fragments, left). With an additional depth buffer lookup, we can discard all potential receiver fragments which are not visible from the camera (leaving only the orange fragments in the mask, right).

fragment lies within the screen-space boundaries and passes the depth test with respect to the camera view. It outputs the test result to a color channel.

```
Fragment ReverseShadowTest(fragin IN,
                           uniform sampler2D depthBuffer)
{
  Fragment OUT;
  // post-projection screen-space position of current fragment
  float4 screenSpacePos = IN.screenSpacePos;
  screenSpacePos /= screenSpacePos.w;

  // the depth of this fragment from the camera
  float fragmentDepth = screenSpacePos.z;
  // the depth of the current pixel from the camera
  float4 depth = tex2D(depthBuffer, screenSpacePos.xy).x;

  // depth comparison: is current fragment visible?
  bool visible = fragmentDepth <= depth + 1e-4f;
  // is fragment inside screen boundaries?
  bool inside = all(saturate(screenSpacePos) == screenSpacePos);

  // if fragment contributes to shading, add to mask
  OUT.color.x = (visible && inside) ? 1.0f : .0f
  return OUT;
}
```

Listing 10.1. The depth buffer of the camera is used to test the visibility of shadow-map fragments. This can be seen as a reverse shadow test that reverses the role of camera and light view.

```
Fragment OcclusionQuery(fragin IN, uniform sampler2D fragMask)
{
  Fragment OUT;
  // post-projection position in receiver mask
  float2 texCoord = IN.maskPos.xy / maskPos.w;
  // lookup corresponding fragment mask value
  float maskVal = tex2D(fragMask, texCoord).x;

  // discard if current fragment not masked
  if (maskVal < .5f) discard;
  return OUT;
}
```

Listing 10.2. Fragment shader for the receiver-mask lookup of an occlusion query.

10.3.3   Render Shadow Casters Using the Mask for Culling

In the shadow-map rendering pass, we rasterize the rest of the geometry as potential shadow casters. The mask is used in this pass to cull those potential shadow
casters that do not contribute to the visible shadows. When issuing a hardware
occlusion query, we use the fragment mask as a lookup texture and discard all
fragments lying outside the mask (as shown in Listing 10.2).

Note that the lookup into the mask creates a minor overhead as compared to
a standard occlusion query, which could be avoided if it were possible to directly
write to the stencil buffer within the fragment shader in order to create a stencil
mask. However, a suitable OpenGL extension (GL_ARB_shader_stencil_export)
is already available and hopefully this feature will be better supported in the
future.

10.4   Optimization: Shadow-Map Focusing

For very large scenes, the shadow-map resolution can become critical for main-
taining a reasonable shadow quality.   Shadow-map warping algorithms like
LiSPSM [Wimmer et al. 04] and shadow-map partitioning algorithms like cascaded shadow maps [Engel 06, Zhang et al. 06] provide a better distribution of
shadow map texels between near and far geometry, and in addition focus the
shadow map in order not to waste shadow-map space on geometry not within the
view frustum. However, if the distance to the far plane is very large compared to
the near plane, the shadow quality can still become unacceptable due to lack of
resolution. While cascaded shadow maps improve shadow quality significantly by
slicing the view frustum and computing a shadow map for each slice individually,
the problem still remains that a lot of shadow resolution can be wasted for areas
that cannot be seen from the camera [Lauritzen et al. 11].

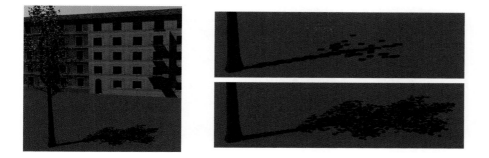

Figure 10.4. The shadow quality of an unfocused shadow map (top) can be greatly improved by focusing the shadow map on the visible geometry (bottom).

Since we collect the geometry visible from the camera in the first step of our algorithm anyway, we get all the information necessary for effectively focusing the shadow map for free. In particular, instead of the usual approach of intersecting the view frustum with the scene boundaries and focusing the shadow map on the resulting polytope, we intersect the view frustum with the union of the bounding boxes of all visible objects.

This algorithm can significantly improve the shadow quality in cases where there is sufficient occlusion (Figure 10.4). Focusing can also improve shadow-map rendering times due to more accurate shadow-frustum culling. However, the increase in the effective shadow-map resolution and the more accurate shadow-frustum culling gained from focusing are both temporally unstable. This temporal instability is potentially manifested by flickering shadow artifacts due to varying shadow-map resolution and incoherent shadow-map rendering times. The former is hard to control, although one could use temporal coherence and careful level design to mitigate the effect. The latter is an example of a non–output-sensitive process and at worst, a single visibility event can make the focused culling dependent on the whole scene. In contrast to simple shadow-frustum culling, our receiver-masking technique is output sensitive and hence the shadow-map rendering times are always predictable. Focusing as a stand-alone algorithm is not a reliable acceleration technique and should always be used in combination with receiver-masking.

10.5 Results

We implemented the presented algorithm in OpenGL and C++ and evaluated it using a GeForce 480 GTX GPU and a single Intel Core i7 CPU 920 with 2.67 GHz. For the camera-view render pass, we used an 800×600 32-bit RGBA render target (to store color and depth) and a 16-bit RGB render target (to store the normals). For the light-view render pass, we used a 32-bit depth texture.

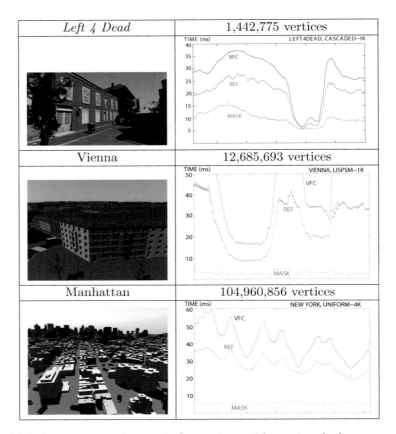

Table 10.1. Test scenes and example frame times with varying shadow parameters.

We compared the proposed receiver-mask algorithm (MASK) to view frustum culling (VFC) and a reference method (REF), which uses our unmodified occlusion culling algorithm for both light and camera views, and we plotted the total frame-rendering times for different test scenes in Table 10.1.

As can be observed from the timings, our algorithm works particularly well in the two city environments: a model of Manhattan and the town of Vienna, which were populated with various scene objects. This is because they are large, containing open scenes with a high cost for shadow mapping. We get a lower speedup of 1.4–2 in the *Left 4 Dead* game scene (rendered at 720p resolution and using four cascaded shadow maps with 1 K resolution each), partially explained by the overall lower geometric complexity. However, keep in mind that a two times speedup in a scene otherwise highly optimized for fast rendering is very worthwhile. The dependence of the algorithm performance on the shadow-map

SM type	LISPSM			UNIFORM		
Shadow size	1K	2K	4K	1K	2K	4K
Scene	Vienna					
Reference	21.6	22.3	22.4	28.7	28.7	29.2
Our method	2.9	3.5	6.1	2.9	3.4	5.9
Scene	Manhattan					
Reference	36.6	35.9	35.1	44.2	43.9	41.8
Our method	4.5	5.4	9.0	4.5	5.3	8.6

Table 10.2. Average frame times for two of the tested scenes (in ms).

resolution (1 K–4 K) and the used shadow-mapping algorithm (LiSPSM [Wimmer et al. 04] and uniform shadow maps) can be seen in Table 10.2.

10.6 Conclusion

We presented an algorithm for fast, output-sensitive shadow mapping in complex scenes. The proposed method generalizes trivially over a wide class of occlusion-culling algorithms as long as they are compatible with receiver masking, a property that holds for all rasterization-based algorithms. The basic principle is easy to integrate into existing game engines, especially if the engine is already using occlusion culling for the main view. We demonstrated the benefits of the algorithm using a reference implementation in the context of large directional light sources and note that the small overhead of generating the receiver mask is easily compensated by the performance gains during shadow-map generation.

10.7 Acknowledgments

We would like to thank Jiri Dusek for an early implementation of shadow map culling ideas; Jason Mitchell for the *Left 4 Dead 2* model; Stephen Hill and Petri Häkkinen for feedback. This work has been supported by the Austrian Science Fund (FWF) contract no. P21130-N13; the Ministry of Education, Youth, and Sports of the Czech Republic under research program LC-06008 (Center for Computer Graphics); and the Grant Agency of the Czech Republic under research program P202/11/1883.

Bibliography

[Cunniff et al. 07] Ross Cunniff, Matt Craighead, Daniel Ginsburg, Kevin Lefebvre, Bill Licea-Kane, and Nick Triantos. "ARB_occlusion_query." *OpenGL Registry.* Available online (http://www.opengl.org/registry/specs/ARB/occlusion_query.txt).

[Engel 06]   Wolfgang Engel. "Cascaded Shadow Maps." In *ShaderX^5: Advanced Rendering Techniques*, edited by Wolfgang Engel, pp. 197–206. Hingham, MA: Charles River Media, 2006.

[Lauritzen et al. 11]   Andrew Lauritzen, Marco Salvi, and Aaron Lefohn. "Sample Distribution Shadow Maps." In *Symposium on Interactive 3D Graphics and Games, I3D '11*, pp. 97–102. New York: ACM Press, 2011.

[Mattausch et al. 08]   Oliver Mattausch, Jiří Bittner, and Michael Wimmer. "CHC++: Coherent Hierarchical Culling Revisited." *Computer Graphics Forum (Proceedings of Eurographics 2008)* 27:2 (2008), 221–230.

[Williams 78]   Lance Williams. "Casting Curved Shadows on Curved Surfaces." *Computer Graphics (SIGGRAPH '78 Proceedings)* 12:3 (1978), 270–274.

[Wimmer et al. 04]   Michael Wimmer, Daniel Scherzer, and Werner Purgathofer. "Light Space Perspective Shadow Maps." In *Rendering Techniques 2004 (Proceedings Eurographics Symposium on Rendering)*, pp. 143–151. Aire-la-Ville, Switzerland: Eurographics Association, 2004.

[Zhang et al. 06]   Fan Zhang, Hanqiu Sun, Leilei Xu, and Lee Kit Lun. "Parallel-Split Shadow Maps for Large-Scale Virtual Environments." In *Proceedings of the 2006 ACM International Conference on Virtual Reality Continuum and its Applications*, pp. 311–318. New York: ACM Press, 2006.

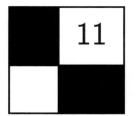

11

Depth Rejected Gobo Shadows
John White

11.1   Introduction

This chapter describes a technique to provide soft shadows using a single texture sample in environments where the objects casting shadows and the objects receiving shadows are disjoint. This is common in games where the lighting on the static environment is prebaked into lightmaps and dynamic objects are later combined into the world.

Note that the soft shadows using this technique will only be cast onto prelit environment surfaces and not on themselves (i.e., self shadowing) or from one dynamic object to another. In these cases you need to use standard soft-shadowing techniques such as percentage closest filtering (PCF), variance [Donnelly and Lauritzen 06] or exponential shadows maps [Salvi 08]; otherwise the object will receive nonfiltered blocky shadows.

11.2   Basic Gobo Shadows

Before we discuss the technique, it is worthwhile to take a step backwards and describe a very simple technique for soft shadows using gobo projected textures.

A gobo is a theatrical term that refers to a cutout shape that can be placed in front of a spotlight light bulb. When the spotlight is turned on, the gobo cutout will partially block some light and the resultant shape will be projected onto the scene.

In games we can apply the same trick by applying a similar black or white texture to a projected light. The result is a soft image that casts onto the world. This texture can therefore be used to fake a shadow from an object. A common example of this in games is to have the light source in a wired cage; the gobo is then used to fake the shadow from the cage onto the world. As in the theater, the trick relies on the fact that any moving objects cannot move in between the light source and the world object from which the gobo is used to fake shadows (see Figure 11.1).

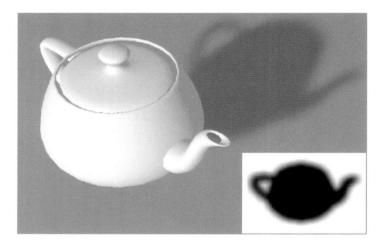

Figure 11.1. A gobo texture and its projection.

In games, this gobo can be generated upfront and loaded in and used statically. It can also be generated per frame by rendering the objects using a black shader onto a white surface, and then applying a blur filter afterwards to smooth the edges to fake the penumbra from the area light source.

Figure 11.2. A correct and an incorrect projection.

The main problem with basic gobo shadowing, especially for infinitely far directional shadowing such as from the sun, is that it is often impossible to guarantee that there is no surface between the light source and the gobo-casting object. This will lead to the gobo incorrectly projecting onto closer objects that should be fully in light. Figure 11.2 shows a wall closer to the light source with an incorrect gobo projection on it.

11.3 Depth Rejected Gobo Shadows

We can now extend the basic projected gobo technique to remove these incorrect projections on objects closer to the light source. We will do this by using standard shadow mapping to store depth values so that we can detect these incorrect back projections.

The basic algorithm in a nutshell is as follows:

1. Render a shadow map as usual but ensure that written pixels are tagged in the stencil buffer or in the second channel of a two-channel texture.

2. Apply a separable blur to the shadow maps to blur the stencil buffer and dilate out the depth values. The output is a two-channel depth + gobo texture.

3. Apply the blurred shadow map to the environment during a forward render pass. Use the depth component as the typical binary depth test with the blurred stencil component as the softness (i.e., penumbra) of the shadow. This shadow map can and should be sampled using a bilinear filter and not a point/nearest filter.

11.3.1 Stage 1: Shadow-Map Rendering

Shadow map rendering is performed as in typical games except that when we clear the depth stencil buffer to `ZFar` we also clear the stencil to zero. On hardware where we cannot read back the depth buffer afterwards, we can render the shadow map into a two-channel 16-bit texture, such as G16R16. The demo in the accompanying web materials renders into a texture of this form.

We then render all objects into the shadow map with the computed depth stored in the R channel and we set the green to 1. In the case of rendering to a depth stencil texture, simply set the stencil states to always set the 8-bit stencil value to 255. This allows for the double speed Z only rendering on the consoles. It is possible to perform standard shadow mapping without the need for a separate channel, but by doing so it allows for a simple blurring stage afterwards.

A difference from common shadowing is that the Z-Buffer runs in reverse; 0.0f is as at the far plane and 1.0 is at the near plane with the depth test changed to a GREATER mode. This is used to allow for some optimizations when later blurring the shadow map in the next stage.

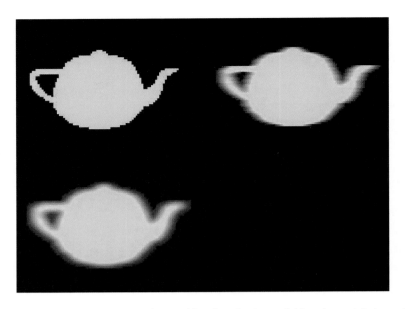

Figure 11.3. Gobo shadow map (top left), after horizontal blur (top right), and after vertical blur (bottom left).

11.3.2 Stage 2: Shadow-Map Blurring

In the next stage, the shadow map is blurred using a modified separable Gaussian blur.

This pass will do a standard Gaussian blur on the gobo component and will perform a weighted average of the depth values for any pixels that are equal to `ZFar`. That is, the blur will dilate out depth values into the initially empty unwritten space. Any pixels that already have a nonzero depth value written out during Stage 1 will not be affected. In the example, I use a G16R16 texture to store this information. You could also use two separate textures to store the depth and gobo components with different bit depths if the hardware allows for such rendering using MRTs.

Figure 11.3 shows the process of blurring the shadow map. Note that the red channel is the depth and these values are dilated out without blurring. The green channel is subject to a Gaussian blur.

11.3.3 Stage 3: Applying Shadows

In the forward render shader, the shadow map is tapped using a bilinear filtered texture sampler. The gobo component is made up of the shadow softness amount and the depth as a binary test to see if we need to use the softness at all, i.e., whether to set the gobo component to zero because the pixel is known to be fully in light. The basic code is given in Listing 11.1.

```
float2 depthGobo = tex2D(shadowSampler, LightSpaceUV)

if(depthGobo.x < lightspaceZ) // Reject gobo if too close
    depthGobo.y = 0.0;

float keylightVisibility = 1.0 - depthGobo.y;
```

Listing 11.1. Applying the gobo shadows.

The value stored in `keylightVisibility` can be used to modulate the key-light $N \cdot L$ result. It is possible to remove the conditional using the code given in Listing 11.2.

```
// Tune the 100 to sharpen the fadeout
depthGobo.y *= saturate((depthGobo.x - lightspaceZ) * 100;
```

Listing 11.2. Removing the conditional.

The best way to think about this new shadowing is that rather than use depth values in the shadow map to identify pixels that are in shadow, the depth is used to indicate which pixels are *not* in shadow.

11.4 Extensions

11.4.1 Variable Penumbra

Instead of doing a binary comparison to see if pixels are in shadow or not, and using the blurriness channel as is for the penumbra amount, the difference between the stored Z value in the shadow map and the Z value from the surface in shadow can be used to adjust the contrast on the softness value. So as the comparison gets smaller, the contrast value increases to sharpen the shadow value. In extreme cases, this can lead to very sharp shadows like shadow volumes. To allow the penumbra to increase further, the prefiltered shadow maps can be mip-mapped. If the distance to the receiver value is over a certain threshold, then an extra tap is read from the mip-chain and this softness value can be used instead. However, in these cases the blurriness value has to be conservatively blurred inwards to avoid hitting failure cases where shadow casters start to overlap more in light space (see Figure 11.4).

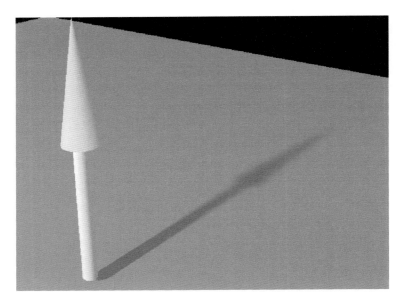

Figure 11.4. Variable penumbra by applying contrast based on the distance from receiver to caster.

11.5   Failure Case

The algorithm works best in large, relatively flat worlds. This is because the technique relies on the premise that shadow-casters are usually disjoint (i.e., not connected) when viewed in light space. There are cases where casters will overlap in shadow-map space with a receiver in-between. In these cases, the receiving surface will receive a blocky shadow from the caster that is overlapping with a more distant caster in light space. Generally these cases are very rare and hence these issues were ignored in games that shipped with this technique. In the demo there is an area where objects are rendered that exhibit this problem. A potential solution to this artifact is to render the world into the shadow map but with the stencil-write off. This will stop the more-distant shadow caster from being written into the shadow map with stencil-writes on.

Bibliography

[Donnelly and Lauritzen 06] William Donnelly and Andrew Lauritzen. "Variance Shadow Maps." Available at http://www.punkuser.net/vsm, 2006.

[Salvi 08] Marco Salvi. Exponential Shadow Maps, GDC 2008.

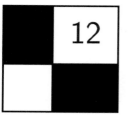

Real-Time Deep Shadow Maps

René Fürst, Oliver Mattausch, and Daniel Scherzer

In offline rendering the algorithm of choice for correctly shadowing transparent objects such as hair or smoke are *deep shadow maps* (DSMs). Algorithms trying to achieve the same effect in *real time* have hitherto always been limited to approximating the solution by depth-peeling techniques. Since the introduction of Direct3D 11, however, it has become feasible to implement the original algorithm using a single rendering pass from the light without introducing any approximations. In this chapter we discuss how to implement a DSM algorithm for rendering complex hair models that runs in real time on Direct3D 11 capable hardware, introducing a novel lookup scheme that exploits spatial coherence for efficient filtering of the deep shadow map.

12.1 Introduction

While real-time (soft) shadows are nowadays routinely used in games, correct shading and rendering of complex hair models, like the ones shown in Figure 12.1, remain nontrivial tasks that are hard to achieve with interactive or even real-time frame rates. The main problem is the complex visibility of hair with super-thin structures that easily creates reconstruction artifacts when using traditional shadow maps. Traditional shadow maps store the distances to the visible front as seen from the light source into each texel of a 2D texture. This means that only the nearest surfaces that block the light are captured. In a second step, a *binary* depth test is performed for each pixel that compares stored texel depth and pixel depth to determine if the pixel is either shadowed or not. While this works well for opaque objects, it has the disadvantage that transparent objects cannot be handled correctly, since every surface behind the visible front is assumed to be fully shadowed.

Shadowing of transparent objects is possible by computing the *percentage of light* that transmits through a material after taking the occlusion of all nearer

Figure 12.1. Hair models rendered with our real-time DSM algorithm.

surfaces along a ray into account. For each texel, a *deep shadow map* (DSM) [Lokovic and Veach 00] stores the transmitted amount of light as a function of depth (shown in Figure 12.2). In reality this amounts to a list of depth values with associated transmittance stored for each texel. When rendering the scene from the camera, the current depth value is searched and used as a lookup into

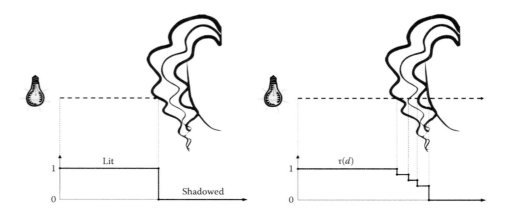

Figure 12.2. Visibility captured for one texel of a shadow map: For traditional shadow mapping (left) only the visible front is captured, while DSMs (right) also account for objects behind it. Here the transmittance function $\tau(d)$ stores the visibility along a ray from the light source.

this transmittance function, and the corresponding remaining light is then used to correctly shade each pixel. A major part of this chapter describes how to store and to sort incoming fragments with Direct3D 11 in order to reconstruct the transmittance function and have a suitable representation that allows a fast lookup of the transmittance.

As with most shadow mapping algorithms, deep shadow mapping is also prone to aliasing artifacts. However, most of these artifacts can be overcome by adapting techniques that are also used for traditional shadow maps, e.g., percentage-closer filtering (PCF) [Reeves et al. 87]. We will show how DSMs can be filtered efficiently by exploiting spatial coherence among neighboring pixels. Furthermore, we extend this concept to allow filtering with *exponential shadow maps* (ESMs) [Annen et al. 08].

12.2 Transmittance Function

The major difference between traditional (binary) shadow maps and deep shadow maps is that for each *deep* shadow map test the transmittance function has to be evaluated for the current pixel's depth. Hence this function has to be created and stored first. Creation is made feasible for rasterization hardware by calculating transmittance out of surface opacities. The idea is to rasterize all geometry as seen from the point of view of the light, storing not only the first depth but also all depths (and associated opacities) in a list for each texel. After sorting these lists by depth, the transmittance at a certain depth d at a given texel location can be calculated out of the opacities α_i of all list entries with depth smaller than d (see Figure 12.2) by

$$\tau(d) = \prod_{i=0}^{n(d)} (1 - \alpha_i), \tag{12.1}$$

where $n(d)$ is the number of fragments before depth d. During shadow lookups, the depth of the current fragment can then be used to look up the correct shading value (i.e., percentage of light transmitted) for shadowing the pixels. In the next section we will show how to create and store such a function efficiently on Direct3D 11 hardware.

12.3 Algorithm

Our algorithm can be divided into the following steps:

- Creating list entries. The scene is rendered from the light source. The alpha value and depth value of *all* incoming fragments are stored in a two-dimensional structure of linked lists. Note that the sizes of the linked lists are only limited by video memory, which allows us to store transmittance functions of varying depth complexity.

- **Processing the fragments.** The fragments are sorted, and the transmittance functions are precomputed for the fragment depths from the individual alpha values (using Equation (12.1)) to allow a fast lookup into the transfer function. Finally the transmittance functions are simplified.

- **Neighbor linking.** For each fragment, the neighboring fragments at the same position in the linked lists are also linked, in order to quickly find those neighboring fragments that are nearest in terms of depth to the light source and achieve quicker filtering.

- **Deferred shadowing.** DSM lookups can become quite expensive for complex hair models (i.e., with big depth complexity and transmittance functions with many stored values). Hence, deferred shading is used to render the scene first and then compute the shading value *only once* for each pixel during deferred shading.

- **Spatial filtering.** At this point, we utilize neighbor links to provide fast lookups for large filter kernels. The DSM idea is combined with two well-known filtering methods for binary shadow maps.

The first three steps can be summarized as building up the DSM structure from the light; the last two steps apply the DSM for the final shading from the camera. Each of these steps will be discussed in more detail in the following sections.

12.3.1   Creating List Entries

One of the main issues for implementing DSMs on a modern GPU is that the amount of per-texel data is dependent on the depth complexity of the scene at the texel position and therefore can vary arbitrarily. In Direct3D 11, this problem can be solved by storing the depth and alpha values of *every* incoming fragment along a light ray in a per-texel linked list. In total each linked list element has the format shown in Listing 12.1. There, `next` represents the index of the next element of a linked list, and it contains −1 if the current element is the last element of the linked list. We also store additional links to the previous element links (making it a double-linked list) to fragments from neighboring pixels that come to use later on.

We create a two-level structure to be able to efficiently insert all fragments into these linked lists during a single rendering pass from the light. All fragments in the linked lists are stored in a structure that we denote as the *list element buffer*. For every pixel, we store the index of the first list element in each linked list in a separate buffer that we denote as the *head buffer*, since it points to the first element of a list. If a linked list corresponding to a shadow map texel is empty, the value −1 is stored in the head buffer. An example is shown in Figure 12.3.

```
struct LinkedListEntry
{
    float depth;
    float alpha;

    int next; // next element in linked list
    int prev; // previous element in linked list

    int right; // right neighbor link
    int upper; // upper neighbor link
};
```

Listing 12.1. Linked list entry structure.

In this example the elements 1 and 6 (2 and 5, respectively) form a single linked list, and the first elements 1 and 2 are stored in the head buffer.

Both structures (head buffer and list element buffer) are stored as Direct3D 11 (RW)`StructuredBuffers` and filled by rendering the geometry once using interlocked operations and the buffer counter in the pixel shader. `InterlockedExchange` is used to exchange the head of the linked list to ensure that we do not face any problems regarding parallelization. The buffer counter is used to "allocate" linked

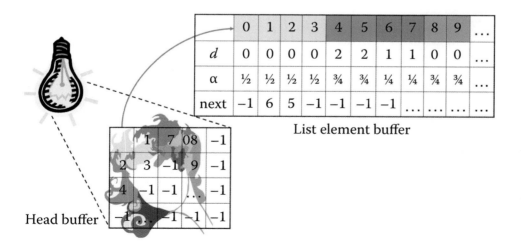

Figure 12.3. We implemented the DSMs as a two-level structure that consists of a per-pixel buffer storing the head of each linked list (head buffer) and the list element buffer for all incoming fragments. For each fragment, we store depth and alpha values, as well as indices of the next and the previous elements, and nearest-depth neighbor links (only the `next` index is shown here for brevity).

```
void ps_main(PS_IN input)
{
    // Allocate a new element in the list element buffer by
    // atomically incrementing the buffer counter.
    int counter = listElementBuffer.IncrementCounter();

    // Store the required information and apply a depth bias.
    listElementBuffer[counter].depth = input.posToShader.z + bias;
    listElementBuffer[counter].alpha = input.alpha;

    // pixel screen coordinate to buffer index
    int index = (int)(input.pos.y * Width + input.pos.x);

    int originalVal;
    // Atomically exchange the element in the head buffer.
    InterlockedExchange(headBuffer[index], counter, originalVal);

    // Create the link to the existing list.
    listElementBuffer[counter].next = originalVal;
}
```

Listing 12.2. Concurrent way of adding a new fragment to the list element buffer and updating the head buffer in a pixel shader.

list elements in parallel. The pixel shader for filling both head buffer and list element buffer with a new incoming fragment is shown in Listing 12.2.

12.3.2   Processing the Fragments

Note that up to now the list entries neither are sorted nor contain the final transmittance. These processing tasks are the purpose of this step. The sorting of all fragments with respect to their depth is done in a separate compute shader (executed for every pixel). We load a single linked list per pixel into a local array and do a local sort, which does not require any shared memory. Since neither compute shaders nor OpenCL support recursion yet, a sorting algorithm like quick sort is not very well suited to the GPU architecture. Instead we use *insertion sort* due to its simplicity and because it is known to be very fast on small arrays (as is the case for models with reasonable depth complexity). This fact was confirmed in our experiments, where insertion sort yielded about two times the performance of a nonrecursive version of quick sort. Next we convert the alpha values in the linked list into a transmittance function according to Equation (12.1). This means that we pre-multiply transmittance for each of the depths d_i from the linked list and store the transmittance at each fragment instead of the alpha values. Note that this step is done to accelerate spatial coherent lookups for filtering later on. Here, having to traverse the list from the head to reconstruct the transmittance for each filter sample is exactly what we want to avoid. Furthermore, the `prev` links are stored in this step of the algorithm in order to create a double-linked list.

To accelerate the lookup time, we have to simplify the transmittance function. In the case of volume data, a sophisticated algorithm for handling the inclination of the transmittance function has been proposed in the original DSM paper [Lokovic and Veach 00]. In the case of hair rendering, however, we deal with a simple, piecewise constant version of the transmittance function. Hence, it turned out that a simple but efficient optimization strategy is to merely cut off the transmittance function after its value does not change significantly any more, i.e., if $\prod_{i=0}^{k+1}(1 - \alpha_i) - \epsilon < \prod_{i=0}^{k}(1 - \alpha_i)$. In our experiments the frame time has been improved by approximately 40% using an ϵ of 0.001, which does not visibly compromise the quality of the shadows. Note that a more sophisticated GPU-friendly compression scheme has been proposed by Salvi et al. [Salvi et al. 10] that limits the transmittance functions to a fixed size and works for shadowing both hair and participating media. This method could alternatively be used instead of the simple truncation, and we believe that it would work well in combination with our neighbor-linking approach (possibly further accelerating the lookup time).

12.3.3 Neighbor Linking

In this step we store links with each entry (fragment) of a linked list to those entries (fragments) in the neighboring linked lists that are closest to it in terms of light-space depth. The reasoning behind this step is that for adjacent pixels in screen space, it's very likely that they have approximately the same depth in light space due to spatial coherence. During filtering, the links enable direct access to the depth-nearest neighbors of a fragment in the DSM. Once we found a fragment corresponding to a given light-space depth, the other corresponding fragments of nearby filter samples can be found very quickly. Note that we only create links for the great majority of pixels where the assumption of coherence of depth values holds.

In order to keep the memory overhead as low as possible, *only* links to the left and upper neighbor are stored. This suffices for computing all other filter samples when starting from the lower-left corner of a rectangular filtering window. For creating the links, in each thread (note that there is one thread for each shadow-map texel) we simultaneously traverse the linked list associated with the texel in question as well as the lists associated with the right texel neighbor and the upper texel neighbor. For each fragment, we traverse each neighboring list until we either find a fragment that is farther in depth or encounter the end of the list. Then, either the last traversed or the previously traversed neighboring fragment will be the one that is closest in depth to the current fragment. We link the current fragment to its depth-nearest neighbors by storing their indices, which we denote `right` and `upper` for each list element. The expense of storing three additional integers per list element (the two neighbor links and the `prev` link) increases the overall memory requirements by about 25%, but this pays off during filtering as will become clear in Section 12.3.5.

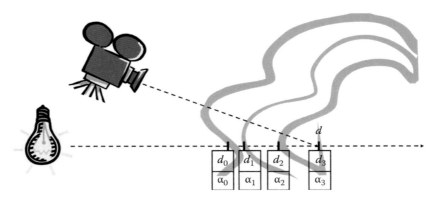

Figure 12.4. To calculate the transmittance for a DSM test evaluation, the opacities α_i of all the surfaces that are nearer than the current pixel's depth d have to be multiplied.

12.3.4   Deferred Shadowing

In the shadowing stage, we search for the depth in the transmittance function, which corresponds to the depth of the current pixel in the eye view (see Figure 12.4). This is done by front-to-back traversal of the linked list corresponding to the current position in the xy-plane. The head of the list is accessed by looking it up in the head buffer. A lookup of the corresponding element in the transmittance function gives the correct transmittance value, which is used to attenuate the shading.

An important point for stabilizing the frame rate and to achieve real-time frame rates is to use a deferred shading pipeline for shadowing. This means that we first render the geometry to store depth and diffuse shading values in render targets before using a single shadow lookup per pixel in the deferred shadowing pass. Consider that with forward rendering, the depth complexity of a hair model potentially requires multiple costly shadow lookups per pixel (and even more when using PCF).

12.3.5   Spatial filtering

Spatial antialiasing is as important for DSM as it is for binary shadow maps in order to achieve high-quality images (see Figure 12.6). Contrary to standard filtering methods for binary shadow maps (e.g., using PCF), we now deal with a list of depth values per pixel. In our case, these depth values are not samples but represent the full transmittance function as it is, which means that we do not need to deal with reconstruction or filtering in z-direction. Therefore we use a 2D filter kernel as in the classical PCF formulation and compare light-space depths of adjacent pixels in screen space.

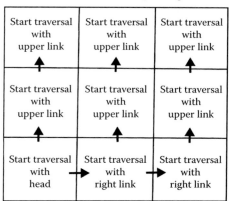

Figure 12.5. We initialize the traversal of the transmittance function using the corresponding link to the closest-depth fragment of the neighboring pixel (going first in y- and then in x-direction).

Since lookup time is slow for DSM, it is essential for DSM filtering to avoid a naive implementation where the overall lookup time grows linearly with the filter size. Searching the whole list of a neighboring pixel for the correct fragment is prohibitively expensive. A binary search would reduce the complexity but is not very suitable for implementation in a compute shader and on linked lists.

Instead we exploit spatial coherence and assume that the neighboring fragment closest in depth has a similar index in its linked list. At this stage we utilize the linking structure from Section 12.3.3, which links list elements closest in depth in order to get a good initial guess for the lookup of a neighboring fragment. This way, the transmittance function has to be traversed from the beginning (the head element) *only once* per pixel, regardless of the used filter size. Once a fragment corresponding to the current depth is found, it is possible to quickly access the neighboring fragments for computing the remaining filter samples.

In our implementation, first the fragment corresponding to the lower-left corner of a filtering window is computed (see Figure 12.5). Next the positions of the fragments linked by `right` and `upper` are used as initial guesses for finding the correct fragment position of a neighboring sample in the DSM (as depicted in Figure 12.4). Then this sample's linked list is traversed by following either `prev` or `next` to determine the correct depth (fragment position in the list). If spatial coherence holds, each traversal only requires a few iterations.

For a filter kernel size of 7×7 and realistic transparency settings, the links speed up the frame times by up to 50% for a frame-buffer resolution of $1{,}280 \times 720$ and up to 100% for a resolution of $1{,}920 \times 1{,}080$ when compared to a brute-force traversal for each filter kernel sample. Note that this technique scales well with the complexity of the hair model (the more complex, the larger the speedup), because the lookup times become roughly constant as long as there is sufficient coherence. Also observe that this technique even scales well with larger filter kernels, since spatial coherence is only required between neighboring pixels. In case of small transmittance functions (e.g., due to high opacity), the gain from the links are minor, which nevertheless only results in a barely noticeable constant overhead due to the links (of about 2%).

Apart from PCF, we also adapted another antialiasing algorithm, exponential shadow mapping, for use with DSM.

Exponential shadow mapping. The standard binary shadow map test causes antialiasing artifacts since it is effectively a step function that jumps between 0 and 1. Hence *exponential shadow mapping* (ESM) [Annen et al. 08] approximates the shadow test with an exponential function (yielding continuous results between [0..1]). This continuous value is subsequently used to attenuate the shading of a pixel.

The DSM algorithm can be combined with ESM in a straightforward fashion, and we denote this combination as *exponential deep shadow mapping* (EDSM). The resulting transmittance is weighted with the continuous shadow test value. As can be seen in Figure 12.6, EDSM performs much better than PCF in terms of visual quality. Note that while the original ESM algorithm supports prefiltering, this feature cannot be used in combination with DSM since the lookup depth along the transmittance function is not known beforehand.

12.4   Results

We computed all our results on an Intel Core i7-2700K Processor (using one core) and using a Geforce GTX 680. All images were rendered in resolution $1{,}280 \times 720$ and using a deferred rendering pipeline with four 32-bit render targets. The hair model used in our experiments has 10,000 individual strands of hairs and about 87,000 vertices.

SM res	SM	DSM	DSM3	DSM5	EDSM	EDSM3	EDSM5
256	222.8	220.9	192.4	160.3	207.2	166.2	121.6
512	121.2	120.2	111.9	98.4	116.0	99.5	79.9
768	70.7	70.2	66.4	61.4	69.2	60.8	51.0

Table 12.1. This table compares typical FPS values for binary shadow mapping by using only the first fragment of a DSM for shading (SM), our method without filtering (DSM) and with PCF (DSM3 and DSM5), and our EDSM algorithm using different filter kernel footprints. The number after the algorithm's name is the filter kernel size (e.g., a 3×3 kernel for EDSM3).

Figure 12.6. DSMs without filtering (left) exhibit resampling artifacts. Smoother shadows can be achieved with PCF (center), while ESM provides even higher quality (right).

In Table 12.1 we compare the timings for a special version of binary shadow mapping (simulated by using only the first fragment of a DSM for shading), DSMs, and DSMs using a 3×3 and a 5×5 PCF kernel size, respectively, and show the comparison for several shadow map resolutions. The comparison to this version of binary shadow mapping demonstrates the overhead of the DSM lookups (using both optimizations, i.e., neighbor links and truncation of the transmittance function). While the overhead is more pronounced for small shadow maps, it becomes small in relation to the DSM creation for increasing shadow map size.

In Figure 12.6 we compare the quality of DSMs without filtering (left), with PCF (center), and using ESM (right). As can be seen, PCF performs solid antialiasing, while EMS improves the rendering quality even more. Furthermore, while all DSM methods require a depth bias to avoid Z-fighting artifacts, ESM needs significantly less bias for artifact-free rendering than unfiltered and PCF rendering.

12.5 Conclusions

We presented an optimized implementation of deep shadow maps for complex hair models that achieves real-time frame rates by employing new features of current graphics hardware. Note that our implementation requires only Direct3D 11 shader features and compute shaders, which makes our algorithm attractive in environments where GPUs from different vendors are used. In our experiments it turned out that the best DSM quality can be achieved by combining it with ESM. While interactive applications are the main target for this algorithm, we also see applications in the movie industry, where such a real-time DSM implementation could save valuable production time and provide immediate feedback to the artists.

12.6   Acknowledgments

We want to thank Cem Yuksel for the permission to use his hair models and
Murat Afsharand for his head model. All models are available at Cem Yuksel's
website, www.cemyuksel.com/research/hairmodels.

Bibliography

[Annen et al. 08] Thomas Annen, Tom Mertens, Hans-Peter Seidel, Eddy Flerackers, and Jan Kautz. "Exponential Shadow Maps." In *Proceedings of
Graphics Interface 2008*, pp. 155–161. Toronto, Canada: Canadian Information Processing Society, 2008.

[Lokovic and Veach 00] Tom Lokovic and Eric Veach. "Deep Shadow Maps." In
*Proceedings of the 27th Annual Conference on Computer Graphics and In-
teractive Techniques*, pp. 385–392. New York: ACM Press/Addison-Wesley
Publishing Co., 2000.

[Reeves et al. 87] William T. Reeves, David H. Salesin, and Robert L. Cook.
"Rendering Antialiased Shadows with Depth Maps." *Computer Graphics
(SIGGRAPH '87 Proceedings)* 21:4 (1987), 283–291.

[Salvi et al. 10] Marco Salvi, Kiril Vidimče, Andrew Lauritzen, and Aaron
Lefohn. "Adaptive Volumetric Shadow Maps." In *Proceedings of the 21st Eurographics Conference on Rendering*, pp. 1289–1296. Aire-la-Ville, Switzerland: Eurographics Association, 2010.

Practical Screen-Space
Soft Shadows
Márton Tamás and Viktor Heisenberger

13.1 Introduction

This chapter describes novel techniques that extend the original screen-space soft shadows algorithm [Gumbau et al. 10] in order to make sure that the speed of rendering is optimal and that we take into consideration overlapping and translucent shadows. We introduce layers, an essential component to filtering overlapping shadows in screen space. We aim to render near one hundred properly filtered, perceptually correct shadows in real time. We also aim to make this technique easy to integrate into existing rendering pipelines.

13.2 Overview

Shadows are important to establish spatial coherency, establish relationships between objects, enhance composition, add contrast, and indicate offscreen space that is there to be explored. As a gameplay element, they are used to project objects onto walls with the intent to create new images and signs that may tell a story. Shadows are often used to either lead the viewer's eye or obscure unimportant parts of the scene.

In computer graphics, light emitters are often represented as a single point with no definite volume. These kinds of mathematical lights cast only hard-edged shadows (a point is entirely obscured by a shadow caster or not) called an *umbra*. However, in the real world, lights usually have volume (like the sun), and therefore they cast soft-edged shadows that consist of an umbra, *penumbra* (a point is partially obscured by shadow caster), and *antumbra* (the shadow caster appears entirely contained by the light source, like a solar eclipse). Figure 13.1 shows a real-world umbra, penumbra, and antumbra.

Figure 13.1. A real-life umbra, penumbra, and antumbra. The objects are lit by a desk spot lamp.

13.3 History

Traditionally, umbras have been represented by either shadow mapping [Williams 78] or shadow volumes [Crow 77]. Shadow mapping works by rendering the scene depth from the point of view of the light source and later in the lighting pass sampling it and comparing the reprojected scene depth to it to determine if a point is in a shadow. Shadow volumes work by creating shadow geometry that divides space into shadowed and unshadowed regions. However, shadow volumes are often bottlenecked by fill rate, leading to lower performance [Nealen 02]. Thus, we use shadow mapping.

While shadow volumes can achieve pixel-perfect hard shadows, shadow mapping's quality depends on the allocated shadow map's (depth texture's) size. If there's not enough shadow map resolution, under-sampling will occur, leading to aliasing. If there's more than enough shadow map resolution, over-sampling will occur, leading to wasted memory bandwidth. Shadow maps also suffer from projective aliasing, perspective aliasing, and erroneous self-shadowing, which needs to be properly addressed.

To simulate penumbra, shadow mapping is often extended with shadow filtering. In order to render soft shadows, percentage closer filtering (PCF) was introduced by [Reeves et al. 87]. This technique achieves soft shadows by implementing blurring in shadow space. Later, PCF was extended by a screen-space

Figure 13.2. Hard shadows (left), a uniform penumbra rendered using PCF (middle), and a perceptually correct variable penumbra rendered using SSSS. When using a variable penumbra, shadow edges become sharper as they approach the shadow caster.

blurring pass [Shastry 05] that enables the use of large filter kernels. However, these techniques can only achieve uniform penumbras. Figure 13.2 shows a comparison of hard shadows, shadows with uniform penumbras, and shadows with variable-sized penumbras.

Percentage-closer soft shadows (PCSS) was introduced to properly render variable-sized penumbras [Fernando 05]. PCSS works by varying the filter size of the PCF blurring. It does a blocker search in order to estimate the size of the penumbra at the given pixel, then uses that information to do variable-sized blurring. However, PCSS still does the blurring step in shadow space, and, depending on the shadow map and kernel size, this step can be a bottleneck, especially when multiple lights are involved. Screen-space soft shadows (SSSS) [Gumbau et al. 10] aims to combat this by deferring the blurring to a screen-space pass so that it will be independent of the actual shadow map size. In screen space, however, we need to account for the varying view angle and therefore we need to use an anisotropic filter. Because the blocker search is still an expensive step ($O(n^2)$), SSSS was extended by [Gumbau et al. 10] with an alternate way to estimate the penumbra size by doing a `min` filter on the shadow map. In addition, this filter is separable and the result only needs to be coarse, so a low-resolution result is acceptable ($O(n + n)$, for much smaller n). [Engel 10] extends SSSS by adding exponential shadow maps and an improved distance function. This allows for self-shadowing, artifact-free soft shadows and better use of the same filter size when viewed from far away.

Mipmapped screen-space soft shadows (MSSSS) [Aguado and Montiel 11] also tries to further improve the speed of filtering. It transforms the shadow map

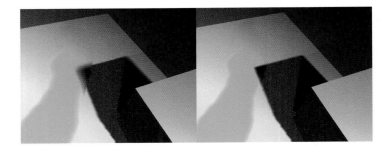

Figure 13.3. Not handling overlapping shadows properly by using layers can lead to artifacts (left), and correct overlapping shadows (right).

blurring problem into the selection of an appropriate mipmap level of a pre-blurred screen-space shadow map based on the estimated size of the penumbra. It also introduces an extension to the algorithm to account for multiple occlusions by using numerous shadow maps.

These screen-space techniques are beneficial because they come with a constant filtering cost, so one does not need to filter the shadows per light source, but the whole screen. Therefore, lights and shadow map filtering are decoupled, and one can employ huge filter kernels resulting in cheap, large penumbras. However, in screen space, another problem surfaces: overlapping shadows of multiple lights. In order to properly account for overlapping shadows, we introduce layered shadow mapping.

The reason we need layers is that if we were to just average the penumbra sizes (storing only one penumbra size per pixel), then we would get incorrect values and artifacts (see Figure 13.3), thus the shadows wouldn't look perceptually correct anymore. With the layers, we can store multiple penumbra sizes and shadow data per pixel, so each light's shadow will be blurred using the correct penumbra size.

In addition, in real-life situations, shadows are often cast by translucent objects, so we also need to take into consideration translucent shadows. The aim of this technique is to render fast, perceptually correct soft shadows with variable penumbra sizes, also accounting for overlapping and translucent shadows. Figure 13.3 shows a comparison between not handling overlapping shadows and handling overlapping shadows.

13.4   Algorithm Overview

13.4.1   G-Buffer Pass

This pass is highly implementation dependent, and while in the original SSSS algorithm this was included in the distances (penumbra) map pass (covered later), we decided to separate this to make sure this technique can be easily integrated into any rendering pipeline. It is possible to go with any G-buffer layout, provided it contains at least the depth buffer and the normals of the scene, as we will need these later. It is important to state that it doesn't matter whether deferred shading or deferred lighting or any of the other popular techniques is being used. We decided to use deferred shading because of its simplicity and speed.

Our G-buffer layout consists of

- D24 depth buffer (stores distance between the viewer and the point being processed),

- RGBA8 view-space normals (RGB channels; alpha channel is free).

13.5 Shadow Map Rendering Pass

In this pass, the standard shadow map rendering is performed, capturing the scene depth from the point of view of the light source. Our technique currently supports spotlights, point lights, and directional lights. Because we are rendering soft shadows, this means that these lights will actually have volume. Note that this will not change the lighting of lit surfaces though.

We consider point lights to be six different shadow casters, and therefore they can be treated the same as spotlights. This means that we can efficiently cull away spotlights, or parts of point lights (that also have shadow maps to be rendered), that do not intersect the camera's frustum as they will not influence the final image. Also, one needs to make sure that projective and perspective aliasing, as well as self-shadowing, is taken care of.

We also extend this pass by considering shadow casters that are not opaque. When this is the case, the shadow caster will allow some light to pass through it, and the shadow may even become colored. Consequently, we need to output an RGBA color per pixel from the point of view of the light. Figure 13.4 shows the contents of a translucency map.

13.6 Introducing Layers and Light Assignment

To allow for multiple overlapping shadows using the original SSSS technique, one could just simply perform all the steps for each light and get correct results. However, this approach is prohibitively expensive, and therefore we looked for a way in which we could perform the screen-space anisotropic blurring for all of the overlapping shadows in one pass.

There was one vital observation (that was also described later in [Anichini 14]): if two lights' volumes don't intersect, their shadows will not overlap either. This means that in screen space, the lights' shadows will not overlap, and because of

Figure 13.4. Contents of the translucency map: a red pole rendered from the point of view of the light source.

this, nonintersecting lights' shadows can be blurred in one pass, independently. However, we also need to consider overlapping shadows from multiple lights.

We observed that this problem (blurring overlapping shadows) is essentially a graph coloring problem, where each graph vertex color represents a shadow layer. In each shadow layer, we store the data of several nonoverlapping lights. In this graph, each light will be a vertex, and there will be an edge between two vertices if the two lights intersect. Because determining the amount of colors needed to color a graph is usually an NP-complete problem, we decided to use a simple greedy algorithm, extended with some rules to help it. For example, since the sun (the directional light) is expected to affect everything, it will be assigned a dedicated layer.

Using the greedy algorithm means that the number of layers (colors) needed equals the maximum vertex degree plus one, and therefore the number of screen-space layers that need to be filtered is only dependent on the maximum number of overlapping shadows produced by different lights (maximum vertex degree). One disadvantage of the greedy vertex coloring is that its quality is highly dependent on the order in which we consider the vertices. Therefore, we use a commonly used vertex ordering scheme, namely, ordering the vertices by their vertex degree in ascending order.

Essentially what we are doing with these layers is trying to minimize the memory and bandwidth costs of overlapping shadows by grouping shadow data into layers instead of storing and filtering them separately for each light source.

It is also advisable to restrict the number of layers for a given scene so that the general coloring problem can be transformed into a k-coloring problem (where k is the predefined number of layers). The shadow filtering will have a predictable cost and artists can be told not to use more overlapping lights than the layer

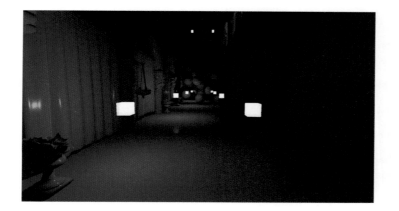

Figure 13.5. Point lights colored according to their respective layer. Each layer is represented by a color (red, green, blue, and yellow). The white cubes illustrate the lights' positions.

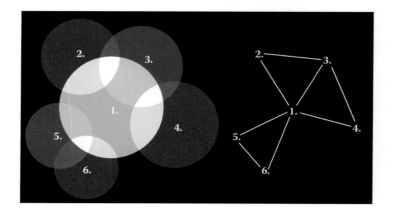

Figure 13.6. Lights are numbered and represented by circles (left), where each color represents a layer (red, green, and blue). Lights and their intersections with each other are represented on a graph (right). We can see that Light 1 has a vertex degree of 5, so we would need a maximum of six layers to render these lights; however, in this case, by using a good graph coloring algorithm, we can reduce the number of needed layers to three.

budget allows for. In addition, in order to speed up the light intersection process, one can use an arbitrary space division data structure such as an octree. The actual layer layout is dependent on the exact technique being used (covered later). Figure 13.5 illustrates the shadow layers and Figure 13.6 illustrates the graph.

13.7   Layered Penumbra Map Pass

In this pass, we calculate all of the needed parameters for the anisotropic Gaussian blur pass, mostly as described in [Gumbau et al. 10]. These parameters include

- distance from the viewer to the point being rendered (scene depth),
- distance of the shadow caster to the point being rendered (penumbra size),
- penumbra mask to determine whether a point needs to be blurred or not,
- shadow buffer (binary value) or exponential shadow buffer (float value, optional),
- translucency map (RGBA values).

13.7.1   Scene Depth

Because we already calculated the scene depth in the G-buffer pass, it is unnecessary to do it again.

13.7.2   Layered Penumbra Map

There are two ways to calculate the penumbra size, as described in [Gumbau et al. 10]:

- using blocker search convolution,
- using a separable `min` filter (covered later).

The first, the blocker search [Fernando 05], is performed by doing a convolution over the shadow map, searching for possible blockers (i.e., where a point is in shadow), then using the average of these blockers' distances (in light projection space) to the light to estimate the penumbra size at a given point. The estimation is done using the following equation, as described in [Gumbau et al. 10]:

$$w_{\text{penumbra}} = \frac{(d_{\text{receiver}} - d_{\text{blocker}})}{d_{\text{blocker}}} \cdot w_{\text{light}},$$

where w_{light} is the size of the light that needs to be tweaked by an artist (empirical value), d_{observer} is the distance to the viewer in light projection space, d_{blocker} is the average blocker distance, and d_{receiver} is the distance to the current point being processed (in light projection space). We can reconstruct the light-projection-space distance (d_{observer}) from a regular depth buffer rendered using a regular OpenGL projection matrix (in Figure 13.7) as shown in Listing 13.1.

It is advisable to store the penumbra size values in at least a 16-bit float value. This means that if we would like to store four layers, we can use an RGBA16F texture. Each of the four layers would be represented by one color channel.

$$
\begin{pmatrix}
\dfrac{n}{r} & 0 & 0 & 0 \\[2mm]
0 & \dfrac{n}{t} & 0 & 0 \\[2mm]
0 & 0 & \dfrac{-(f+n)}{f-n} & \dfrac{-2fn}{f-n} \\[2mm]
0 & 0 & -1 & 0
\end{pmatrix}
$$

Figure 13.7. The (symmetric perspective) OpenGL projection matrix, where n is the near plane distance, f is the far, $t = n \times \tan(\text{fov} \times 0.5)$, and $r = \text{aspect} \times t$.

```
//# of bits in depth texture per pixel
unsigned bits = 16;
unsigned precision_scaler = pow(2, bits) - 1;
//generates a perspective projection matrix
mat4 projmat = perspective(radians(fov), aspect, near, far);
//arbitrary position in view space
vec4 vs_pos = vec4(0, 0, 2.5, 1);
//clip-space position
vec4 cs_pos = projmat * vs_pos;
//perspective divide
vec4 ndc_pos = cs_pos / cs_pos.w;
float zranged = ndc_pos.z * 0.5f + 0.5f; //range: [0...1]
//this goes into the depth buffer
unsigned z_value = floor(precision_scaler * zranged);

//helper variables to convert back to view space
float A = -(far + near) / (far - near);
float B = -2 * far * near / (far - near);

//get depth from the depth texture, range: [0...1]
float depth = texture(depth_tex, texcoord).x;
float zndc = depth * 2 - 1; //range: [-1...1]
//reconstructed view-space z
float vs_zrecon = -B / (zndc + A);
//reconstructed clip-space z
float cs_zrecon = zndc * -vs_zrecon;
```

Listing 13.1. Reconstructing clip space z from the depth buffer.

We have two options for generating penumbra information for many lights:

- We can generate them separately and blend them together additively.

- We can batch them and generate all of them at once (covered later).

When generating the penumbra information for each light in a separate pass, at each pixel there will be multiple layers in the penumbra map; therefore, we need to store the penumbra information of each layer separately. We can achieve this by using additive hardware blending.

13.7.3   Layered Penumbra Mask

The penumbra mask essentially stores whether we found a blocker in the blocker search or not. We can notice that the penumbra size calculated previously is in essence just a value that tells us how much we should blur the shadows at a point. In other words, this will scale the effective filter size of the anisotropic Gaussian blurring. Therefore, we can store the penumbra mask in the penumbra size by setting it to zero if the penumbra mask would be zero. Then we can just check when doing the anisotropic blurring if the penumbra size is greater than zero and only blur in that case.

13.7.4   Layered Shadow Buffer

There are two options on what to store in the shadow buffer:

- a binary value that only tells if the point is in shadow or not,

- an exponential shadow map, as described in [Engel 10].

If we are storing the binary shadow value, we can just perform a regular shadow test by sampling the shadow map, reprojecting the scene depth, and comparing the two. This way we can represent each shadow layer in just one bit, so we can store 32 shadow layers in an R32U texture.

Otherwise, if we decide to do exponential shadow mapping, we need to store the result on at least 8 bits so that four layers could fit into an RGBA8 texture. The value that needs to be stored is defined by

$$\text{tex}(z, d, k) = e^{k \cdot (z-d)},$$

where z is the scene depth from the point of view of the viewer, d is the scene depth from the point of view of the light source, and k is an empirical value (scale factor) that is used to tweak the exponential shadow map.

13.7.5   Layered Translucency Map

In order to represent a penumbra in shadows that translucent objects cast, we need to blur the translucency maps computed in the shadow rendering pass, too. Therefore, we accumulate these maps into a layered translucency map. We can represent each layer as an RGBA8 color value that we can pack into an R32F float; so in an RGBA32F texture that has 128 bits, we can store four layers. The packing is done as shown in code Listing 13.2.

13.8   Anisotropic Gaussian Blur Pass

Now we will need to blur the shadows to generate variable-sized penumbras. We will sample the penumbra information generated in the previous pass.

```
//input: float value in range [0...1]
uint float_to_r8( float val )
{
   const uint bits = 8;
   uint precision_scaler = uint(pow( uint(2), bits )) - uint(1);
   return uint(floor( precision_scaler * val ));
}

uint rgba8_to_uint( vec4 val )
{
   uint res = float_to_r8(val.x) << 24;
         res |= float_to_r8(val.y) << 16;
         res |= float_to_r8(val.z) << 8;
         res |= float_to_r8(val.w) << 0;
   return res;
}
```

Listing 13.2. A function to pack an RGBA8 value into an R32F float.

```
float threshold = 0.25;
float filter_size =
   //account for light size (affects penumbra size)
   light_size *
   //anisotropic term, varies with viewing angle
   //added threshold to account for diminishing filter size
   //at grazing angles
   sqrt( max( dot( vec3( 0, 0, 1 ), normal ), threshold ) ) *
   //distance correction term, so that the filter size
   //remains constant no matter where we view the shadow from
   ( 1 / ( depth ) );
```

Listing 13.3. Implementation of the variable filter size.

In order to account for various viewing angles, we need to modify the filter size. To do this, we approximate the filter size by projecting the Gaussian filter kernel into an ellipse following the orientation of the geometry. We used the method described in [Geusebroek and Smeulders 03], which shows how to do anisotropic Gaussian filtering while still keeping the kernel separable. We also need to consider that if we are viewing the shadows from far away, the filter size needs to be decreased to maintain the effective filter width. Because of the nature of the dot product, the filter size can diminish at grazing angles, so we need to limit the minimum filter size. The value that we are comparing to is chosen empirically (usually 0.25 works well). Listing 13.3 shows how this variable filter size is implemented.

Next, all we need to do is evaluate the Gaussian filter. Because this is separable, the blurring will actually take two passes: a horizontal and a vertical. We will modify the filter size by the anisotropy value. We also need to sample all layers at once at each iteration and unpack the individual layers. The layer

```
float unpack_shadow( vec4 shadow, int layer )
{
    //4 layers
    uint layered_shadow = uint(16.0 * shadow.x);
    return ( ( layered_shadow & ( 1 << layer ) ) >> layer );
}

vec4 hard_shadow = texture( layered_shadow_tex, texcoord );
float layer0 = unpack_shadow( hard_shadow, 0 );
```

Listing 13.4. Unpacking shadow data.

```
vec4 uint_to_rgba8( uint val )
{
    uint tmp = val;
    uint r = (tmp & 0xff000000) >> 24;
    uint g = (tmp & 0x00ff0000) >> 16;
    uint b = (tmp & 0x0000ff00) >> 8;
    uint a = (tmp & 0x000000ff) >> 0;
    return vec4( r / 255.0, g / 255.0, b / 255.0, a / 255.0 );
}
```

Listing 13.5. A function to unpack an RGBA8 value from an R32F float.

unpacking is done as shown in Listing 13.4. Because this is a screen-space filter, we need to take into consideration that the shadows might leak light if the filter size is large. Therefore, if the depth difference between the center of the filter and the actual sampled point is greater than a threshold (usually 0.03 works great), then we don't consider the sample.

If we decide to do the Gaussian blurring at half resolution, we can take advantage of the fact that we still have the hard shadow map information available at the original resolution; therefore, if we sample the hard shadow map in a grid pattern (four samples using texture gather), then we can eliminate some of the aliasing artifacts (essentially super-sampling the layered shadow map). We can also decide to use exponential shadow mapping, which will reduce some of the self-shadowing artifacts.

If there are translucent shadow casters, then we need to blur them, too. We need to do the same as for the opaque casters, only the unpacking will be different. The unpacking is done as shown in Listing 13.5.

13.9 Lighting Pass

Finally, we need to apply lighting to the scene. This pass is also highly implementation dependent, but one can still easily integrate SSSS into one's lighting process. We use an optimized tiled deferred shader.

When lighting, one needs to find out which layer the light belongs to, sample the blurred shadow maps accordingly, and multiply the lighting with the shadow value. Note that you only need to sample the screen-space soft shadows once for each pixel and then use the appropriate layer.

13.10 Performance Considerations

There are various ways to speed up the SSSS rendering process. For example, we can do the anisotropic Gaussian blurring at lower (practically half) resolution. This essentially lowers the memory bandwidth requirement of the blurring.

In addition, we can do the penumbra generation at a lower resolution, too; however, this will cause some aliasing near the shadow casters (where the penumbra size is low), which can be eliminated using the super-sampling method described above.

We can also implement the `min`-filter approach. When using this, we need to generate a low-resolution `min`-filtered shadow map, after the shadow-map generation pass. Then we substitute the blocker search result with this value. We can also implement the penumbra mask by checking if this value is below a certain threshold (the anisotropic Gaussian filter width would be negligible anyway). This way we don't need to store the penumbra sizes in screen space in layers, because these `min`-filter maps are small enough to sample each of them in the anisotropic blurring pass, so in the penumbra map pass we only calculate the layered shadow buffer and layered translucency map. The rest of the algorithm remains the same. However, as we observed at 4 layers and 16 lights, this approach is usually around 0.2 ms slower than storing the penumbra size as usual. This may not be the case with more layers, though.

Additionally, instead of generating penumbra information for each light separately and blending them together additively, we can also batch the lights and generate the penumbra information for all of them in one pass. However, if we decide to go this way, then all the shadow map and `min`-filtered shadow map information needs to be available at once. This means that in one pass we need to sample all of the shadow maps of all the visible lights. These can be passed to a shader using texture arrays or texture atlases.

We can also adjust the kernel size of the Gaussian blurring. Usually a 11×11 filter works well, but you can also implement huge filters like a 23×23 filter, which will allow for enormous penumbras, or use an efficient 5×5 filter.

13.11 Results

The tests were run on a PC that has a Core i5 4670 processor, 8-GB DDR3 RAM, and a Radeon 7770 1-GB graphics card. We used an untextured Sponza scene

Figure 13.8. Shadows rendered using SSSS (left), and reference image rendered with Blender (right).

with 16 colored lights each having a 1024×1024 shadow texture to illustrate overlapping shadows.

13.12   Quality Tests

We generated reference images with Blender using path tracing and compared them with the output of the quality tests to make sure that the results were correct. Figure 13.8 shows these comparisons.

As you can see, our results closely match the reference; however, the Gaussian filter size may affect the result. Because the blurring is done in screen space, we can easily afford huge filter sizes. Note that we needed to adjust the light sizes empirically to match the reference images.

Figure 13.9 shows additional examples from the Sponza scene.

13.13   Performance Analysis

Table 13.1 lists the performance results obtained by rendering the Sponza scene with 16 shadow casting lights from the same point of view using our technique, PCSS, PCF, and hard shadows. In the reference image, in our technique, and in the PCSS case, the shadows have variable penumbras. In the PCF version, they have uniform penumbras, and in the hard shadows version, they don't have penumbras.

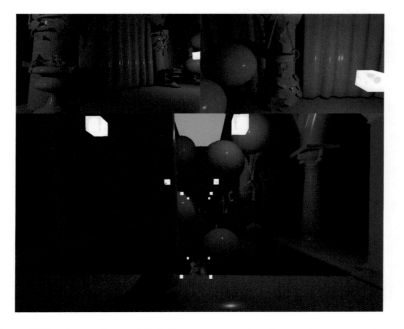

Figure 13.9. Screenshots with light sources rendered over the scene as boxes.

Technique/Resolution	720p	1080p
Lighting only	1.6 ms	3.7 ms
Hard shadows	22.1 ms	25.6 ms
PCF 5×5	25.8 ms	34.1 ms
PCF 11×11	33.9 ms	51.6 ms
PCF 23×23	67.4 ms	126.6 ms
PCSS $5 \times 5 + 5 \times 5$	30.1 ms	43.4 ms
PCSS $5 \times 5 + 11 \times 11$	44.4 ms	75.1 ms
PCSS $5 \times 5 + 23 \times 23$	70.6 ms	133.7 ms
SSSS blocker $5 \times 5 + 5 \times 5$	33.4 ms	50.3 ms
SSSS blocker $5 \times 5 + 11 \times 11$	33.8 ms	51.1 ms
SSSS blocker $5 \times 5 + 23 \times 23$	34.6 ms	52.2 ms
SSSS min *filter* 5×5	26.4 ms	31.7 ms
SSSS min *filter* 11×11	27.0 ms	33.0 ms
SSSS min *filter* 23×23	28.2 ms	35.8 ms
SSSS optimized 5×5	24.7 ms	27.9 ms
SSSS optimized 11×11	24.9 ms	28.4 ms
SSSS optimized 23×23	25.4 ms	29.8 ms

Table 13.1. Performance results (frame times) from the Sponza scene.

We included various versions of our technique, like the `min`-filter optimization and the blocker search variant. We also included an optimized version that uses the `min`-filter optimization, half-resolution Gaussian blurring, and penumbra generation, plus the mentioned super-sampling to maintain the quality. All of the variants use the batching method to generate the layered penumbra data.

You can see that SSSS outperforms PCSS and delivers roughly the same performance as PCF. It can be observed that while the techniques based on shadow-space blurring (PCF and PCSS) took a severe performance hit when increasing the resolution, the SSSS version didn't suffer from this. In addition, increasing the kernel size also had a great impact on the performance of the shadow-space techniques, but the SSSS version still didn't suffer from this problem.

13.14   Conclusion

We showed, that using layered shadow buffers, we can correctly handle overlapping shadows and that we can use layered translucency maps to allow for colored shadows cast by translucent shadow casters. We also showed that this technique can be implemented in real time while still being perceptually correct.

Bibliography

[Aguado and Montiel 11] Alberto Aguado and Eugenia Montiel. "Mipmapped Screen-Space Soft Shadows." In *GPU Pro 2: Advanced Rendering Techniques*, edited by Wolfgang Engel, pp. 257–274. Natick, MA: A K Peters, 2011.

[Anichini 14] Steve Anichini. "Bioshock Infinite Lighting." *Solid Angle*, http://solid-angle.blogspot.hu/2014/03/bioshock-infinite-lighting.html, March 3, 2014.

[Crow 77] Franklin C. Crow. "Shadow Algorithms for Computer Graphics." *Computer Graphics: SIGGRAPH '77 Proceedings* 11:2 (1977), 242–248. 1977

[Engel 10] Wolfgang Engel. "Massive Point Light Soft Shadows." Presented at Korean Game Developer Conference, September 14, 2010. (Available at http://www.slideshare.net/WolfgangEngel/massive-pointlightsoftshadows.)

[Fernando 05] Randima Fernando. "Percentage-Closer Soft Shadows." In *ACM SIGGRAPH 2005 Sketches*, Article no. 35. New York: ACM, 2005.

[Geusebroek and Smeulders 03] Jan M. Geusebroek and Arnold W. M. Smeulders. "Fast Anisotropic Gauss Filtering." *IEEE Transactions on Image Processing* 12:8 (2003), 99–112.

[Gumbau et al. 10] Jesus Gumbau, Miguel Chover, and Mateu Sbert. "Screen Space Soft Shadows." In *GPU Pro: Advanced Rendering Techniques*, edited by Wolfgang Engel, pp. 477–491. Natick, MA: A K Peters, 2010.

[Nealen 02] Andrew V. Nealen. "Shadow Mapping and Shadow Volumes: Recent Developments in Real-Time Shadow Rendering." Project Report for Advanced Computer Graphics: Image-Based Rendering, University of British Columbia, 2002.

[Reeves et al. 87] William T. Reeves, David H. Salesin, and Robert L. Cook. "Rendering Antialiased Shadows with Depth Maps." *Computer Graphics: Proc. SIGGRAPH '87* 21:4 (1987), 283–291.

[Shastry 05] Anirudh S. Shastry. "Soft-Edged Shadows." *GameDev.net*, http://www.gamedev.net/page/resources/_/technical/graphics-programming-and-theory/soft-edged-shadows-r2193, January 18, 2005.

[Williams 78] Lance Williams. "Casting Curved Shadows on Curved Surfaces." *Computer Graphics: Proc. SIGGRAPH '78* 12:3 (1978), 270–274.

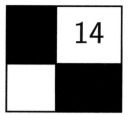

14

Tile-Based
Omnidirectional Shadows
Hawar Doghramachi

14.1 Introduction

Rendering efficiently a massive amount of local light sources had already been solved by methods such as *tiled deferred shading* [Andersson 09], *tiled forward shading* [Billeter et al. 13], and *clustered deferred and forward shading* [Olsson et al. 12]. However, generating appropriate shadows for a large number of light sources in real time is still an ongoing topic. Since accurate shadows from direct lights significantly improve the final image and give the viewer additional information about the scene arrangement, their generation is an important part of real-time rendering.

This chapter will demonstrate how to efficiently generate soft shadows for a large number of omnidirectional light sources where each light casts individual shadows. It will be further shown that this is accomplished without introducing new artifacts, such as shadow flickering. The underlying algorithm is based on *shadow mapping*, introduced in [Williams 78], thus it benefits from the architecture of current rasterizer-based graphics hardware as well as from a wide range of existing techniques to provide high-quality soft shadows.

For this, the concepts of *programmable draw dispatch* [Riccio and Lilley 13] and *tetrahedron shadow mapping* [Liao 10] are combined via a novel usage of the programmable clipping unit, which is present in current consumer graphics hardware. For each light source a separate shadow map is generated, so a hierarchical quad-tree is additionally utilized, which efficiently packs shadow maps of all light sources as tiles into a single 2D texture map. In this way, significantly more shadow maps can be stored in a limited amount of texture memory than with traditional shadow mapping methods.

14.2   Overview

The main target of this work is to utilize recently available features of common consumer graphics hardware, exposed by the OpenGL graphics API, to accelerate the computation of high-quality soft shadows for a high number of dynamic omnidirectional light sources.

Traditional shadow map rendering typically first determines the meshes that are overlapping the volumes of all relevant light sources which is already an $O(nm)$ time complexity task. After this information has been computed, for each relevant mesh and light source, one GPU draw command is dispatched. For omnidirectional lights, the situation is even more problematic: e.g., for a cube map-based approach [Gerasimov 04], we need do the visibility determination for six cube map faces and dispatch up to six GPU draw commands per mesh and light source. The large amount of submitted draw calls can cause a significant CPU overhead. The first part of the proposed algorithm bypasses this problem by using the concept of programmable draw dispatch [Riccio and Lilley 13]. In this way, the entire visibility determination and draw command generation process is shifted to the GPU, avoiding almost the entire CPU overhead of traditional methods.

The second part of the proposed technique makes use of the idea that for omnidirectional light sources it is not necessary to subdivide the 3D space into six view volumes, as done for cube map–based approaches [Gerasimov 04]. According to tetrahedron shadow mapping [Liao 10], it is entirely enough to subdivide the 3D space into four view volumes by a regular tetrahedron to produce accurate shadows for omnidirectional light sources. In this way up to a third of the draw call amount of cube map–based approaches can be saved. In contrast to the tetrahedron shadow mapping algorithm as proposed in [Liao 10], the entire process of creating shadow maps for four separate view directions is efficiently moved to the GPU by introducing a novel usage of the programmable clipping unit, which is part of current consumer graphics hardware. Furthermore, the original method is extended in order to provide soft shadows.

Finally, this work takes advantage of the observation that the required shadow map resolution is proportional to the screen area that the corresponding light source influences—i.e., the smaller the radius of the light source and the larger its distance to the viewer camera, the smaller the required shadow map resolution. After determining the required resolution, the shadow maps of all relevant light sources are inserted as tiles into one large 2D texture map, which will be called the *tiled shadow map*. To make optimal use of the available texture space, a hierarchical quad-tree is used. This concept not only saves memory bandwidth at writing and reading of shadow maps, but further enables the use of a large amount of shadow-casting light sources within a limited texture space.

The entire process of *tile-based omnidirectional shadows* can be subdivided into four distinct steps:

- In a first preparation step, it is determined which meshes and light sources are relevant, i.e., influence the final image. This can be done, for example, by view frustum culling and GPU hardware occlusion queries. For all relevant meshes and light sources, a linear list is written into a GPU buffer that contains information about each mesh and each light source, respectively. This process has an $O(n + m)$ time complexity and is done on the CPU.

- On the GPU, a compute shader takes the previously generated buffers as input and tests each mesh for overlap with each relevant light source. This process has an $O(nm)$ time complexity and thus is spread over a large amount of parallel computing threads. As a result of this overlap test, the corresponding draw commands are written into a GPU buffer, which will be called the *indirect draw buffer*.

- By the use of a single indirect draw call submitted from the CPU, all GPU-generated draw commands within the indirect draw buffer are executed. In this way, shadow maps are generated for all relevant light sources and written into corresponding tiles of the tiled shadow map.

- Finally, the tiled shadow map is sampled during the shading process by all visible screen fragments for each relevant light source to generate soft shadows.

14.3 Implementation

In the following subsections, each step will be described in detail. All explanations assume a column-major matrix layout, right-handed coordinate system with the y axis pointing upward, left-bottom corner as texture and screen-space origin, and clip-space depth-range from -1.0 to 1.0. This work only focuses on generating shadows for point lights, but as will be demonstrated in Section 14.5.2, it can be easily extended to additionally support spotlights.

14.3.1 Preparation

In this step, it is first determined which lights are relevant for further processing. Typically these are all shadow-casting light sources that are visible to the viewer camera—that is, their light volume overlaps the view frustum and is not totally occluded by opaque geometry. This can be accomplished by view frustum culling and GPU hardware occlusion queries.

Tile resolution. After finding all relevant light sources, we need to determine how large the influence of each light source on the final image is. For this, we first compute the screen-space axis-aligned bounding box (AABB) of the spherical light volume. Care must be taken not to clip the AABB against the boundaries

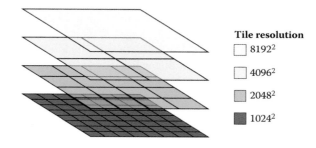

Tile resolution

□ 8192^2

□ 4096^2

▨ 2048^2

■ 1024^2

Figure 14.1. First four levels of a quad-tree that manages the tiles of a 8192×8192 tiled shadow map.

of the screen; for example, a large point light that is near to the viewer but only a small portion of which is visible on the screen still requires a high-resolution shadow map tile. After finding the width and height of the AABB, the larger of these two values will be taken as an approximation for the required shadow map tile resolution. However, to avoid extremely small or large values, the acquired resolution should be clamped within a reasonable range. For the case that more shadow-map tiles will be inserted than the tiled shadow map can handle, the lights are sorted relative to their acquired tile resolution. In this way, light sources with the smallest tile resolution will be at the end of the sorted light list and are the first to be excluded from shadow-map rendering when the tiled shadow map runs out of space.

Tile management. A typical texture resolution that should suffice in most cases for a tiled shadow map is 8192×8192. When using a 16-bit depth buffer texture format at this resolution, we can keep the required amount of video memory under 135 MB, which should be a reasonable value on modern graphics cards.

For the quad-tree implementation, a cache-friendly approach is chosen, where all nodes are stored in a preallocated linear memory block. Instead of pointers, indices are used to identify each node. Keeping all nodes in a linear list has the further advantage that resetting the quad-tree is a very fast operation, since we only have to iterate linearly over the node list. Each level of the quad-tree corresponds to a power-of-two shadow map tile resolution and each node holds the texture-space position of a tile in the tiled shadow map (Figure 14.1). To increase runtime performance, the quad-tree nodes are already initialized with the corresponding position values for a user-specified number of levels. The previously acquired tile resolution should be clamped within a reasonable range since, on the one hand, too small values would increase runtime performance for finding an appropriate node and, on the other hand, too large values would rapidly occupy the available texture space.

At runtime, each light source requests, in the order of the sorted light list, a tile inside the quad-tree with the calculated tile resolution. For this, first we must determine the lowest quad-tree level that has a tile resolution that is still higher than the specified value:

$$\text{level} = \log_2(s) - \text{ceil}(\log_2(x)),$$

where s is the resolution of the entire tiled shadow map and x the specified resolution. However, after finding a corresponding free tile node, the initially acquired resolution is used instead of the power-of-two node value. Thus, popping artifacts at shadow edges can be avoided, which would otherwise occur when the distance of the viewer camera to the light source changes. Performance-wise, the costs for the tile lookup are negligible; on an Intel Core i7-4810MQ 2.8 GHZ CPU for 128 light sources, the average required time is about 0.16 ms. Lights that cannot acquire a free tile due to an exaggerated light count are flagged as non–shadow casting and ignored during shadow generation. Because such lights have the smallest influence on the output image anyway, in general, visual artifacts are hard to notice.

Matrix setup. After all relevant lights are assigned to a corresponding shadow map tile, for each light source, the matrices that are used during shadow-map rendering and shading have to be correctly set up. As initially described, a regular tetrahedron is used to subdivide the 3D space for omnidirectional shadows. Because this part of the system builds upon tetrahedron shadow mapping as proposed in [Liao 10], only the modifications introduced here will be described in detail.

First, for each of the four tetrahedron faces, a view matrix needs to be found that consists of a rotational and a translational part. The rotational part can be precomputed since it is equal for all lights and never changes; yaw, pitch, and roll values for constructing these matrices are listed in Table 14.1.

The translational part consists of the vector from the point light center to the origin and must be recalculated whenever the light position changes. Concatenating the translation matrix with each of the rotation matrices yields the final four view matrices.

In the next step, appropriate perspective projection matrices have to be calculated. For this, the far plane is set to the radius of the point light. Table 14.2 shows the horizontal and vertical field of view (FOV) for each tetrahedron face.

Face	Yaw	Pitch	Roll
A	27.36780516	180.0	0.0
B	27.36780516	0.0	90.0
C	−27.36780516	270.0	0.0
D	−27.36780516	90.0	90.0

Table 14.1. Yaw, pitch, and roll in degrees to construct the rotation matrices for the four tetrahedron faces.

Face	Horizontal FOV	Vertical FOV
A	$143.98570868 + \alpha$	$125.26438968 + \beta$
B	$125.26438968 + \beta$	$143.98570868 + \alpha$
C	$143.98570868 + \alpha$	$125.26438968 + \beta$
D	$125.26438968 + \beta$	$143.98570868 + \alpha$

Table 14.2. Horizontal and vertical FOV in degrees to construct the perspective projection matrices for the four tetrahedron faces. As can be seen, faces A and C and, respectively, faces B and D share the same values. In order to provide soft shadows, the values from the original paper have to be adjusted by α and β.

```
vec3 centers[4] = {vec3(-1,0,-1),vec3(1,0,-1),vec3(0,-1,-1),
                   vec3(0,1,-1)};

vec3 offsets[4] = {vec3(-r,0,0),vec3(r,0,0),vec3(0,-r,0),
                   vec3(0,r,0)};
for(uint i=0; i<4; i++)
{
  centers[i] += offsets[i];
  v[i] = normalize(invProjMatrix * centers[i]);
}
dilatedFovX = acos(dot(v[0], v[1])) * 180/PI;
dilatedFovY = acos(dot(v[2], v[3])) * 180/PI;
alpha = dilatedFovX - originalFovX;
beta = dilatedFovY - originalFovY;
```

Listing 14.1. Pseudocode for computing α and β that is used to extend the original FOV values in order to provide soft shadows.

Because the original paper [Liao 10] did not take into account that soft shadows require a slightly larger texture area for filtering, the original horizontal and vertical FOV values must be increased by α and β (Table 14.2). These two angles can be computed by first offsetting the center points of each clip-space edge at the near plane with a dilation radius r. Using $r = 0.0625$ provides in practice enough space for reasonable filter kernels while avoiding an unnecessary reduction of the effective texture resolution. The offset center points are transformed into view space with the inverse projection matrix of tetrahedron face A, which is built with the original FOV values and normalized to form the vectors $\mathbf{v}_0, \ldots, \mathbf{v}_3$ that point from the view-space origin to the transformed points. With the help of these vectors, α and β can be calculated as shown in Listing 14.1.

Fortunately, the projection matrices are equal for all lights and never change; thus, they can be precomputed.

Finally, the texture transformation matrices have to be calculated, which will position the projected tetrahedron views correctly within the tiled shadow map. Because the projected view area of each tetrahedron face correspond to a triangle (Figure 14.2), these areas can be packed together into squared tiles, which

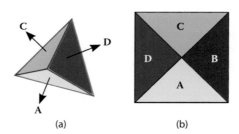

(a)   (b)

Figure 14.2. (a) A perspective view of the used tetrahedron, where face B is facing away from the camera. (b) The triangular-shaped projected views of the four tetrahedron faces packed together into a squared tile.

perfectly fits to the proposed quad-tree–based partitioning scheme. All we need for computing these matrices are the previously computed position coordinates (p_x, p_y) and the size s of each shadow map tile in texture space:

$$M_A = \begin{pmatrix} s & 0 & 0 & p_x \\ 0 & s/2 & 0 & p_y - s/2 \\ 0 & 0 & 1 & 0 \\ 0 & 0 & 0 & 1 \end{pmatrix}, \quad M_B = \begin{pmatrix} s/2 & 0 & 0 & p_x + s/2 \\ 0 & s & 0 & p_y \\ 0 & 0 & 1 & 0 \\ 0 & 0 & 0 & 1 \end{pmatrix},$$

$$M_C = \begin{pmatrix} s & 0 & 0 & p_x \\ 0 & s/2 & 0 & p_y + s/2 \\ 0 & 0 & 1 & 0 \\ 0 & 0 & 0 & 1 \end{pmatrix}, \quad M_D = \begin{pmatrix} s/2 & 0 & 0 & p_x - s/2 \\ 0 & s & 0 & p_y \\ 0 & 0 & 1 & 0 \\ 0 & 0 & 0 & 1 \end{pmatrix},$$

where $M_A, \ldots, M_D$ are the texture transformation matrices for the tetrahedron faces $A, \ldots, D$.

Concatenating the texture, projection and view matrices finally gives the four matrices that are required to render and fetch each shadow map tile and are called *shadow matrices*.

Light buffer. In the order of the sorted light list, the position, radius, and four shadow matrices of each light source have to be uploaded to the GPU, for which a `GL_SHADER_BUFFER_STORAGE` buffer is used.

Mesh-info buffer. Similar as for the light sources, one first needs to determine which meshes are relevant for further processing. Typically these are all shadow-casting meshes that overlap the volumes of the point lights that are found to be visible to the viewer camera. Because the actual light-mesh overlap test will be done later on the GPU, at this stage, only a fast preexclusion of irrelevant meshes should be performed. This could be done for instance by testing the

AABB of the meshes for overlap with the AABB that encloses all relevant light sources. An important prerequisite of the proposed technique is that commonly processed meshes have to share the same vertex and index buffer. However, this is strongly recommended anyway, since frequent switching of GPU resources has a significant impact on the runtime performance due to a driver CPU overhead [Riccio and Lilley 13]. According to the light buffer, the required information for each relevant mesh is written into a `GL_SHADER_BUFFER_STORAGE` type GPU buffer. For each mesh, its first index into the common index buffer, number of indices required to draw the mesh, and minimum and maximum corners of the enclosing AABB have to be uploaded.

14.3.2   Indirect Draw Buffer Generation

In this step, a compute shader takes the previously generated light and mesh-info buffers as input and generates a command buffer with which the shadow maps of all relevant light sources will be rendered later on. For this, two additional `GL_SHADER_BUFFER_STORAGE` buffers are created, into which the results are written.

Indirect draw buffer. The first required output buffer is the command buffer itself. The first member of this buffer is an atomic counter variable that keeps track of the number of indirect draw commands that are stored subsequently. The indirect draw command structure is already predefined by the OpenGL specification and contains the number of required mesh indices (`count`), number of instances to be rendered (`instanceCount`), first index into the bound index buffer (`firstIndex`), offset to be applied to the indices fetched from the bound index buffer (`baseVertex`), and offset for fetching instanced vertex attributes (`baseInstance`).

Light-index buffer. The second required output buffer stores the indices of all relevant lights that overlap the processed meshes. Corresponding to the indirect draw buffer, an atomic counter variable keeps track of the number of subsequently stored light indices.

Computation. A compute shader is dispatched to generate the indirect draw and light-index buffers, whereby for each relevant mesh one thread group is spawned. For each thread group, a multiple of 32 threads is used.

While each thread group processes one mesh, all threads within a thread group iterate in parallel over all relevant lights and perform a sphere-AABB overlap test between the volume of each point light and the AABB of each mesh. For this, a fast overlap test is used as proposed in [Larsson et al. 07]. Each time an overlap is detected, an atomic counter is incremented and the corresponding light index is written into a light-index list. Both the atomic counter variable as well as the light-index list are located in the fast shared thread group memory of the GPU, thus avoiding frequent atomic writes into the global video memory, which would be more expensive [Harada et al. 13]. After all relevant lights are processed for a mesh, a new indirect draw command is added to the indirect draw buffer, but only if at least one light overlaps the AABB of the processed mesh. This is done by incrementing the atomic counter of the indirect draw buffer and writing the new draw command to the corresponding location. At this point, we additionally increment the atomic counter of the light-index buffer with the number of overlapping lights. This will return a start index into the light-index buffer, which resides in the global video memory, from where the acquired light indices in the shared thread group memory can be copied into the light-index buffer. The copying process is done in parallel by each thread of a thread group at the end of the compute shader.

Besides passing the `firstIndex` and `count` of the current mesh to the new indirect draw command, the number of overlapping lights is forwarded as `instance Count`—i.e., later on, when the indirect draw command is executed, for each light source a new mesh instance will be rendered. However, at that stage it is necessary to acquire for each instance the corresponding light index. For this, we write the obtained start index, which points into the light-index buffer, into the `baseInstance` member of the draw command. This member will be only used by the OpenGL pipeline if instanced vertex attributes are utilized—that is, vertex attributes with a nonzero divisor. Since traditional instancing (e.g., to create multiple instances of the same mesh at various locations) does not make much sense in the proposed method, we can relinquish instanced vertex attributes, which enables the use of the valuable `baseInstance` parameter. Fortunately, in the context of OpenGL 4.4, the `GL_ARB_shader_draw_parameters` extension has been introduced, which allows a shader to fetch various draw command related parameters such as the `baseInstance` one. In this way, when the indirect draw commands are executed later on, for each instance, an offset into the light-index buffer can be retrieved in the vertex shader by summing the OpenGL supplied draw parameters `gl_BaseInstanceARB` and `gl_InstanceID`. At this offset, the corresponding light index can be fetched from the light-index buffer. This approach significantly reduces the required amount of video memory space in contrast to generating for each overlapping light source a new indirect draw command, which requires five times more space than a single light index. Listing 14.2 shows how this can be done for OpenGL in GLSL.

```
#define MAX_NUM_LIGHTS 1024
#define LOCAL_SIZE_X 256

shared uint groupCounter;
shared uint groupLightIndices[MAX_NUM_LIGHTS];
shared uint startLightIndex;

layout(local_size_x=LOCAL_SIZE_X) in;
void main()
```

```
{
  // initialize group counter
  if(gl_LocalInvocationIndex == 0)
    groupCounter = 0;
  barrier();
  memoryBarrierShared();

  // iterate over all relevant light sources
  uint meshIndex = gl_WorkGroupID.x;
  for(uint i=0; i<uniformBuffer.numLights; i+=LOCAL_SIZE_X)
  {
    uint lightIndex = gl_LocalInvocationIndex+i;
    if(lightIndex < uniformBuffer.numLights)
    {
      vec3 lightPosition = lightBuffer.lights[lightIndex].position;
      float lightRadius = lightBuffer.lights[lightIndex].radius;
      vec3 mins = meshInfoBuffer.infos[meshIndex].mins;
      vec3 maxes = meshInfoBuffer.infos[meshIndex].maxes;

      // perform AABB-sphere overlap test
      vec3 distances = max(mins-lightPosition, 0.0) +
                       max(lightPosition-maxes, 0.0);
      if(dot(distances, distances) <= (lightRadius*lightRadius))
      {
        // For each overlap increment groupCounter and add
        // lightIndex to light-index array in shared thread
        // group memory.
        uint index = atomicAdd(groupCounter, 1);
        groupLightIndices[index] = lightIndex;
      }
    }
  }
  barrier();
  memoryBarrierShared();

  // In case at least one overlap has been detected, add new
  // indirect draw draw command to indirect draw buffer and
  // determine start index into light-index buffer. Both
  // buffers reside in global video memory.
  if(gl_LocalInvocationIndex == 0)
  {
    if(groupCounter > 0)
    {
      uint cmdIndex = atomicAdd(drawIndirectCmdBuffer.counter, 1);
      startLightIndex = atomicAdd(lightIndexBuffer.counter,
          groupCounter);
      drawIndirectCmdBuffer.cmds[cmdIndex].count =
          meshInfoBuffer.infos[meshIndex].numIndices;
      drawIndirectCmdBuffer.cmds[cmdIndex].instanceCount =
          groupCounter;
      drawIndirectCmdBuffer.cmds[cmdIndex].firstIndex =
          meshInfoBuffer.infos[meshIndex].firstIndex;
      drawIndirectCmdBuffer.cmds[cmdIndex].baseVertex = 0;
      drawIndirectCmdBuffer.cmds[cmdIndex].baseInstance =
          startLightIndex;
    }
  }
  barrier();
  memoryBarrierShared();

  // Copy light indices from shared thread group memory into
  // global video memory.
  for(uint i=gl_LocalInvocationIndex; i<groupCounter; i+=LOCAL_SIZE_X)
  {
```

```
        lightIndexBuffer.lightIndices[startLightIndex+i] =
            groupLightIndices[i];
    }
}
```

Listing 14.2. Compute shader for generating indirect draw buffer.

For the Crytek Sponza scene with 103 meshes and 128 processed light sources, the GPU time taken for this computation task was about 0.02 ms on an NVIDIA GeForce GTX 880 Mobile.

Finally, care must be taken to reset the atomic counters of the indirect draw and light-index buffers at the beginning of each frame, which can be done by using the OpenGL command `glClearBufferSubData()`.

14.3.3   Indirect Shadow Map Rendering

At this stage, the previously generated indirect draw buffer is executed by the OpenGL draw command `glMultiDrawElementsIndirectCountARB()`. This draw call has been introduced in the context of OpenGL 4.4 with the `GL_ARB_indirect_parameters` extension and is an improved version of the previously available `glMultiDrawElementsIndirect()`. Since we have no idea on the host side how many draw commands the GPU has generated and a corresponding query would be very inefficient (since it introduces a synchronization point between CPU and GPU), previously the only possibility was to execute `glMultiDrawElementsIndirect()` with a maximum number of elements and discard draws by writing zero to the `instanceCount` member of the indirect draw command. However, discarding draws is not free [Riccio and Lilley 13]. With the new draw call `glMultiDrawElements IndirectCountARB()`, the number of executed elements will be determined by taking the minimum of the value specified in the draw command itself and a value that is sourced from a `GL_PARAMETER_BUFFER_ARB` type GPU buffer, for which the atomic counter of the indirect draw buffer is used.

Programmable clipping. There is still one major obstacle that needs to be solved prior to being able to render indirectly all shadow map tiles into the tiled shadow map. As demonstrated, the previously generated shadow matrices will create triangular projected areas that can be theoretically tightly packed as squared tiles, but since we are rendering into a 2D texture atlas, these areas will overlap and cause major artifacts. One possible solution could be the use of a viewport array. However, since the maximum number of simultaneously set viewports is usually limited to a small number, typically around 16, and the viewports are rectangular and not triangular, this approach is not viable. Another possible solution could be to discard in a fragment shader all fragments outside the projected triangular areas, but this would be far too slow to be feasible. Fortunately, with programmable clipping there exists another hardware-accelerated approach that,

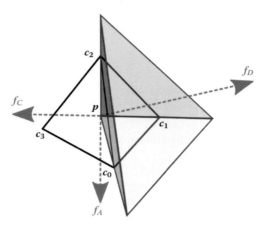

Figure 14.3. The green arrows show the tetrahedron face vectors f_A, f_C, and f_D. Face vector f_B is pointing away from the camera. The four corners of the tetrahedron are marked as $c_0, \ldots, c_3$, and the center of the tetrahedron that coincides with the point light position is shown as p. The three clipping planes that separate the view volume of tetrahedron face D from its neighbors are depicted in blue, green, and yellow.

to the knowledge of the author, had previously not been used in this context. The clipping unit of current consumer graphics hardware allows the user to insert custom clipping planes inside shaders. This algorithm will take advantage of this feature to efficiently render indirectly all shadow map tiles into the tiled shadow map. Even though on the GPU a triangle setup that uses custom clipping planes is slower than a regular setup, this will not have a significant performance impact since only triangles that are actually clipped at the border of each tetrahedron view volume are affected.

As stated at the beginning of this section, a regular tetrahedron is used to subdivide the 3D space into four view volumes. Hence, each view volume is separated from its neighbors by exactly three planes, as shown in Figure 14.3. In order to clip against these planes, first the plane normals have to be calculated. This can be done by using the four normalized tetrahedron face vectors as given in [Liao 10] (Table 14.3).

With the help of the tetrahedron face vectors $f_A, \ldots f_D$, the vectors $v_0, \ldots, v_3$ can be calculated, which point from the tetrahedron center p to the tetrahedron corners $c_0, \ldots, c_3$ (Figure 14.3):

$$v_0 = -f_A, \quad v_1 = -f_C, \quad v2 = -f_A, \quad v_3 = -f_D.$$

In Listing 14.3, the normal of the yellow clipping plane illustrated in Figure 14.3 will be calculated, which separates the view volumes of faces A and D. All other clipping plane normals can be calculated correspondingly.

Face	x	y	z
A	0.0	−0.57735026	0.81649661
B	0.0	−0.57735026	−0.81649661
C	−0.81649661	0.57735026	0.0
D	0.81649661	0.57735026	0.0

Table 14.3. The x, y, and z components of the four normalized tetrahedron face vectors.

```
normal = normalize(cross(v1, v));
rotationAxis = normalize(cross(fA, fD));

// quat(rotationAxis, alpha) is a quaternion that rotates alpha
// degrees around rotationAxis
rotatedNormal = quat(rotationAxis, alpha) * normal;
```

Listing 14.3. Pseudocode for calculating clipping plane normal.

Since later on it should be possible to generate soft shadows by applying, e.g., *percentage closer filtering* (PCF), the plane normals have to be adjusted appropriately. For this the plane normals are rotated in order to increase the aperture of the tetrahedron view volumes. The angle α used for this is the same as derived in the section "Matrix setup" on page 197; this angle ensures, on the one hand, that a sufficient amount of primitives pass the clipping stage to account for shadow map filtering and, on the other hand, that the projected tetrahedron view areas do not overlap in the effective sampling area. Since the resulting 12 clipping plane normals are equal for all lights and never change at runtime, they can be precalculated and added as constants into the corresponding shader.

At runtime, the precalculated normals are combined each time with the position of the processed light source to construct the appropriate clipping planes.

Vertex processing. To render indirectly the shadow maps, a simple vertex shader is required to fetch the vertex attributes (typically the vertex position), to calculate the light index (as already described in the section "Computation" on page 200), and to pass this value to a subsequent geometry shader.

Primitive processing. After the vertex shader, a geometry shader is invoked to perform clipping with the precalculated plane normals. Depending on which of the four view volumes of the tetrahedron the processed triangle intersects, up to four new primitives have to be generated. Against all expectations, it has proven to be far more performant to run a loop over four primitives in a single geometry shader invocation than using geometry shader instancing and invoking the geometry shader four times. The reasons for this can be that, in a high percentage of cases, less than four primitives have to be emitted and that the light buffer data has to be fetched only once for each incoming primitive in the loop-based approach.

An alternative strategy would be to cull the AABBs of the relevant meshes against the four tetrahedron view volumes for each light in the indirect draw buffer generation step and add for each overlap a new indirect draw command, thus avoiding later the use of the geometry shader. However, it has shown that this approach not only requires more video memory for storing the increased amount of indirect draw commands, but also runs notably slower than the geometry shader approach. A reason for this can be that the geometry shader performs culling on a per-triangle basis, in contrast to culling AABBs of the relevant meshes.

Since back-face culling as implemented by the graphics hardware is performed after the vertex and primitive processing stage, it is done manually at the beginning of the geometry shader. By reducing the amount of processed primitives, runtime performance can be further increased [Rákos 12]. This can be an additional reason why geometry shader instancing is performing more slowly, because the back-face culling code has to be performed four times in contrast to the loop-based solution, where this code is shared for all four primitives.

Though the clip distances are passed via `gl_ClipDistance` to the clipping unit of the graphics hardware, it has proven that additionally culling primitives in the shader further improves runtime performance. This can be done by only emitting a new primitive when at least one of the calculated clip distances of the three processed triangle vertices is greater than zero for all three clipping planes of the processed tetrahedron face.

Finally, transforming the incoming vertices boils down to performing for each relevant tetrahedron face one matrix multiplication with the matching shadow matrix. Listing 14.4 shows the corresponding GLSL geometry shader.

```
float GetClipDist(in vec3 lightPos, in uint vertexIndex, in uint
              planeIndex)
{
   vec3 normal = planeNormals[planeIndex]; //clipping plane normal
   return (dot(gl_in[vertexIndex].gl_Position.xyz, normal)
         +dot(-normal, lightPosition));
}

layout(triangles) in;
layout(triangle_strip, max_vertices = 12) out;
void main()
{
   const uint lightIndex = inputGS[0].lightIndex;
   const vec3 lightPosition = lightBuffer.lights[lightIndex].position;

   // perform back-face culling
   vec3 normal = cross(gl_in[2].gl_Position.xyz-gl_in[0]
                           .gl_Position.xyz,
                       gl_in[0].gl_Position.xyz-gl_in[1]
                           .gl_Position.xyz);
```

```
        vec3 view = lightPosition-gl_in[0].gl_Position.xyz;

    if(dot(normal, view) < 0.0f)
        return;

    // iterate over tetrahedron faces
    for(uint faceIndex=0; faceIndex<4; faceIndex++)
    {
        uint inside = 0;
        float clipDistances[9];

        // Calculate for each vertex distance to clipping planes and
        // determine whether processed triangle is inside view
        // volume.
        for(uint sideIndex=0; sideIndex<3; sideIndex++)
        {
            const uint planeIndex = (faceIndex*3)+sideIndex;
            const uint bit = 1 << sideIndex;

            for(uint vertexIndex=0; vertexIndex<3; vertexIndex++)
            {
                uint clipDistIndex = sideIndex*3+vertexIndex;
                clipDistances[clipDistIndex] = GetClipDist(lightPosition,
                    vertexIndex, planeIndex);
                inside |= (clipDistances[clipDistIndex] > 0.001) ?
                    bit : 0;
            }
        }

        // If triangle is inside volume, emit primitive.
        if(inside == 0x7)
        {
            const mat4 shadowMatrix =
                lightBuffer.lights[lightIndex].shadowMatrices[faceIndex];

            // Transform vertex positions with shadow matrix and
            // forward clip distances to graphics hardware.
            for(uint vertexIndex=0; vertexIndex<3; vertexIndex++)
            {
                gl_Position = shadowMatrix*gl_in[vertexIndex].gl_Position;
                gl_ClipDistance[0] = clipDistances[vertexIndex];
                gl_ClipDistance[1] = clipDistances[3+vertexIndex];
                gl_ClipDistance[2] = clipDistances[6+vertexIndex];
                EmitVertex();
            }
            EndPrimitive();
        }
    }
}
```

Listing 14.4. Geometry shader for indirect shadow map rendering.

Tiled shadow map. After the draw commands in the indirect draw buffer are executed, the shadow map tiles of all relevant light sources are tightly packed together into the tiled shadow map. Figure 14.4 shows this texture that was generated for the scene in Figure 14.5.

As can be seen in Figure 14.4, the shadow map tiles of all light sources in the processed scene are tightly packed; thus, shadow maps for significantly more

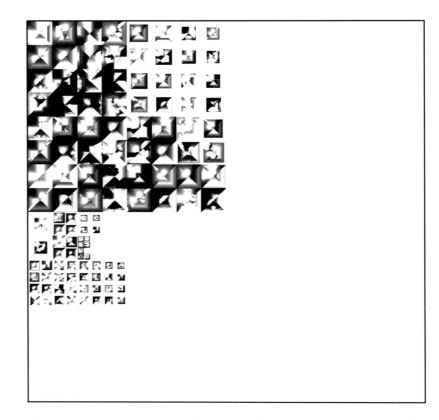

Figure 14.4. A tiled shadow map (generated for the scene in Figure 14.5) with a resolution of 8192 × 8192. The tile size is clamped between 64 and 512. Since the scene is rendered with view frustum culling of invisible light sources, for 117 out of the 128 medium-sized moving point lights, an individual shadow map tile is generated. With this texture and clamped tile resolution, in the worst case, shadow map tiles for 256 light sources can still be stored in the tiled shadow map.

omnidirectional light sources can be stored in a limited texture space than with traditional shadow mapping systems.

14.3.4 Shading

Finally, the tiled shadow map can be used in the shading stage to produce high-quality soft shadows. Shading methods such as tiled deferred shading [Andersson 09], tiled forward shading [Billeter et al. 13], or clustered deferred and forward shading [Olsson et al. 12] require the shadow maps for all relevant light sources to be created prior to the shading process as the proposed algorithm does. How-

```
// matrix of tetrahedron face vectors
mat4x3 faceMatrix;
faceMatrix[0] = faceVectors[0];
faceMatrix[1] = faceVectors[1];
faceMatrix[2] = faceVectors[2];
faceMatrix[3] = faceVectors[3];

// determine face that is closest to specified light vector
vec4 dotProducts = -lightVecN*faceMatrix;
float maximum = max (max(dotProducts.x, dotProducts.y),
          max(dotProducts.z, dotProducts.w));
uint index;
if(maximum == dotProducts.x)
      index = 0;
else if(maximum == dotProducts.y)
    index = 1;
else if(maximum == dotProducts.z)
    index = 2;
else
    index = 3;

// project fragment world-space position
vec4 projPos =
    lightBuffer.lights[lightIndex].shadowMatrices[index]*position;
projPos.xyz /= projPos.w;
projPos.xyz = (projPos.xyz*0.5)+0.5;

// calculate shadow term with HW-filtered shadow lookup
float shadowTerm = texture(tiledShadowMap, projPos.xyz);
```

Listing 14.5. Generating the shadow term with a tiled shadow map.

ever, lighting methods such as deferred shading [Hargreaves and Harris 04] that theoretically can reuse shadow map textures for multiple lights by alternating between shadow map rendering and shading, can profit as well from the proposed method, since frequent switching of render states and GPU resources can be an expensive operation.

Generating shadows with the help of a tiled shadow map is straightforward and follows [Liao 10]. After acquiring the world-space position of the currently shaded screen fragment, for each relevant light source it is first determined inside which of the four tetrahedron view volumes the processed fragment is located. The acquired fragment position is then multiplied with the corresponding shadow matrix to yield the projected fragment position with which a shadow comparison is done. See Listing 14.5 for details.

Besides performing a hardware-filtered shadow comparison, various filtering approaches such as PCF [Reeves et al. 87] or percentage-closer soft shadows (PCSS) [Fernando 05] can be used to produce high-quality soft shadows. Since, as already described earlier in this section, the shadow projection matrices and tetrahedron clipping plane normals are properly adapted, such filtering techniques will not produce any artifacts by sampling outside of the appropriate shadow map areas.

14.4   Results

To capture the results, the Crytek Sponza scene was used, which contains without the central banner 103 meshes and ~280,000 triangles. The test machine had an Intel Core i7-4810MQ 2.8 GHZ CPU and an NVIDIA GeForce GTX 880 Mobile GPU and the screen resolution was set to 1280×720. For the lighting system, tiled deferred shading [Andersson 09] is used.

A layered cube map–based shadowing solution is used as the reference for the proposed technique. For this, the shadow maps of each point light are rendered into a cube map texture array with 128 layer and a 16-bit depth buffer texture format; each cube map face has a texture resolution of 256×256. For each point light, the 3D space is split up into six view frustums that correspond to the six faces of a cube map. Each mesh is tested for overlap with each of the six view frustums. Every time an overlap is detected, a new indexed draw call is submitted to the GPU. To speed up rendering performance, all meshes share the same vertex and index buffer and the cube map face selection is done in a geometry shader. For a large number of light sources, it has proven to be more performant to submit for each overlap a separate draw call rather than always amplifying the input geometry in the geometry shader six times and using one draw call. To improve the quality of the generated shadows, `GL_TEXTURE_CUBE_MAP_SEAMLESS` is enabled, and besides performing hardware shadow filtering, 16× PCF is used for soft shadows. In the remaining part of this section, the reference technique will be referred to as the *cube solution*.

For the proposed method, a 8192×8192 tiled shadow map is used with a 16-bit depth buffer texture format. The tile size is clamped between 64 and 512 (see Figure 14.4). According to the reference method, hardware shadow filtering in combination with 16× PCF is used to produce soft shadows. In the remaining part of this section, this proposed technique will be referred to as the *tiled technique*.

It can be seen in the comparison screenshots in Figure 14.5 that the quality of both images is nearly equal while the proposed method runs more than three times faster than the reference solution. In the close-up comparison screenshots shown in Figure 14.6, we can also see that quality-wise the technique described here comes very close to the reference solution.

For the performance measurements, the same scene configuration was used as in Figure 14.5 with the exception that view frustum culling of invisible lights was disabled; hence, for all 128 point lights in the scene, shadow maps were generated. The measured frame times in Figure 14.7 show that the tiled technique gets significantly faster compared to the reference cube solution as the number of shadow-casting point lights increases. Figure 14.8 shows the number of draw calls that were submitted for each frame from the CPU to render the shadow maps. In the proposed method, the number of draw calls is constantly one due to the indirect shadow map rendering, whereas the number of draw calls rapidly

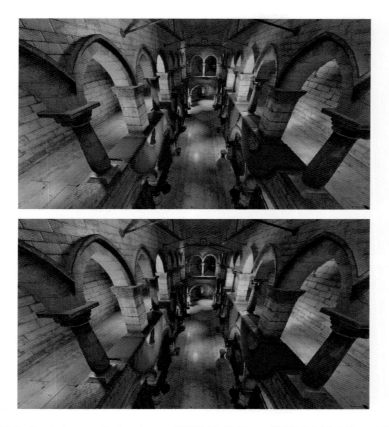

Figure 14.5. Real-time rendering (on an NVIDIA GeForce GTX 880 Mobile at 1280×720 resolution) of the Crytek Sponza scene (~280,000 triangles) with 128 medium-sized moving point lights, which all cast omnidirectional shadows via shadow maps. The upper image is rendered with the proposed tiled method at 28.44 fps; the lower image is the reference with the cube approach at 8.89 fps. Both methods use hardware shadow filtering in combination with 16× PCF for providing high-quality soft shadows.

increases in the reference technique. Finally, in Table 14.4, CPU and GPU times for shadow map rendering and shading are compared.

According to Table 14.4, the CPU times for rendering shadow maps with the proposed technique are at a constant low value since only one indirect draw call is submitted each frame. However, the CPU times for the reference technique are drastically increasing with the light count due to the rising number of CPU draw calls. When comparing the times taken by the GPU to render the shadow maps, the proposed technique is significantly faster than the reference method, which can be primarily attributed to the reduced number of primitives processed in the

Figure 14.6. One shadow-casting point light is placed directly in front of the lion-head model in the Crytek Sponza scene. The images on the left are rendered with the tiled technique, and the images on the right with the reference cube technique. While the images at the bottom show the final shading results, the images at the top visualize the partitioning of the tetrahedron and cube, respectively, volumes. As can be seen, the shadow quality of the proposed solution comes close to that of the reference method.

tiled solution. Considering the times taken by the GPU to shade all visible screen fragments using tiled deferred shading, it first seems unexpected that the cube solution would have higher execution times than the tiled technique. Though

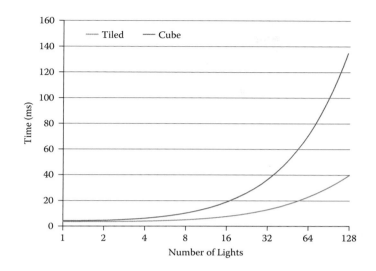

Figure 14.7. Frame times of tiled versus cube technique with an increasing number of shadow-casting point light sources.

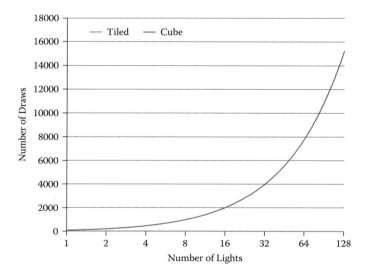

Figure 14.8. Number of CPU submitted draw calls to render shadow maps in tiled and cube technique with an increasing number of shadow-casting point lights.

doing a hardware texture lookup in a cube map is faster than doing the proposed lookup, this is not true for performing PCF to produce soft shadows. While for

| Number | Shadow CPU | | Shadow GPU | | Shading GPU | |
of Lights	Tiled	Cube	Tiled	Cube	Tiled	Cube
1	0.09	0.12	0.49	0.79	0.15	0.18
2	0.09	0.21	0.68	1.45	0.15	0.19
4	0.09	0.41	1.01	3.03	0.16	0.21
8	0.09	0.65	1.65	5.70	0.23	0.35
16	0.09	1.38	3.76	12.98	0.34	0.56
32	0.09	2.89	8.24	29.46	0.70	1.22
64	0.09	5.42	15.59	58.17	1.36	2.52
128	0.09	11.06	33.75	119.94	2.18	4.04

Table 14.4. Comparison of CPU and GPU times (ms) for shadow map rendering and shading with an increasing number of shadow-casting point lights.

the tiled method it is enough to apply 2D offsets to the lookup coordinates, for the cube technique a 3D direction vector, which is used for the texture lookup, has to be rotated in 3D space.

According to the presented performance values, the proposed technique is in all aspects and for all number of shadow-casting point lights faster than the reference technique. On the one hand, the driver CPU overhead, present in the reference method due to the high number of draw calls, can be nearly completely eliminated; on the other hand, the time taken by the GPU to render the shadow maps is significantly reduced.

14.5   Discussion

We now discuss some important aspects related to this technique and relevant for real-time applications such as computer games.

14.5.1   Shadow Map Caching

To further improve runtime performance, it is possible to cache shadow map tiles for certain lights. Every time a light does not move and the shadow-casting geometry in its influence area remains unchanged, the corresponding shadow map tile does not need to be cleared and recomputed. However, this should only be the case when the corresponding tile size does not change significantly in order to avoid popping artifacts at shadow edges and to better utilize the limited amount of available texture space.

To achieve this in the indirect draw buffer generation step, such lights are ignored and the associated tile nodes in the quad-tree are not reset. However, clearing the tiled shadow map can no longer be done by simply calling `glClear()`. One possibility to selectively clear the used texture atlas is to render a list of quadrilaterals that correspond to the tiles of the light sources that are not cached.

14.5.2 Spotlights

Though this chapter focuses on point lights, it is trivial to include support for spotlight shadows as well. Actually, it is easier to handle spotlight sources since only one view volume that corresponds to the view frustum of the spotlight has to be taken into account. However, when clipping the primitives while rendering into the tiled shadow map, the clipping planes must be set to the four side planes of the spotlight view frustum.

14.5.3 Dynamic, Skinned Meshes

Neither CPU- nor GPU-skinned meshes are an issue in the proposed method. For CPU-skinned meshes, the one thing to keep in mind is that the same vertex and index buffers should be used for all meshes. GPU-skinned dynamic meshes are easy to handle as well. In addition to writing the light indices for each light into the light-index buffer when the indirect draw buffer is generated, a unique mesh ID is added prior to the light indices for each relevant mesh. Later on, when the indirect draw commands are executed, according to the light index, the unique mesh ID can be acquired and the corresponding transformation and skinning matrices can be looked up in a GPU buffer. Due to the usage of a geometry shader to render into the four faces of a tetrahedron, each mesh only needs to be transformed and skinned once per point light source.

14.5.4 Alpha Testing

One aspect that needs to be discussed is handling meshes with alpha-tested materials since this involves a texture lookup into an alpha map. This problem can be solved by three different approaches. The first solution is to simply render each alpha-tested mesh separately into the tiled shadow map, hence omitting the indirect draw pipeline but still using the proposed clipping-based geometry shader approach. The second possibility is to pack all alpha maps into a common texture atlas. The third option is to make use of the `GL_ARB_bindless_texture` extension, with which theoretically an arbitrary number of alpha maps can be used simultaneously. However, it should be noted that this extension is not supported by all graphics hardware that otherwise would support the proposed technique.

For the above discussed cases, the indirect draw buffer generation as well as the indirect shadow map rendering step should be handled separately where applicable to avoid dynamic shader branching. In most cases, this only means dispatching the compute shader for generating the indirect draw buffer and submitting an indirect draw call a few times per frame, which will have only a slight negative impact on the driver CPU overhead. Nevertheless, in all cases, one unique tiled shadow map can be used.

14.6   Conclusion

This chapter presented a comprehensive system for generating high-quality soft shadows for a large number of dynamic omnidirectional light sources without the need of doing approximations as merging shadows of multiple lights. It has been demonstrated that this method is competitive quality-wise to a reference cube map–based approach and performs with any tested number of shadow-casting point lights faster. Furthermore, due to the usage of a tiled shadow map, significantly more shadow maps can be stored for point light sources in a limited amount of texture space than with a cube map–based approach.

14.7   Acknowledgments

I would like to thank Nikita Kindt for porting the accompanying demo application to Linux (available in the book's web materials).

Bibliography

[Andersson 09] J. Anderrson. "Parallel Graphics in Frostbite: Current and Future." Beyond Programmable Shading, SIGGRAPH Course, New Orleans, LA, August 3–7, 2009. (Available at http://s09.idav.ucdavis.edu/talks/04-JAndersson-ParallelFrostbite-Siggraph09.pdf.)

[Billeter et al. 13] M. Billeter, O. Olsson, and U. Assarsson. "Tiled Forward Shading." In *GPU Pro 4: Advanced Rendering Techniques*, edited by Wolfgang Engel, pp. 99–114. Boca Raton, FL: CRC Press, 2013.

[Fernando 05] R. Fernando. "Percentage-Closer Soft Shadows." In *ACM SIGGRAPH 2005 Sketches*, Article no. 35. New York: ACM, 2005.

[Gerasimov 04] P. S. Gerasimov. "Omnidirectional Shadow Mapping." In *GPU Gems*, edited by Randima Fernando, pp. 193–203. Reading, MA: Addison-Wesley Professional, 2004.

[Harada et al. 13] T. Harada, J. McKee, and J. C. Yang. "Forward+: A Step Toward Film-Style Shading in Real Time." In *GPU Pro 4: Advanced Rendering Techniques*, edited by Wolfgang Engel, pp. 115–135. Boca Raton, FL: CRC Press, 2013.

[Hargreaves and Harris 04] S. Hargreaves and M. Harris. "Deferred Shading." Presented at NVIDIA Developer Conference: 6800 Leagues Under the Sea, San Jose, CA, March 23, 2004. (Available at http://http.download.nvidia.com/developer/presentations/2004/6800_Leagues/6800_Leagues_Deferred_Shading.pdf.)

[Larsson et al. 07] T. Larsson, T. Akenine-Möller, and E. Lengyel. "On Faster Sphere-Box Overlap Testing." *Journal of Graphics, GPU, and Game Tools* 12:1 (2007), 3–8.

[Liao 10] H.-C. Liao. "Shadow Mapping for Omnidirectional Light Using Tetrahedron Mapping." In *GPU Pro: Advanced Rendering Techniques*, edited by Wolfgang Engel, pp. 455–475. Natick, MA: A K Peters, 2010.

[Olsson et al. 12] O. Olsson, M. Billeter, and U. Assarson. "Clustered Deferred and Forward Shading." In *Proceedings of the Fourth ACM SIGGRAPH/Eurographics Conference on High Performance Graphics*, pp. 87–96. Aire-la-Ville, Switzerland: Eurographics Association, 2012.

[Rákos 12] D. Rákos. "Massive Number of Shadow-Casting Lights with Layered Rendering." In *OpenGL Insights*, edited by Patrick Cozzi and Christophe Riccio, pp. 259–278. Boca Raton, FL: CRC Press, 2012.

[Reeves et al. 87] W. T. Reeves, D. H. Salesin and R. L. Cook. "Rendering Antialiased Shadows with Depth Maps." *Computer Graphics: Proc. SIGGRAPH '87* 21:4 (1987), 283–291.

[Riccio and Lilley 13] C. Riccio and S. Lilley. "Introducing the Programmable Vertex Pulling Rendering Pipeline." In *GPU Pro 4: Advanced Rendering Techniques*. edited by Wolfgang Engel, pp. 21–38. Boca Raton, FL: CRC Press, 2013.

[Williams 78] L. Williams. "Casting Curved Shadows on Curved Surfaces." *Computer Graphics: Proc. SIGGRAPH '78* 12:3 (1978), 270–274.

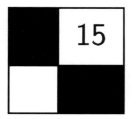

Shadow Map Silhouette Revectorization

Vladimir Bondarev

Shadow Map Silhouette Revectorization (SMSR) is a two-pass filtering technique inspired by MLAA [Jimenez et al. 11] that aims to improve the visual quality of a projected shadow map by concealing the perspective aliasing with an additional umbra surface. In most cases under-sampled areas result in a higher shadow silhouette edge quality.

SMSR is based on the idea of reducing the perceptual error [Lopez-Moreno et al. 10] by concealing the visible perspective aliasing around the shadow silhouette edge.

15.1   Introduction

Shadow mapping [Williams 78] is known for its compatibility with rasterization hardware, low implementation complexity, and ability to handle any kind of geometry. However, aliasing is also a very common problem in shadow mapping. This chapter introduces a shadow map filtering technique that approximates an additional umbra surface (space completely occluded from the direct light) based on linear interpolation in projected view space.

Projection and *perspective aliasing* [Lloyd et al. 08] are the two main discontinuity types that deteriorate the quality of a projected shadow. Since the introduction of shadow mapping, many algorithms have been developed to reduce or even completely remove shadow map aliasing. Most algorithms that are developed to remove aliasing are not compatible to run in real time [Johnson et al. 05] and in some cases propose additional hardware changes to allow for real-time application [Lloyd et al. 08].

Most real-time shadow-mapping techniques can be divided in two main categories: sample redistribution (PSM, TSM, LiSPSM, and CSM) and filter-based techniques (VSM, PCF, and BFSM). Shadow Map Silhouette Revectorization

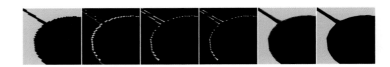

Figure 15.1. From left to right, the shadow silhouette revectorization process.

Figure 15.2. An uncompressed image (left), and the encoded shadow discontinuity buffer (right). See Table 15.1 for color definition.

is a filtering technique that improves upon the conventional two-pass shadow-mapping technique [Williams 78] by concealing the visible aliasing and yet remaining inside an acceptable performance range. In some scenes, SMSR can get away with a much lower shadow-map resolution and at the same time is capable of providing a high-quality umbra.

SMSR achieves a comparable result to shadow silhouette maps (SSM) [Sen et al. 03], however with a very different approach. To generate a silhouette map, SSM rasterizes the edges of all elements as quadrilaterals. In contrast to SMSR, SSM will prove to be more performance intensive with a high polygon-count scene.

15.2   Implementation

The SMSR technique consists of two fullscreen passes and requires access to the depth buffer, shadow map, lighting buffer, view matrix, light matrix, and inverse of the light matrix.

15.2.1   First Pass

The first pass searches for the exterior side of the shadow silhouette edge and compresses the relative edge discontinuity directions into a two-component output vector (Figure 15.1, second image, and Figure 15.2).

In screen space (camera view), we are looking for a shadow discontinuity (edge). The kernel of the first pass compares the current shadow state with the neighboring shadow-map sample state (left, top, right, and bottom). The discontinuity is distinguished into two main types: *exterior discontinuity*, where

Value	Red Channel	Green Channel
0.00	No discontinuity	No discontinuity
0.50	Left	Bottom
0.75	Left and right	Bottom and top
1.00	Right	Top

Table 15.1. Value definition of the two-channel discontinuity encoding.

the current fragment sample is inside the umbra and the next neighboring sample is outside the umbra, and *interior discontinuity*, where the current fragment sample is outside the umbra and the next neighboring sample is inside the umbra.

SMSR is only concerned with the exterior discontinuity of the shadow silhouette edge. When an exterior discontinuity is detected, the direction from the current fragment sample toward the discontinuity is encoded into one of the output channels (used in the second pass to determine discontinuity orientation). Horizontal discontinuities are stored into the red channel and vertical discontinuities are stored into the green channel. Each channel has four possible states: for example, the red channel uses the value 0.0 to indicate no discontinuity, 0.5 discontinuity to the left, 0.75 discontinuity to the left and right, and 1.0 discontinuity to the right. The green channel uses the value 0.0 to indicate no discontinuity, 0.5 discontinuity to the bottom, 0.75 discontinuity to the bottom and top, and 1.0 discontinuity to the top.

To reduce the memory footprint, the discontinuity encoding can be stored in a 4-bit channel. However, for the sake of simplicity, we are not doing it in this implementation.

15.2.2 Second Pass

The second pass consists of five major steps and uses a shadow-map depth buffer, a camera-view depth buffer, and the encoded data gathered by the first pass.

First, we have to find the *discontinuity length* (the length of the exterior discontinuity along the shadow map on the same axis) of the current projected camera-view fragment. To find the discontinuity length, we have to find the relative offset in the projected camera-view space to the neighboring shadow-map sample on the same axis. This is done by transforming the current fragment's world-space position into the light-view space, applying an xy-offset to the neighboring center of the next shadow map sample, replacing the z-vector component by the depth value of the matched shadow map sample and then projecting the coordinate back onto the projected camera-view space.

Second, after we have determined where in the screen space our neighboring shadow-map sample is located, we repeat the step from the new location until we find a break in discontinuity. The discontinuity break is initiated by exceeding the delta-depth threshold, by reaching the maximum search distance, or by find-

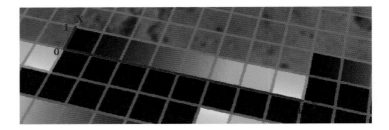

Figure 15.3. Orientated normalized discontinuity space (ONDS) stretches from 0.0 to 1.0 on the y-axis over eight shadow-map samples and on x-axis over just one. The last ONDS sample located near $y = 1.0$ indicates the discontinuity end.

ing a discontinuity on the opposite axis. By performing this iteration in screen space, we approximate the length of the exterior discontinuity along the shadow silhouette.

Third, we need to find a discontinuity contained in both channels (red and green) that indicates a *discontinuity end* (see Figure 15.3). The discontinuity end is used to determine the orientation of the *exterior discontinuity* along the shadow silhouette edge.

Fourth, knowing the discontinuity length and the discontinuity end, we will construct a normalized 2D space that stretches along the exterior discontinuity of the shadow silhouette (*orientated normalized discontinuity space* (ONDS)).

Fifth, after ONDS is constructed, it's normalized coordinate system is used to interpolate a new additional umbra into the lighting buffer.

15.3   Results

SMSR successfully hides the visual perspective aliasing (see Figure 15.1, rightmost image, and Figure 15.4) in under-sampled areas of the shadow map, and the unoptimized version takes less than 1.5 ms to process on GTX 580, regardless of the shadow-map resolution in full HD.

15.3.1   Inconsistencies

SMSR doesn't come without its drawbacks, which are categorized into special cases, absence of data, and mangled silhouette shape.

15.3.2   Special Cases

The technique is unable to handle exterior discontinuities with a parallel umbra spacing of a single shadow-map sample, causing visual artifacts (see Figure 15.5,

Figure 15.4. Configuration of the Crytek Sponza scene with a 1024×1024 shadow map: without SMSR (top) and with SMSR (bottom).

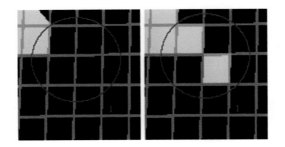

Figure 15.5. A closeup with SMSR (left) and without SMSR (right). Point 1 is the discontinuity in more than two directions, a special case that makes it hard for SMSR to handle. The current solution is to fill those areas completely with an umbra.

right image). SSM suffers from the same problem. The SMSR kernel has a dedicated portion of code that fills all single shadow-map spacing with an additional umbra, yielding less visually noticeable artifacts (see Figure 15.5, left image).

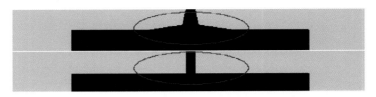

Figure 15.6. A mangled silhouette shape with SMSR (top) and without SMSR (bottom). Due to edge generalization and lack of shape understanding, SMSR changes the desired object shape.

15.3.3 Absence of Data

In this specific scenario, the shadow discontinuity is prematurely interrupted by an occluder or the search function goes outside the viewport boundaries. These cases result in a varying or incorrect edge discontinuity length during the search step, which results in a visible silhouette artifact.

15.3.4 Mangled Silhouette Shape

A typical MLAA approach distinguishes discontinuities into L-, Z-, and U-shaped patterns. Taking the shape pattern into account helps to increase the precision of the edge reapproximation and results in higher image quality. The current approach of SMSR is unable to distinguish shape patterns and processes all discontinuities as L-shaped patterns. This inability to recognize shape patterns leads to a coarse edge approximation and, particularly on low-resolution shadow maps, will often change the shape of the object's shadow (see Figure 15.6).

15.4 Future Work

Shadow Map Silhouette Revectorization effectively reduces the perceptual error by concealing the perspective aliasing of an under-sampled shadow map area. Unfortunately, projection and temporal aliasing remain unaddressed.

By saving the triangle edge data into the shadow map sample [Pan et al. 09], it's possible to approximate a more accurate shadow silhouette edge and at the same time reduce temporal aliasing.

15.5 Conclusion

Shadow Map Silhouette Revectorization particularly shines in scenes with many large polygons, where it has the ability to utilize a lower shadow-map resolution (to reduce the GPU memory footprint) without sacrificing a great portion of visual quality and effectively helps to conserve the GPU fill rate. However, the technique is in its early stage and can be improved in many different areas such as interpolation based on shape patterns (to improve edge revectorization), soft shadows (to improve realism), and temporal aliasing (to reduce jagged edges). It can also be combined with other sample-redistribution techniques such as cascade shadow maps (to optimize the use of shadow sample density where it is needed).

Bibliography

[Jimenez et al. 11] J. Jimenez, B. Masia, J. Echevarria, F. Navarro, and D. Gutierrez. "Practical Morphological Antialiasing." In *GPU Pro 2: Advanced Rendering Techniques*, edited by Wolfgang Engel, pp. 95–114. Natick, MA: A K Peters, 2011.

[Johnson et al. 05] Gregory S. Johnson, Juhyun Lee, Christopher A. Burns, and William R. Mark. "The Irregular Z-Buffer: Hardware Acceleration for Irregular Data Structures." *ACM Transactions on Graphics* 24:4 (2005), 1462–1482.

[Lloyd et al. 08] D. Brandon Lloyd, Naga K. Govindaraju, Cory Quammen, Steven E. Molnar, and Dinesh Manocha. "Logarithmic Perspective Shadow Maps." *ACM Transactions on Graphics* 27:4 (2008), Article no. 106.

[Lopez-Moreno et al. 10] Jorge Lopez-Moreno, Veronica Sundstedt, Francisco Sangorrin, and Diego Gutierrez. "Measuring the Perception of Light Inconsistencies." In *Proceedings of the 7th Symposium on Applied Perception in Graphics and Visualization*, pp. 25–32. New York: ACM Press, 2010.

[Pan et al. 09] Minghao Pan, Rui Wang, Weifeng Chen, Kun Zhou, and Hujun Bao. "Fast, Sub-pixel Antialiased Shadow Maps." *Computer Graphics Forum* 28:7 (2009), 1927–1934.

[Sen et al. 03] Pradeep Sen, Mike Cammarano, and Pat Hanrahan. "Shadow Silhouette Maps." *ACM Transactions on Graphics* 22:3 (2003), 521–526.

[Williams 78] Lance Williams. "Casting Curved Shadows on Curved Surfaces." *Computer Graphics: Proc. SIGGRAPH '78* 12:3 (1978), 270–274.

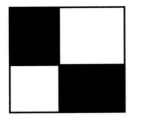

About the Contributors

Jiri Bittner is an assistant professor of electrical engineering of the Czech Technical University in Prague. He received his PhD in 2003 at the same institute. His research interests include visibility computations, real-time rendering, spatial data structures, and global illumination. He has also participated in creating commercial projects that deal with real-time rendering of complex scenes.

Vladimir Bondarev is a senior graphics programmer at Confetti Interactive Inc. He graduated with honors from NHTV Breda University of Applied Sciences. He worked on CPU optimizations for the new Futuremark Benchmark and GPU optimizations for *Dirt 4*, and he is currently working on Super Evil Megacorp's title *Vainglory*.

Hawar Doghramachi studied dental medicine at the Semmelweis University in Budapest and received in 2003 the doctor of dental medicine (DMD) title. After working for a while as a dentist, he decided to turn his lifetime passion for programming into his profession. After he studied 3D programming at the Games Academy in Frankfurt, from 2010 he worked as an Engine-Programmer in the Vision team of Havok. Currently he is working as a Graphics-Programmer in the R&D team of Eidos Montreal. He is particularly interested in finding solutions for common real-time rendering problems in modern computer games.

René Fürst is a graduate student of visual computing at Vienna University of Technology. He is interested in various GPGPU topics, for example, shadowing, global illumination, and fluid simulation in real time.

Holger Gruen ventured into creating real-time 3D technology over 20 years ago writing fast software rasterizers. Since then he has worked for games middleware vendors, game developers, simulation companies, and independent hardware vendors in various engineering roles. In his current role as a developer technology engineer at NVIDIA, he works with games developers to get the best out of NVIDIA's GPUs.

Viktor Heisenberger is a software engineer at GRAPHISOFT, working on CAD software for the AEC industry. He graduated with a master's degree in information technology engineering at Budapest University of Technology and Economics. His professional interests include computer graphics and web development. In his free time, he enjoys photography and various sports.

Andrew Lauritzen is a software engineer on the Advanced Rendering Technology team at Intel. He received his M.Math in computer science from the University of Waterloo in 2008, where his research was focused on variance shadow maps and other shadow filtering algorithms. His current research interests include lighting and shadowing algorithms, deferred rendering, parallel programming languages, and graphics hardware architectures.

Aaron Lefohn is a senior graphics architect at Intel, where he is a research lead in the advanced rendering technology team, creating new interactive rendering algorithms, pipelines, and programming models. Aaron previously led Intel's involvement in OpenCL, where he contributed significantly to OpenCL's heterogeneous parallel coordination API. Before joining Intel he designed parallel programming models for rendering on Sony PlayStation3 at the startup Neoptica. Aaron spent three years at Pixar working on interactive rendering tools for artists and GPU acceleration of RenderMan. He received his PhD in computer science from UC Davis in 2006 and holds MS and BA degrees from the University of Utah and Whitman College.

Hung-Chien Liao is a graduate of Full Sail University. He is very interested in graphics programming, which he considers a puzzle to a beautiful world. Currently, he is working at Tencent Boston as a senior engine programmer.

Oliver Mattausch is currently employed as a post doctorate in the VMML Lab of the University of Zurich, working on processing and visualizing large datasets. Previously he worked as a computer graphics researcher at the Vienna University of Technology and at the University of Tokyo/ERATO. He received his MSc in 2004 and his PhD in 2010 from Vienna University of Technology. His research interests are real-time rendering, visibility and shadows, global illumination, and geometry processing.

Matt Pharr is a principal engineer at Intel and the lead graphics architect in the Advanced Rendering Technology group. He previously co-founded Neoptica, worked in the Software Architecture group at NVIDIA, co-founded Exluna, worked in Pixar's Rendering R&D group, and received his PhD from the Stanford Graphics Lab. With Greg Humphreys, he wrote the textbook *Physically Based Rendering: From Theory to Implementation*. He was also the editor of *GPU Gems 2*.

Marco Salvi is a senior graphics engineer in the Advanced Rendering Technology group at Intel, where he focuses his research on new interactive rendering algorithms and sw/hw graphics architectures. Marco previously worked for Ninja Theory and LucasArts as a graphics engineer on multi-platform and PS3-exclusive games where he was responsible for architecting renderers, developing new rendering techniques and performing low-level optimizations. Marco received his MSc in physics from the University of Bologna in 2001.

Daniel Scherzer is professor of visual computing at the University of Applied Sciences Ravensburg-Weingarten. He has also worked at MPI, KAUST, the University of Applied Sciences Hagenberg, the Ludwig Boltzmann Institute for Archaeological Prospection and Virtual Archaeology, and the Institute of Computer Graphics and Algorithms of the Vienna University of Technology, where he received an MSc in 2005, an MSocEcSc in 2008, and a PhD in 2009. His current research interests include global illumination, temporal coherence methods, shadow algorithms, modeling, and level-of-detail approaches for real-time rendering. He has authored and coauthored several papers in these fields.

Michael Schwärzler is a PhD student, researcher, and project manager in the field of real-time rendering at the VRVis Research Center in Vienna, Austria. In 2009, he received his master's degree in computer graphics and digital image processing at the Vienna University of Technology, and his master's degree in computer science and management at the University of Vienna. His current research efforts are concentrated on GPU lighting simulations, real-time shadow algorithms, image-based reconstruction, and semantics-based 3D modeling techniques.

Ari Silvennoinen is Principal Programmer and Research Lead at Umbra Software, where he is focusing on next generation rendering technology research and development. His primary areas of interest include visibility algorithms, real-time shadow techniques, global illumination, and rendering optimization in general. Ari holds a MS degree in computer science from the University of Helsinki and has previously worked with the 3D graphics research group at Helsinki University of Technology (now Aalto University School of Science and Technology).

Wojciech Sterna has been an avid programmer since 2002. He started with simple programs made in Delphi but quickly moved towards C++, games, and graphics programming. From that time on, he has continuously (co-)worked (mostly) on private game projects. In 2011 he graduated with a Bachelor's degree in computer science from Wrocław University of Technology, writing a thesis on software rendering using CUDA. This led him to a three-month internship as a DevTech Engineer Intern at NVIDIA London's office. He had a short stint in Sweden, studying computer graphics for six months. Since that time he has worked professionally mostly on engine/rendering development at Madman Theory Games in Wrocław and most recently at Flying Wild Hog in Warsaw. He also co-runs a game and middleware company, Blossom Games.

Márton Tamás is currently studying computer engineering at Budapest University of Technology and Economics. His interests include real-time rendering, GPU programming, and engine development. Follow him on twitter @0martint.

Kiril Vidimče is a senior software architect and researcher at Intel's Advanced Rendering Technologies group. His research and development interests are in the area of real time rendering, cinematic lighting, physically-based camera models, and computational photography. Previously he spent eight years at Pixar as a member of the R&D group working on the in-house modeling, animation, lighting, and rendering tools, with a brief stint as a Lighting TD on Pixar's feature film, *Cars*. In his previous (academic) life he did research in the area of multiresolution modeling and remeshing. His research work has been published at SIGGRAPH, EGSR, IEEE Visualization, IEEE CG&A, and Graphics Interfaces.

John White was, until recently, a Senior Rendering Engineer at Electronic Arts Black Box working on *Need For Speed: The Run*. He works in all areas of rendering development and specializes in both low-level GPU optimizations and high-level rendering architecture. Having previously presented at GDC, his current focus is on post-processing techniques, local and global lighting, shadowing, and level-of-detail techniques. Prior to working at EA, John worked at Deep Red Games in the UK, where he architected and developed the in-house rendering run-time and tool-chain that powered their PC-based strategy games. Before this, John worked in the R&D department at Gremlin Interactive, where he developed their in-house low-level rasterization, math, and Win32 libraries. Published games include *Need For Speed: Hot Pursuit, Skate 2, Skate 1, NBA Live 07, NBA Live 06, Vegas Tycoon, Monopoly Tycoon, Risk II, Actua Soccer 3*, and *Actua Tennis*.

Michael Wimmer is an associate professor at the Institute of Computer Graphics and Algorithms of the Vienna University of Technology, where he received an MSc in 1997 and a PhD in 2001. His current research interests are real-time rendering, computer games, real-time visualization of urban environments, point-based rendering, and procedural modeling. He has coauthored many papers in these fields, was papers cochair of EGSR 2008 and of Pacific Graphics 2012, and is associate editor of the journal *Computers & Graphics*.